NAKED
EMPERORS

NAKED EMPERORS

★ ★ ★ ★ ★ ★ ★ ★ ★ ★ ★ ★ ★ ★ ★

THE FAILURE OF THE
REPUBLICAN
REVOLUTION

★ ★ ★ ★ ★ ★ ★ ★ ★ ★ ★ ★ ★ ★ ★

SCOT M. FAULKNER

ROWMAN & LITTLEFIELD PUBLISHERS, INC.

Lanham • Boulder • New York • Toronto • Plymouth, UK

ROWMAN & LITTLEFIELD PUBLISHERS, INC.

Published in the United States of America
by Rowman & Littlefield Publishers, Inc.
A wholly owned subsidary of The Rowman & Littlefield Publishing Group, Inc.
4501 Forbes Boulevard, Suite 200, Lanham, Maryland 20706
www.rowmanlittlefield.com

Estover Road
Plymouth PL6 7PY
United Kingdom

British Library Cataloguing in Publication Information Available

Library of Congress Cataloging-in-Publication Data:
Faulkner, Scot M., 1953–
  Naked emperors : the failure of the Republican revolution / Scot M. Faulkner.
    p. cm.
  ISBN-13: 978-0-7425-5881-6 (cloth : alk. paper)
  ISBN-10: 0-7425-5881-9 (cloth : alk. paper)
  1. Republican Party (U.S. : 1854–) 2. United States. Congress. House.
3. Conservatism—United States. 4. Political ethics—United States. 5. United States—
Politics and government—1993–2001. 6. United States—Politics and government—
2001– I. Title.
  JK2356.F37 2008
  324.273609'049—dc22   2007029666

Printed in the United States of America

♾™ The paper used in this publication meets the minimum requirements of
American National Standard for Information Sciences—Permanence of Paper for
Printed Library Materials, ANSI/NISO Z39.48-1992.

★ CONTENTS ★

★ ACKNOWLEDGMENTS ★

This book is, itself, an acknowledgment to all those who fought for and implemented the historic reforms of the 104th Congress. Your individual and collective contributions changed democracy for the better. May this book pay you proper homage.

I also want to acknowledge all those who seek to reform government at all levels. Your individual acts of heroism go unreported, but you are the ones who battle against the odds while keeping the flame of democracy and liberty alive. May this book inspire you to continue your good works.

This book is also for every American who harbors a growing concern that our democracy is at risk. May this book ignite a passion for action.

I owe an eternal debt of gratitude to my family and friends who supported me through the most arduous period of my life. I wish to thank Pam Leigh for guiding me into the literary world and having faith in this project. I also thank Sarah A. H. Morgan for her research and the publishers for their contributions to the final product. Expert advice made the reforms, and this book, possible.

★ CAST OF CHARACTERS ★

Scot M. Faulkner—Chief Administrative Officer (CAO)

Irene M. Faulkner—Mother

Vicki C. Hunter—Fiancée

Clarence "Ki" Faulkner—Father

THE A RING

Jackie Aamot—Executive Secretariat

Jane Bennett—Customer Service

Bill Crain—Support Services

Mike Dorsey—General Counsel

Kay Ford—Human Resources

Debora Hansen—Facilities Liaison

Phil Kiko—Procurement

Ben Lusby—Publishing and Distribution

Don Mutersbaugh—Information Services

Tom Simon—Internal Control

Tom Anfinson—Finance

Jennifer Borcherdling—House Information Resources

James Davison—Media Services

Rick Endres—House Information Resources

John Garbett—Support Services

Terri Hasdorff—Executive Assistant

Carole Kordich—Support Services

Ken Miller—Information Services

Bill Norton—Procurement

Bill Sturdevant—Internal Control

Paul Sweetland—Facilities

Donna Wiesner—Executive Secretariat

Wendy Younk—Training

Edith "Edie" Vivian—ONECall

Gloria Wright-Simmonds— Chief of Staff

CAO TEAM MEMBERS

John Atkinson—Webmaster

Lynn Borkon—Media

Dwight Comedy—Photographer

Doug Fehrer—HR

Barbara Hanrahan—ONECall

John Hitzel—Food Services

Susan Marone—Assistant to CAO

Chad Mosley—House Information Resources

Don Rice—Finance

Tom Van Dyke—Furnishings

Bern Beidel—Employee Assistance

Trent Coleman—Webmaster

Joan DeCain—ONECall

Scott Granieri—HR

Gail Henkin—Assistant to CAO

Carol Kresge—Internal Control

Joan McEnery—Attorney

Cosmo Quattrone—Furnishings

Joe Simpson—Publications

Susan Zeleniak—Telephone Services

NEWTWORLD

Pam Ahearn—Protocol

Arnie Christiansen— Deputy Chief of Staff

Joe Gaylord—GOPAC

Rep. Newt Gingrich (R-GA)—Speaker

Dan Meyer—Chief of Staff

Tony Blankley— Communications

Jeff Eisenach—GOPAC

Ed Gillespie—Assistant

Jack Howard—Assistant

Sue Wadel—General Counsel

COMMITTEE ON HOUSE OVERSIGHT

Rep. John Boehner (R-OH)

Dan Crowley—Legal Counsel

Rep. Jennifer Dunn (R-WA)

Mary Sue England— Deputy Director

Stacy Carlson—Staff Director

Rep. Lincoln Diaz-Balart (R-FL)

Rep. Vern Ehlers (R-MI)

Rep. Vic Fazio (D-CA)— Ranking

Rep. Sam Gejdenson (D-CT)
Rep. William Jefferson (D-LA)

Scott Montrey—Media
Rep. Ed Pastor (D-AZ)
Rep. Pat Roberts (R-KS)
Rep. Bill Thomas (R-CA)—
  Chairman
Chris Wright—Parking

Rep. Steny Hoyer (D-MD)
Tom Jurkovich—Min. Staff
  Director
Rep. Bob Ney (R-OH)
Perry Pockros—Min. Staff
Reynolds Schweickhardt—IT
Otto Wolff—CAO Liaison

LEGISLATIVE APPROPRIATIONS SUBCOMMITTEE

David Coggins—Staff Liaison
Rep. Vic Fazio (D-CA)—
  Ranking
Ed Lombard—Staff Director
Rep. Ron Packard (R-CA)—
  Chairman
Rep. Ray Thornton (D-AR)
Rep. C. W. Bill Young (R-FL)

Rep. Julian Dixon (D-CA)
Rep. Bob Livingston (R-LA)—
  Chairman, Full Committee
Rep. Dan Miller (R-FL)
Rep. Charles Taylor (R-NC)

Rep. Roger Wicker (R-MS)

THE GANG OF SEVEN

Rep. John A. Boehner (R-OH)
Rep. Scott L. Klug (R-WI)
Rep. Frank D. Riggs (R-CA)
Rep. Charles Taylor (R-NC)

Rep. John T. Doolittle (R-CA)
Rep. Jim Nussle (R-IA)
Rep. Rick Santorum (R-PA)

OFFICERS OF THE HOUSE

Robin Carle—Clerk
John Lainhart—Inspector
  General
Linda Nave—Assistant Clerk

Dr. James Ford—Chaplain
Bill Livingood—Sergeant at Arms

Jeff Trandahl—Assistant Clerk

MEMBERS OF CONGRESS

Rep. Dick Armey (R-TX)
Rep. Bud Brown (R-OH)

Rep. John Ashbrook (R-OH)
Rep. Dick Chrysler (R-MI)

Rep. Tom DeLay (R-TX)
Rep. Bill Emerson (R-MO)
Rep. Tom Foley (D-WA)
Rep. Ben Gilman (R-NY)
Rep. Dennis Hastert (R-IL)
Rep. John Kasich (R-OH)
Rep. Bob Michel (R-IL)
Rep. David Obey (D-WI)
Rep. Don Ritter (R-PA)
Rep. Chris Shays (R-CT)
Rep. Bob Walker (R-PA)

Rep. David Drier (R-CA)
Rep. Mark Foley (R-FL)
Rep. Richard Gephardt (D-MO)
Rep. Dan Glickman (D-KS)
Rep. Peter Hoekstra (R-CA)
Rep. John Linder (R-GA)
Rep. John Murtha (D-PA)
Rep. Nancy Pelosi (D-CA)
Rep. Charlie Rose (D-NC)
Rep. Jerry Solomon (R-NY)
Rep. Frank Wolf (R-VA)

OTHER PLAYERS

Jack Abramoff—Lobbyist
Gerald Carmen—Mentor
Stan Evans—Mentor
Justin Logsdon—Mentor
Ron Kessler—Author
Dan Muhollan—Dir.,
 Congressional Research
 Service
Marvin Runyon—
 Postmaster General
Jim Stephens—Compliance
 Office
George M. White—
 Architect of the Capitol
Three Audit Teams
Three California Businessmen

Charles Bowsher—GAO
Philip Crosby—Mentor
Gene Hedberg—Mentor
Prof. Larry Longley—Mentor
Randall Medlock—NLFS
Brad Nash—Mentor

Rick Shapiro—Dir., Congressional
 Management Foundation
General Leonard Wishart—Dir.,
 NLFS
Barbara Wolanin—Curator

★ INTRODUCTION ★

History, like life, is a collection of choices and their consequences. Every day there are paths taken and others left unexplored. The ripple effects of these innumerable selections spread out into the future, shaping events for years to come.

This book is about a moment in American history when the choices were more fundamental than during any other period in the last century. The 1994 election broke apart the grand political Pangaea of Washington, D.C. The various continental plates of American politics—House and Senate members, interest groups, lobbyists, the media, academia, and the bureaucracy—were in a massive and sudden state of flux. It was a historic window of opportunity for rethinking and reinventing everything about representative democracy before the plates locked back in place for generations to come. What happened next, what was done, and what was left undone is still shaping America's political landscape. Those who venture into this book will gain new insights and understandings about how it happened, why it happened, and what is still to come.

This window of opportunity, when everything and everyone was responding to a sudden turn of events and anything was possible, lasted for only a brief moment. Powerful forces from the established order soon rallied. Equally powerful and pervasive flaws among the leaders of the insurgency diffused and ultimately diminished the Republican majority's ability to carry out its dream of fundamental reform. By the autumn of

1996, less than two years after the historic Republican victory, the passion was spent. By the summer of 1997, the Republican Party in the House was destroying itself in a fratricidal orgy. In the years that followed, even the most committed leaders for reform succumbed to the old ways, finding ever more innovative ways to abandon their principles. In the end, a small minority of members preserved their commitment to reform and retained a glimmer of what could have been. America and representative democracy continue to suffer new indignities to this day.

For sixty-four years (1931–1995), the Democratic Party dominated Washington, D.C. During this time, control of the House of Representatives became a virtual "birthright" for generations of Democrats. Except for two isolated Congresses, the Eightieth and the Eighty-third, when the Republicans temporarily broke the Democrats' hold, the Democrats in the House were the foundation of Washington's culture of governance. During this period the various power blocs and power players of Washington developed and institutionalized a complex web of relationships. The last Republican Speaker of the House, Joseph W. Martin Jr. of Massachusetts, stepped aside in January 1955. This meant that for the forty years prior to 1995, this web of relationships was able to evolve in an environment devoid of partisan disturbance.

This sixty-four-year period did much to change the size and role of government in America, but had surprisingly little impact on the machinery of governance. As 1994 began, the House of Representatives would have been a familiar place to those who met in the Continental Congress or even the House of Burgesses. While America had grown into a world power, and while the basis of its economy had shifted from agriculture to industry to information, the structure, processes, and culture of the House remained a nearly perfect time capsule of the eighteenth century.

All of this had the potential to change in November 1994.

As a result of a critical mass of new personalities calling for reform, many of the old dysfunctional methods of doing the "people's business" were to be changed forever. Yet some of the old ways proved extremely resilient to change and instead changed the "revolutionaries" into the same kind of people they had run against. The enticements of power, perks, and money were a siren's song luring even the most committed reformers onto the rocks of abuse and scandal.

It did not have to end up this way. Over 50 percent of the new Republican majority were freshman or sophomore members. Nearly a third of the diminished Democrats in the new minority were freshman or sophomore members. Significantly, 26 percent of the entire membership of the House had come to Washington from business backgrounds.[1]

On the morning of November 9, 1994, the world changed for all of them. Except for one Republican member who had been a page, none had ever served in a Republican-run House. Many were not old enough to remember the last Republican House majority. Those who were born after 1954 had lived their entire lives in the world of a Democratic-run House.

For this historic group of people, service in the House represented an opportunity to make a difference. Coming from outside the Capital "Beltway" and from outside of politics, they, as a group, approached the House very differently from those wedded to the established order. Their perceived mandate, and their campaign promises, inspired them to pry open the time capsule of the eighteenth-century-based House and let the air of the late twentieth century pour into every niche of this ancient chamber.

This story proves, once again, that the forces of change are always racing the clock. This race is repeated over and over again as the idealism of opposition and the exhilaration of initial victory give way to the petty issues and jealousies of governance. A person changes from wanting change, to just holding on to what he or she has. Power for a purpose becomes power for its own sake. The enjoyment of sitting in the inner circles of power, with its elitist charms and its seductive privileges, is a pervasive force of gravity that brings revolutions and revolutionaries crashing to earth. Time is always the enemy of change.

This story of opportunities lost will be instructive to all who desire change. First, the 1994 revolution did, in fact, usher in many positive, substantive, and lasting changes. How these changes occurred, even in the face of widespread opposition and deteriorating support, provides a template of hope for those who remain committed to reform at all levels of government.

Second, the story of opportunities lost, and how they were lost, proves that fundamental change is required in the way America is governed in the twenty-first century.

These fundamental changes—"direct democracy"—will empower everyone in America to take control of government using the tools of the information age. These changes will happen only if America can summon the will and focus to topple the power elite of Washington, D.C. America won its independence on the battlefield, but it assured its democracy by creating a new capital away from the established centers of power at the time—Boston, Philadelphia, and New York. For America to reestablish true democracy, it must find ways to once again move its system of government away from the current center of power—Washington, D.C. The Internet, and the multitude of other technologies, will allow America to end the oligarchy of the K Street lobbyists, the career politicians, and their career staff. This revolutionary shift away from the current established power center will give democracy a fighting chance for centuries to come. Our public processes must actually be public. Public documents must really be public. Public information must be truly public. In the end, our leaders must directly hear the public voice and be held accountable for how well they listen.

This is a narrative about the management of democratic processes in the U.S. Congress. Although this is the most political of environments, the struggles are about management principles and techniques that are as old as humankind. The first group of humans, who successfully hunted as a team, established the groundwork for modern management. Those first hunters had a clear objective (find food), created and perfected appropriate tools, effectively communicated, worked as a team, measured and documented (cave drawings) their results, learned from their experiences, and continually improved upon all of this to achieve sustained success.

It is always amazing how leaders, whether in government or corporations, find ways to complicate and confuse these management basics.

This book is told from the perspective of a group of committed change agents who applied these basic management principles and kept their eyes on the prize to make real and lasting change happen. All around them swirled the passions and pettiness of political Washington. Their challenge was to leverage this passion, and avoid the pettiness, to achieve their change agenda. How they went about this, how they initially succeeded, and how, ultimately, they were undone is the prism through which the reader will view the rise and fall of the Republican revolution.

This is a story about people and their choices. It unfolds the same way these people experienced it. Not everything is known from the start, including which side people are really on or shift to later. They are all "mere mortals." The story chronicles how these change agents grappled with rescuing American democracy from those who no longer believed in their own mortality but postured as gods or emperors. We are all naked before our maker and history, yet they still paraded in their imaginary finery.

This book is also about how both the Republicans and the Democrats failed America. The Democrats' failure was one of governance. They perverted the basic mechanisms of government and institutionalized their exploitation. The Republicans' failure was one of leadership. They allowed individuals to exploit the system and lost sight of their goals.

The material in this book comes from primary and official sources. All quotations and summations of documents are from the original materials. Unless otherwise documented in endnotes, all dates, summations, and transcriptions of conversations come from my personal diaries, notes, and meeting logs.

★ PROLOGUE ★

June 17, 1991

"**N**ewtworld is in trouble," deadpanned Dan Meyer followed by a round of laughter. The quality management awareness session was going well. This four-hour module was tailored for Gingrich's three major organizations, collectively called "Newtworld." Gingrich's staff described "Newtworld" as a large amusement park with various theme areas: the Grand Old Party Action Committee (GOPAC), the minority whip's staff, and his personal office. The awareness module was from Philip Crosby Associates' (PCA's) curriculum. It mixed fun with brutal insight. From the fun came a comfort among attendees to identify and deal with their "awkward realities." From dealing with these realities came commitment to do something about them.

Thirty minutes into the session with the minority whip's staff, the room was energized. "We've got work to do," noted Tony Blankley. Everyone nodded in emphatic agreement. Linda Nave and Hardy Lott quietly made notes based on the flip chart at the front of the room.

The list on the flip chart, generated through a structured brainstorming approach, was indeed stark. It had been developed first from individual worksheets, which lead to a brief discussion among groups of twos and threes, and then from the entire group of eleven identifying and explaining their "biggest problems" facing the whip's organization.

NEWTWORLD'S BIGGEST PROBLEMS

JUNE 17, 1991

* Unplanned projects—exceeds resources
    no priorities
    telephone tag
    no time/no answers
* Too many organizations
    lack of coordination
    lack of scheduling
    lack of time allocation
* No time management
* Poor communications
    to leadership
    to committees
    making sure right people know!
* Interruptions
* No follow through
* Lack of FOCUS!! (especially on District)
* No coordination/much duplication

Source: Flip chart from Gingrich awareness session, June 17, 1991.

"The good news," I began, "is that your list is similar to the problems facing every type of organization and corporation worldwide. Remember the firefighting cycle we started with":

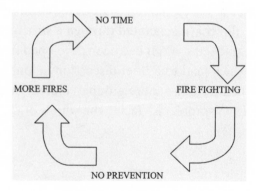

"We find ourselves in this vicious cycle of being surprised by the unexpected and the unplanned. We cease to manage. We only react. We don't have time to manage because we are always firefighting. Because we are firefighting, we don't have time to solve the underlying problems that may help us prevent future fires. Guess what? By not taking the time to prevent problems, even more fires break out! The cycle then begins again, with even less time to do what we want. This constant firefighting costs us time and money, it lowers morale, and it ultimately impacts our organization's ability to meet our goals and the needs of our customers.

"Only by using prevention methods can we ever stop this cycle. We are going to learn how prevention is one of the main principles of quality management. These principles have given others the ability to break free of this firefighting cycle. You can do the same thing here."

"What happens when the boss is a pyromaniac?" Dan Meyer queried. The room resounded in applause and laughter.

★

The merger of the quality-management revolution and the reform of House operations began eight years before "Newtworld" wrestled with its applications. At that time, Representative Don Ritter (R-PA) introduced Newt Gingrich to Dr. W. Edwards Deming, the foremost developer and theorist of quality management. Those early meetings evolved into a close friendship and deep respect between the "father of quality management" and the future leader of the Republican Congressional "revolution."

Ritter, an enthusiastic and articulate proponent of quality management, was the first to see how these principles could apply to House operations. He recommended that Gingrich follow up his discussions with Dr. Deming by attending formal training classes in quality management. Ritter also noted that one of the most successful American companies to apply quality management was the Milliken Company in Georgia. Milliken, a large fabric mill, was one of the first winners of the Malcolm Baldrige National Quality Award in 1988. The company became a national role model for anyone implementing quality principles.

Its management classes were based on the work of another major figure in the quality movement, Philip Crosby.

Gingrich immediately grasped the importance of the quality revolution and made it a key element in his "Renewing American Civilization." This set of principles would become both a series of lectures at Kennesaw State College in 1993 and the foundation for the Republican effort to retake the House in 1994.[1]

Before "Renewing American Civilization" took shape, there was Gingrich's first version of an integrated approach to leadership and to rebuilding America: "Process for a Successful America." After his first introduction to Deming and his attendance at the Milliken training, Gingrich corresponded regularly with both Deming and Crosby to develop major elements of this first version. From these dialogues, Gingrich shaped his own unique blend of Republicanism, conservatism, and quality management.[2]

Pulling together various themes and actions from the quality movement, Gingrich drew heavily from Deming's concept of "14 points," which defined quality, and Crosby's "14 steps," which implemented quality.[3]

Gingrich also adopted the lexicon "Listen, Learn, Help, and Lead," which drew from the works of Stephen Covey. These principles became the banner for Gingrich's successful rise to be minority whip for the Republicans at the beginning of the 101st Congress (1989–1990).

My association with this merging of management and politics began on September 17, 1990, when Representative Ritter met with me to discuss bringing quality management to Capitol Hill. I had known Don from our days of helping the Committee for a Free Afghanistan. I particularly remember the handwoven carpet that dominated his personal office. It was made by Afghan refugees, and depicted Soviet helicopters attacking villages.

The meeting went very well. Don explained the history of the quality movement as it related to his introducing Newt Gingrich to Deming and Crosby. "This could be one of the most important things we could do for America," said the congressman. He went on to state the case that once Congress began using quality-management principles, Congress could then use these same principles in conducting better oversight and guidance of the executive branch. "Once the government gets on board the quality revolution, America will get better laws and that will help everyone." Don's strengths included seeing the big picture and enthusiastically selling others on his vision.

"Scot," said Don, "the next steps are very important. You need to link up with the Congressional Management Foundation. Rick Shapiro [the foundation's executive director] and you will get along famously. He has been trying to improve Hill operations for years. The two of you, along with Crosby, can launch something special." His two assistants, Patty Sheetz and Carol Kresge, took notes and offered to help in this effort. "The other key action is that you have got to see Newt. He can make things happen."

Time passed. Representative Ritter and other House members completed the 1990 election cycle and the organization of the 102nd Congress (1991–1992). The House quality effort went to the back burner.

Finally, at the end of March 1991, the opportunity for launching quality management in the House presented itself. Dan Meyer, Newt Gingrich's chief of staff in the minority whip's office, had begun reading books by Crosby and Deming. Ritter said Gingrich was working on a major address on quality management to be presented on the floor of the House.

Dan Meyer and I traded telephone calls to set up some meetings. As Dan put it, "we need to find ways for Newtworld to practice what Newt is now preaching." At the end of normal House business on April 24, Gingrich stepped into the "well" of the House (the place on the House floor where members use lecterns to present formal remarks) and conducted a sixty-minute special order on his "Process for a Successful America." It was just before 5:00 p.m., and the C-SPAN audience heard something very different from the usual political speech. They heard a scholarly lecture on how the principles of Frederic Taylor, Dr. Deming, and Philip Crosby would save America. "I wonder," said Gingrich, "what our customers, the taxpayers, want. I wonder how we should deal with quality as defined by the taxpayer?"[4]

Gingrich's speech was breathtaking in scope. He discussed how Japan had applied quality principles. He reviewed the history of the quality movement. He outlined what made corporations successful. He discussed the Milliken Company and how it involved employees in suggesting improvements:

> Let us now focus these ideas on the Post Office. What if our goal was not thirty-nine suggestions per employee, the Toyota standard; was not twenty-three suggestions per employee, the Milliken standard; what if our goal for the Post Office was two recommendations per employee for 1991? That would come to about 1,500,000 recommendations. . . . We would accept twenty percent for the first year. That is 300,000 changes in the postal system. That would currently be illegal. We would have to rethink the union contracts. . . . We would have to rethink the whole process of the way in which we manage personnel in the federal government. It would be a totally different approach.
>
> Yet, you are never going to get to the kind of productivity . . . to deliver the mail as efficiently and as effectively as is possible technically in the modern world. You will never get there without going to some kind of process of quality and some kind of encouragement. . . . Mr. Speaker, I believe we have an opportunity to create a successful America with this process. . . . I want to encourage every one of my colleagues, and everyone who is listening, to develop personally their own movement for a successful America that applies these principles so that together we can create a successful 21st century America.[5]

On May 24, I had my first face-to-face meeting with Dan Meyer and Len Swinehart, another Gingrich staffer. Meyer went into a general discussion that "Newtworld" needed to learn about quality management and apply it to everything they do. "Newt really wants us to use this stuff. He wants us to be a role model for others in the House," explained Dan.

Dan and I reviewed what Ritter had envisioned—that eventually the entire House could have quality training and the institution could move toward putting quality principles into practice. "We can be the first pilot effort, but then we will need to run the gauntlet of the Committee on House Administration," Dan explained.

The Committee on House Administration (CHA) was like a board of directors that directly ran all administrative functions of the House. It was well known that the committee was a group of members who saw their role as protecting the House's patronage system. During the 207-year history of the House, this system had fully politicized all management of the institution.

"That will be a bridge we will have to cross later," continued Dan. "For now, let us work on making quality happen within Newtworld." We scheduled a series of preliminary training sessions. "You should meet some of the other key players around Newt, especially Gaylord and Eisenach." With schedule books at the ready, we mapped out the summer months.

Ritter's staff arranged my first meeting with Rick Shapiro and the staff of the Congressional Management Foundation. The positive chemistry between Rick and me was immediate. He considered himself a voice in the wilderness, trying to bring rational, private-sector, and professional practices to congressional operations. He saw Ritter and Gingrich's crusade for quality as a major opportunity. Never before had such highly placed members been interested in major changes to the House.

We discussed rolling out quality training to the House after Newtworld's effort was underway. Rick explained that professional training was not authorized in the House. His foundation provided services by having his own staff hired as staff to the offices they trained for the duration of the service. "No one has ever raised the issue of having tuition or training fees paid for from official funds. Congress has yet to understand professional development."

Rick and I exchanged large packages of each other's training materials. A long-term alliance and friendship began, as we each saw the other as a strong advocate of overdue reform.

PCA authorized my providing pro bono training sessions to Newtworld. I also discovered that former senator Paula Hawkins (R-FL), an advisor to PCA's board of directors and to its parent company, Alexander Proudfoot, had been talking to Gingrich directly about a similar effort.

The June 17 training of the whip's office went well, as did the session with the personal staff on July 7. Dan then set up a meeting to brief the staff of the Republican Conference on July 25.

On July 18, I joined Senator Hawkins for a day of meetings on Capitol Hill. The first stop was a one-hour meeting with Representative

Nancy Johnson (R-CT). We then walked from the Cannon House Office Building across to the Capitol.

The minority whip's office in the Capitol could be described as "cozy." H-219 was near the House floor, had high ceilings, and wonderful chandeliers, but was "intimate" compared with the other leadership offices. Still, Gingrich used every inch of space to display his wide range of interests. This was not your usual congressional office with "grip and grin" photographs filling up wall space. Instead, dinosaur bones (real ones!) and books on dinosaurs and books on many other topics (including quality) were everywhere.

Gingrich walked out from his inner office and greeted Senator Hawkins with great enthusiasm. Paula then turned and introduced me. Gingrich vaguely recognized me, and I reminded him that I had been Representative John Ashbrook's (R-OH) legislative assistant when Newt was a freshman.

We settled back into our seats in the front reception area and Gingrich pulled up a chair. Senator Hawkins recounted her earlier conversations with him regarding PCA. Newt leaned forward and interjected in mid-sentence: "Absolutely, absolutely. That is exactly what I have been talking about," he began energetically. "I have always said that quality management must be part of this country's future if we have any hope of being a leader in the next century."

"Well, Newt," Paula continued, "that is why we are here. We want to work with you to show the Congress how quality management applies, even up here."

"You are already talking to Dan on this?" Newt looked around the group. I nodded affirmatively. "That is the first step. I want everyone who works for me to understand what quality management is and how it relates to the broader agenda of making America a success in the next century. I want us to practice quality in all we do so that we can say to everyone else that this is real, and it works. Unless we make the effort to use it ourselves, we have no hope of expanding this to the rest of government."

The talk turned to next steps. Paula led the conversation, reviewing how PCA works with clients. "Scot is our man in Washington and will work with your staff to move things along."

"Good . . . good," agreed Gingrich. "I want us to look into bringing this to every office on Capitol Hill. Even the Democrats should be part of this. This is something everyone should have."

After further pleasantries, Gingrich stood up and bid us good luck. "Keep Dan informed on how things are going. Let me know what else we can do. This is important." The meeting ended.

The meeting had gone well. Gingrich had liked the idea for testing quality management in pilot programs in members' personal offices. The next day this commitment to a quality effort was furthered during a lunch meeting with Dan Meyer at the Capitol Hill Club, the private club for Republicans located at the corner of First and C streets S.E., kitty-corner to the Cannon House Office Building. Dan brought along Mary Brown from Gingrich's personal office and two new players from GOPAC: Joe Gaylord and Jeff Eisenach. Over a working lunch in the basement grill, we assessed the quality effort, to date, and what needed to happen next.

"This all ties together," began Gaylord. "Newt sees quality as the vehicle for bringing the House into the twentieth century. Once members and staff use these principles, we can run the House far more efficiently."

"In addition," interjected Eisenach, "we see quality as a key part of Newt's 'Circle of American Success.' We can use these principles for campaign management. We can use them as part of his platform to replace the welfare state."

The discussion turned to GOPAC and how Gingrich saw all parts of "Newtworld" working together to help the Republican Party, to help Republican candidates, and to be the vehicle to bring revolutionary change to the House. Woven through it all were four basic principles: quality management, technology, economic reform, and a core of traditional cultural values. "We will take the House," assured Gaylord. "Maybe not in 1992, but soon, and we want to have a unified operation to do it right."

Dan knew through Tony Blankley and others of my role in planning and implementing the personnel aspects of the Reagan presidential transition of 1980–1981. He urged me to open up about the shortcomings of the Reagan "revolution" and how conservatives, like myself, were overruled by moderates around the president, which resulted in the placement of people in key positions who were not loyal or not focused on the conservative agenda during Reagan's first term. I explained that the result of not properly planning for personnel hiring and policy control in 1980 affected the entire eight years of the Reagan administration. The Reagan years witnessed a rapid diffusion of political energy and outright sabotage of the Reagan administration's mandate by many people we recruited and placed on the administration's own payroll.

"We need to make sure that never happens to us. Too much is at stake," Eisenach added.

"One way," I continued, "is to bring key people on board and train them well. If you prepare enough in advance, you can avoid the traps encountered in the Reagan revolution."

"That is what we are already doing, and this quality stuff can help us," certified Gaylord.

Joe and I decided that the quality training for GOPAC staff would wait until strategy for the 1992 election was set. That way all the efforts of 1992 could be directly related to quality principles and vice versa. In the meantime, a proposal from PCA for bipartisan quality training would be rolled out. Under House rules, committees could hire consultants. If the CHA approved of the training, then PCA could work with member offices. The groundwork could be laid for bringing business principles to the House.

On July 29, I sent Dan Meyer a proposed strategy for "congressional management." In it, I proposed two options. Option one was to train five offices, two Republican and three Democratic. Option two was more extensive, providing training for five offices from each party.

Dan sent the proposal to Representative Bill Thomas (R-CA), the ranking Republican on the CHA. He also sent one to Mary Sue England, the minority staff director of the committee. In both cases he added a note that Gingrich endorsed the effort. I sent copies of the proposal to Ritter and to Shapiro, hoping they would approach Thomas as well.

Almost immediately the quality proposal for the House seemed to fall into a black hole. Although Dan Meyer and Don Ritter returned my calls and were encouraging, nothing moved forward. My own calls to

Thomas's office and the CHA were never returned. This lack of progress was unusual for a proposal launched with such fanfare.

I finished training "Newtworld." On December 12, 1991, in the woodland resort of Coolfont, near Berkeley Springs, West Virginia, I conducted a lively session for the GOPAC national staff on how quality principles could apply to the political environs of "Newtworld." Jeff Eisenach was impressed and pledged to help try to move the House proposal out of the black hole. True to his word, Dan Meyer called before the Christmas holidays and said that he had finally set up a meeting for me with Mary Sue England to discuss the administration committee's concerns with the quality proposal.

Tucked away on the third floor of the Capitol (H-330) was an office filled with desks. Except for a great view of the Mall, it was like the offices I squeezed myself into during my own years working in the House. It was January 8, 1992, and events were occurring that should have sparked interest in bringing a new work culture to the House.

The General Accounting Office (GAO), now the Government Accountability Office, considered an ineffective lapdog of the ruling House Democrats, had finally had enough. During the fall of 1991, the GAO showed that it could break free of political pressure as it published a series of devastating audits. These audits outlined major scandals in the way the House bank, House post office, and House restaurants conducted their operations. In each case, there was the potential for dozens of members to have personally benefited, to the detriment of the American taxpayer.

It was my hope that this explosion of scandal involving House administrative operations would help sell a quality process. Quality management could provide problem-solving and measurement tools that would prevent such abuses from happening again. I went over these ideas with Ms. England.

"That might be so," she began tentatively, "but we have never hired trainers for the House. I don't see how we can do it now."

I went through the precedents developed by Rick Shapiro and explained that ultimately, it would be the committee that would lead the effort, not PCA.

"I still don't see why anybody would be interested in spending House funds on such a program," she challenged. I walked her through the fact that quality management is a long-term approach to doing things differently, that it was not a "program" that comes and goes. I explained that the investment in quality would be a pittance compared with the savings to taxpayers if quality principles solved the management problems of the House.

"That is the issue," she continued. "Mr. Thomas does not see how quality management applies to the House. After all, isn't it just a fad? Isn't it getting mixed reviews by businesses that have tried it?" I quickly explained that quality management was hardly a "fad," and that there were countless examples of its success in different work environments. I referenced places as tradition-bound as the Smithsonian Institution, which were now using Crosby methods.

"Well, this is the House," she countered, "and I still don't see how any of this can relate to us. We are, after all, a political body, not a business. The matter is closed. Quality will never happen here. Mr. Thomas does not plan any further consideration of this."

★ THE GANG OF SEVEN ★

October 1, 1991

The member of Congress tore the paper bag from his head. "Mr. Speaker, it is time to take the mask off this institution. It is time to expose the check-writing scandal that I like to call Rubbergate. It is time to bring some honor back to this institution."

Representative Jim Nussle, a freshman from Iowa's Second District, seconds earlier had strode the "well" of the House with a paper bag over his head. Two eyeholes were cut so he could see and another hole for his mouth. It could have been a send-up of the "unknown comic" routine, but today there was no laughter.

> Nine months ago, I stood on this Floor with other freshmen and took the oath of office for the first time in my career, and it was probably one of the most important days of my entire life. I have never been so proud; but to go home to my district over this weekend and to have people laughing at Congress, laughing at Congressmen, laughing at this institution, brings dishonor on all of us.[1]

Nussle recounted the ridicule he was encountering. "I was out at a Pizza Hut this weekend with my son, Mark, my daughter, Sarah, and my wife, Leslie. A gentleman from the booth behind me asked me, 'Are you going to pay for this with a check, congressman?'"

There was a spattering of supportive applause from the "Gang of Seven." Representative Sonny Montgomery, in the chair as Speaker pro tempore, lightly scolded Nussle for using a paper bag: "The gentleman is not supposed to use the exhibit as he did." Though the chamber's reaction was low key, this short bit of "street theater" had an electrifying reaction across the nation. The film clip led the national news and became an icon among editorial cartoonists.

This was one more memorable moment for the Gang of Seven. This group of freshman House members was waging a siege on the abuses of power within the House. They brought to this task tireless fervor and energy, born from their all being freshmen and most being fairly young. Their mix of backgrounds and geography created a formidable team that helped focus public attention on a variety of management issues during the 102nd Congress (1991–1992).

Two of its leaders would emerge as key players in the reform movement. Representative John A. Boehner (R-OH) was born in 1949 and was one of the wealthiest House members. He had served six years in the Ohio state legislature prior to entering Congress. Nussle (R-IA) was the youngest of the "gang," but became its leader through his own audacious speaking style. He had honed his investigative skills while serving as a county prosecutor.

Along with the other Republican freshmen elected in November 1990, the "gang" spent most of 1991 learning the basics of being an elected representative. They also learned how to cope with being in the minority. The Democratic Party had perfected governing the House over its thirty-six years in power, however, this perfection was leading to complacency. Many members were focusing more on "perks" than on policy.

This all began to change. The General Accounting Office (GAO), now the Government Accountability Office, after having spent years being content to have the parameters of its reviews dictated by House leadership, found abuses that could not be ignored. In August 1988, the GAO pressed for written rules on honoring checks. When no rules were implemented, Charles Bowsher, comptroller general of the GAO, sent a letter to Speaker Thomas S. Foley (D-WA) on December 19, 1989, stating that the GAO's audit had uncovered six hundred bad checks, totaling more than $462,000, that had been written in the previous nine months. Foley quietly took some internal, superficial actions, hoping that this would placate the GAO. This time the GAO would not be placated, releasing a report on the House bank in February 1990.[2]

This first report on the House bank ignited criticism among Republicans and media critics. Foley, along with his chief of staff and wife Heather Foley, continued to work on the issue internally. They kept trying to find ways to make minor refinements to the existing system instead of disrupting member services by implementing major reforms. However, the GAO kept up the pressure. In early 1991, the GAO initiated another audit of the bank, finding once again that abuses existed and that no substantive action had been taken to resolve the matter.[3]

House Minority Leader Robert Michel (R-IL) knew about the persisting bank problem, but chose, consistent with his nonconfrontational manner, to communicate behind the scenes with Foley. This traditional Republican low-key response was to change when the "Gang of Seven" made the bank a major issue. Unlike the usual feisty freshmen of previous classes, the "gang's" goal was to focus on institutional integrity issues instead of policy issues. They were well positioned to vigorously pursue the House bank when the second GAO report was issued in September 1991. In that report, the GAO reported that more than 8,000 bad checks had been written against members' House bank accounts in a one-year period ending June 30, 1990. The following month, the accounting agency disclosed that about 250 members owed $250,000 in overdue bills in the House members' dining room. Another GAO report outlined extensive embezzlement and drug dealing involving postal funds in the House-run post office.

Reality was finally crashing the Democrats' perk party.

THE HOUSE BANK[4]

The House bank was an unusual institution whose roots could be traced back to the earliest days of the House. When the House moved to Washington in 1791, there had to be some way to pay members. First, the House sergeant at arms, the only House official supplied with a horse and a gun, was pressed into service to ride to the Treasury and pick up the gold needed to pay members.

Once the gold was brought to the House, it was handed over to the Speaker. There was an unofficial agreement between the Speaker and the Treasury that money for members' pay would be advanced to him so that he could pay the members himself. Later, this arrangement was delegated by the Speaker's office to the sergeant at arms, who created a House bank, which maintained members' pay accounts. The bank evolved into a more formal disbursing office in which members could deposit money, cash checks, and sometimes arrange personal loans.

During the years of Democratic rule in the House, the House bank began to regularly honor personal checks written on members' no-interest accounts, even if they did not have the funds to cover them. These bounced checks were simply absorbed by the bank using tax dollars drawn from general operational accounts.[5] In essence, members could use tax dollars to live beyond their means. This was not just a temporary issue; in some cases, members were never required by the House bank to make good on their deficit bank balances. This lack of limits and discipline was compounded by the traditional policy of not disclosing the financial transactions of House members. The results were financially catastrophic.

The GAO reports sent several shock waves through the House, which echoed into the national news media. On September 25, 1991, Speaker Foley moved to limit the damage. In typical Washington fashion, he embraced the modest recommendations of the GAO report and pledged to seek confidential repayment of bounced checks by negligent members. Foley strode the House floor declaring, "This is now a matter that is over and done with," and after describing the minor changes, which included not honoring any more bad checks, he stated that all House members were starting over "with a clean slate."[6]

This preemptive action only inflamed those who wanted the House bank closed and the names of the three hundred congressmen who had bounced checks, along with their bank statements, to be publicly released. The issue brought the Gang of Seven to the center stage of congressional politics. Their contention was that the bank was the "tip of the iceberg" of abuses and ethical lapses that had become pervasive in the House. Representatives Boehner, Rick Santorum (R-PA), and Scott L. Klug (R-WI) began making daily speeches on the House floor, calling for a public airing of the names of those who abused check-writing privileges.[7]

When asked why they were doing this, the freshmen stated that they had formed the Gang of Seven to clean up the House. This was key to giving focus and momentum to the bank scandal. The national media now had a group of articulate and idealistic freshmen willing to go to the microphones and demand simple actions that the average American could understand. Their cry for disclosure made the bank scandal tangible. Columnists used the banking scandal as an example of a larger pattern of abuse by the House. *New York Times* columnist William Safire fired away on September 30: "At large are officials who willfully and frequently abused their privilege. All should be exposed; some should be made to pay substantial taxes with penalties; a few deserve censure."[8] The next day, Jim Nussle went to the House floor with the paper bag on his head. Now there was a strong visual to add to the strong words.

The Nussle move crystallized the bank scandal and forced immediate action to be taken. On October 3, two days after Nussle's "paper bag" speech, the House passed House Resolution 236 by a vote of 390–8. This resolution called for the end of all bank and check-cashing operations in the office of the sergeant at arms no later than December 31, 1991. One day short of this deadline, the House bank was no more. From that moment onward, members had to use the Wright Patman Congressional Federal Credit Union, an independent bank run like any other employee credit union and open to all who worked in the House.

Nussle's action and the passage of House Resolution 236 opened the media floodgates. *Time* magazine led with a story titled "Washington Perk City"[9] and *U.S. News & World Report* led with "Day of the Living Deadbeats."[10] The public was exposed to the secret world of House "perks."

The chorus continued to mount, both in and out of the House, for true reform and full disclosure. House Resolution 236 also instructed the House Committee on Standards of Official Conduct (often referred to as the ethics committee) to review the GAO audit records to determine if there were abuses and patterns of abuse. On March 10, 1992, the ethics committee recommended releasing the names of those members guilty of the most blatant check-bouncing behavior. This meant that only nineteen members who were serving at the time would have been named, along with five former members.

This did not put the issue to rest. The pressure from the media and the Gang of Seven continued. On March 12, the House voted 391–36 to release the names of the top twenty-four abusers within ten days, recessed, and then reconvened to vote 426–0 at 1:15 a.m. to release all names within twenty days. Attorney General William P. Barr then appointed a special counsel to investigate whether crimes had been committed.

On April 16, all 303 names, and the checking-account records corresponding to the period of the GAO audit, were publicly released. The list included 188 Democrats and 114 Republicans, showing that abuses were rooted in the institutional culture, not in partisan politics.[11]

The numbers were startling. The pattern of abuse was unlike the behavior of the average citizen who may occasionally bounce a small check because of misprojecting cash flow in his or her account. Representative Stephen Solarz (D-NY) wrote 743 bad checks totaling $594,646 and was overdrawn for thirty months. Representative Carl Perkins (D-KY) wrote 514 bad checks totaling $565,651 and was overdrawn for fourteen months. In terms of numbers of checks, former representative Tommy F. Robinson (D-AR) led the list with 996 bad checks with a total value of $251,609, and Representative Robert J. Mrazek (D-NY) led the list of serving members with 920 bad checks with a total value of $351,609.[12]

Another sideshow of the bank scandal was the decline and fall of a pillar of the perquisite and power monopoly of the House—the sergeant at arms, Jack Russ. On March 1, 1992, Russ was shot in the face. He contended that three assailants had done the shooting, but the general view was that it was a suicide attempt.[13] With the old world collapsing around him, he resigned on the same day as the House voted to release the names. As overseer of the bank, Russ himself had $56,300 in bad checks. He would later plead guilty to three felonies, including embezzling $75,300 from the federal government, and be sentenced to two years in prison.

Following the release of the 303 member names, the special counsel, Malcolm Wilkey, subpoenaed the House bank records. This ignited another battle over the prerogatives and protections of the House versus the investigative needs of the executive branch. The Gang of Seven pressed the case that the need of the public to know the truth outweighed institutional concerns. "What are we hiding from?" asked Nussle during the April 28 debate on the subpoena. "This is an issue of credibility to the people we represent."[14]

"Public opinion be damned," countered Representative Dave Nagle (D-IA). "I refuse to be a leaf driven by a political wind. I came here to defend the Constitution, and I came here to defend the right of the members." The battle lines were drawn, but the forces of openness won, with the House voting 347–64 to comply with the subpoena.[15]

The total victory on the bank was a major vindication for the Gang of Seven and other House reformers. There was rising optimism that the end of the House bank would be the first of many victories to clean up the House. "It is absolutely essential," said Representative Frank D. Riggs (R-CA), "to make Congress work again before we can break the policy gridlock that we have back in Washington and start dealing with the problems that confront our country."[16]

Unfortunately, like many other operational issues in the House, the damage from the bank cut through both political parties. Two "gang" members, Klug and Riggs, were found to have bounced three checks each. Compared with others, these were minor infractions, but it was enough to defeat Riggs for reelection. Other Republicans, notably rising star Representative Vin Weber (R-MN), decided not to seek reelection and retired from the House. The bank's bipartisan fallout prevented some Republicans from making the scandal a symbol of Democratic abuse. Instead, the bank scandal showed that there was an institutional culture of abuse dating back to 1791. It all stemmed from integrating politics into the administrative operation of the House.

HOUSE RESTAURANTS

In September 1991, news stories began to surface that 250 House members owed a total of $255,000 in unpaid bills for food and catering services they received from the members' dining room and other House restaurants. The shortfall came from the practice of allowing members to sign their meal tabs and be billed later, the way most private clubs operate.

The public response was swift and negative. Early news leaks put the figure substantially higher. The idea of members freeloading meals on the taxpayer in exclusive dining facilities outraged activist groups and radio talk-show hosts. Later the numbers were refined downward, and it was shown that a portion of the unpaid bills came from outside groups who used Capitol facilities and services under the auspices of members.

The Committee on House Administration (CHA) chairman, Representative Charlie Rose (D-NC), moved swiftly to repair the damage. On October 1, 1991, the CHA, which ran the restaurants, announced that members could no longer sign for meals and that meal costs had to be paid for immediately. Outside groups would have to pay for catering services in advance.

However, the damage was done. The Democrats lost additional credibility when a group of highly-touted consultants was hired to help improve the food service. It was discovered that one of the consultants was a former member who had served three months in jail for tax evasion and for lying to the Federal Election Commission (FEC).[17]

The House restaurant scandal provided a sordid picture of privilege and power to the American public. The feeling that something major must be done to the institution of the House began to deepen among a growing number of members and voters.

HOUSE POST OFFICE

Prior to 1977, House rules allowed members to convert unused office allowances into cash. The stationery account, then about $6,500, and the stamp account, then around $1,100, were the usual allowances cashed out for other purposes. These were only a few of the dozens of accounts that made up the members' overall allowance for running their personal offices.

The cash-for-stamps procedures were not well documented or clear. This allowed members to press the boundaries of House rules and eventually, to sail over the cliff of corruption. During the 1994 transition, House post office employees outlined this evolution:

Scene I: Member A walks into the House post office and orders $100 worth of stamps. Under House rules, members are allowed to print and use envelopes with their names printed where the stamp would otherwise go. A member's signature on the envelope is considered a "stamp" for purposes of official mailings. This is what is known as the Congressional "frank" and renders unnecessary the use of individual postage stamps. Yet with crates of these franked envelopes stored in each office, a stamp account still existed. Why members needed to buy stamps with tax dollars was never explained.

Scene II: Member B walks back into the House post office with $100 worth of stamps, stating he really did not need them after all. The post office employee takes back the stamps, but instead of crediting the member's account (something logic and accountability would dictate), gives cash to the member (an option allowed under then House rules). The accounting documentation does not reflect this exchange. The record still shows that stamps were purchased.

Scene III: Member C, not wanting to go through the activity of buying stamps and returning them, simply shows up in the House post office, hands over a voucher reflecting the purchase of $100 worth of stamps, and asks for $100 in cash. This final scenario became so popular that House post office employees told the transition teams that drawers stuffed with cash were required to meet member demand.

The stamp account of $1,100 under House rules should have limited this practice to, at worst, embezzlement of $1,100 per year. However, everything was relative in the House. Members, if they asked the right person on the Committee on House Administration (which then directly ran all House administrative operations), could reallocate their allowances to meet the needs of their spending patterns. Under the highly prescriptive system prior to 1994, members required waivers from the CHA to move these allowances up, down, and around. Thanks to the delegation of signature authority to staff and the autopen, up to four thousand such waivers happened each month. Unless the effort was made to clearly document these transactions in the Clerk of the House

Report (the quarterly accounting of the House's expenditures), spending for "stamps" could grow well beyond $1,100 per year.

Unfortunately, the Clerk of the House Report was, at best, a work of fiction. There were many ways to move undocumented money among accounts. Many high-dollar operations of members' offices were funded through general House accounts. Most member transactions, although requiring purchase orders, contracts, and vouchers, rarely had any of these. There was no way even the most dedicated outsider could ever find out what it really cost to run a member's office. The result was the ability of a member with less-than-high morals to pour taxpayer money into his or her own wallet without any fear of being discovered.

In 1980, the U.S. Postal Service's (USPS) Postal Inspection Service conducted a probe of the House post office, based on anonymous tips that cash-for-stamps abuse was rampant. At that time, the House postmaster, Robert V. Rota, and his account supervisor, Mary C. Bowman, falsely denied the accusations. Years later it would be revealed that Rota had instructed Bowman to make these denials in order to protect the members involved.

Rota's misleading testimony to postal inspectors delayed the inevitable day of reckoning by nearly eleven years. Rumors of the House post office being a haven for theft, embezzlement, drug dealing, interest-free loans, and illegal check cashing circulated among reform-minded staff and members. Various journalists, like Paul M. Rodriguez of the *Washington Times*, probed these stories and were met with stonewalling. Then on April 26, 1991, a House post office employee was reported missing, along with approximately $10,000 in office funds. Rota called in the U.S. Capitol Police to investigate the disappearance. A few days later, on May 1, the missing employee resurfaced, admitted to taking funds, and began disclosing that other employees of the House post office had also been stealing funds.[18]

These disclosures opened the door for the U.S. Capitol Police, the U.S. attorney's office, the U.S. Postal Inspection Service, and the U.S. Department of Justice to conduct a thorough review of House postal operations. In September 1991, an audit found a shortfall of nearly $35,000 in cash and stamps. Three House postal clerks pleaded guilty to embezzlement and agreed to cooperate with prosecutors. Their evidence, along with the onslaught of federal investigators, unearthed illegal loans, drug trafficking, the cashing of personal and campaign checks for members, and obstruction of justice.

News of the postal scandal added fuel to the fire already burning from the House bank and House restaurants scandals. The Gallup Organization documented a steady plummeting of approval of the institution of Congress from 44 to 19 percent.[19]

The fallout from the post office scandal ranged far and wide. Rota resigned as postmaster on March 19, 1992, and later pleaded guilty to embezzlement.[20] Members' names began to float among investigative journalists as federal investigators focused on who benefited from those drawers full of cash.

As the election year of 1992 began, Majority Leader Richard Gephardt (D-MO) was fighting holding actions against vigorous Republican assaults. Even nonconfrontationalist Republicans, like Minority Leader Michel, sensed vulnerability in the majority party and became more aggressive. Resolutions calling for independent probes and institutional reforms were used to hammer away at the Democrats and to stoke public outrage. On February 5, 1992, Gephardt prevailed on a vote of 254–160 for a more restrained course. His House Resolution 340 mandated that the CHA, the committee that presided over the scandals in the first place, investigate the House post office.

On February 19, 1992, the CHA named a task force to investigate the post office. Chairman Charlie Rose (D-NC) and ranking Republican Bill Thomas (R-CA) headed the effort. As calm seemed to settle over the post office scandal, the GAO found continued mismanagement and cash shortages.[21]

Speaker Foley, not wanting to cede control of the House post office to the independent U.S. Postal Service, moved swiftly to a middle ground. He appointed Michael Shinay acting postmaster of the House. Shinay was a veteran of the U.S. Postal Service and had recently served as senior assistant to the U.S. postmaster general. This attempt to retain independence succeeded for just nine days.

On April 9, 1992, the House overwhelmingly passed House Resolution 423, known as the Administrative Reform Resolution, which established the Office of Nonlegislative and Financial Services (NLFS). That same resolution abolished the independence of the postmaster and placed him under this new office. The new office was an attempt, within the existing administrative culture of the House, to consolidate some operations and create a manager who could act with limited political supervision. This move was trumpeted as a major House reform, and the postal scandal abated.

The 102nd Congress limped toward the 1992 elections with great trepidation. The public's view of the institution had dramatically soured. Two House officers had resigned under clouds and both were facing criminal charges. The chief of the U.S. Capitol Police had retired early out of his own frustration with the lack of cooperation from House members. Two independent investigations from the Justice Department, one for the bank and one for the post office, were moving toward indicting members. A number of lower-level House employees had already pleaded guilty to criminal conduct and were helping with the investigations.

"As of today," ethics committee member Representative Fred Grandy (R-IA) told his colleagues (about the release of members who bounced checks), "your talk show hosts have a topic, your opponent has an issue, and your constituents have a reason to support term limits."[22]

THE 103RD CONGRESS

The election of 1992 did not go well for the ruling Democrats. While Bill Clinton was sailing across the finish line to become president, the ruling Democrats saw their majority shrink by nine seats. This was only the second time in history such a split mandate had occurred.[23] In addition, the rash of retirements by members of both parties in the wake of the scandals created a larger-than-normal freshman class.

For the 103rd Congress there would be sixty-four Democratic and forty-six Republican freshmen. A generational shift away from the old ways had begun.

As important as these numbers were, the 1992 elections also brought in a new brand of aggressive Republican freshmen. The Gang of Seven, except Riggs, had all survived their races. They now welcomed the new freshmen into the 103rd Congress. The new freshmen, many of whom ran on "clean up Congress" platforms, were eager to continue the pressure for real reform.

Each year, the House Republican members conduct a policy retreat to review the previous year and to plan through the next election cycle. There was a restive mood during their February 1993 policy retreat. The new freshmen were bonding with the Gang of Seven. They saw Michel and his inner circle as having been too lenient on the Democrats. This leniency led to less-aggressive and less-public confrontations with Speaker Foley and the House majority. In the view of the "gang" and the freshmen, an opportunity to retake the House had been squandered.

For Michel and his supporters, such thinking was severely flawed. There are many ways a majority can completely freeze out the minority. Their traditional low-key approach had maintained some Republican voice and input into the legislative process.

The insurgent Republicans countered that such thinking had locked the Republicans into a permanent minority in the House. It was time for new thinking, new tactics, and new leaders. The "gang," and its supporters, looked for someone who could embody all their hopes and channel their zeal into an effective takeover strategy. They increasingly turned to Newt Gingrich.

Representative Newt Gingrich (R-GA) was a member of the feisty House freshman class of 1978 who helped lob bombs on the deteriorating Carter Democrats. As many conservatives followed Reagan into pressing their agenda in the executive branch, Gingrich had formed the Conservative Opportunity Society (COS) to become a rallying point for those who still wanted to make the House Republicans stand for something.

COS members took the skills learned from Representative John Ashbrook (R-OH) and the older conservative "street fighters" and added their own knowledge of using the media. Live coverage of House sessions had only been available to cable television audiences since March 1979, when C-SPAN began to broadcast the House signal. Through ingenious use of the one-minute speeches that led the daily sessions and the special orders which ended the legislative day, Gingrich and the COS began to build a television audience. In the days before Rush Limbaugh and other conservative media personalities, the COS shows obtained a conservative "cult" following. The COS members became popular icons to a new generation of young conservative activists. Speaker Tip O'Neill, in an attempt to humiliate the COS, ordered the House cameras to show the empty chamber that the COS was addressing late at night. This only added to the COS mystique, as activists outside Washington saw the empty chamber as a metaphor for COS members standing courageously alone against the powerful forces of big government.

In 1988, Gingrich launched an ethics complaint against then Speaker Jim Wright (D-TX). He questioned the financial arrangements around Wright's book, *Reflections of a Public Man*. Controversy swelled around Gingrich as Democrats attacked him for similar problems with his own 1977 book deal. Such attacks only added to Gingrich's following among "grassroots" conservatives outside Washington.

The election of George H. W. Bush as president in 1988 led to a historic opportunity for Gingrich. Representative Dick Cheney (R-WY) had been tapped to become secretary of defense in the wake of the unsuccessful confirmation fight for former senator John Tower (R-TX). With Cheney leaving the minority whip's position in March 1989, the opportunity presented itself for a conservative insurgency against Michel's candidate, Representative Edward Madigan (R-IL). Madigan had been the chief deputy minority whip and was viewed as the natural successor to Cheney. Republicans tended to reward people in turn and to shy away from insurgency candidates. This tradition of planned succession was symbolized by having conservative Representative Tom DeLay (R-TX) act as Madigan's campaign manager against Gingrich.

On March 22, 1989, the tradition was shattered as Gingrich was elected by a two-vote margin. "The issue is not ideology; it's active versus passive leadership," said Representative Weber.

Gingrich immediately set about reshaping the opposition of the House. Along with the organizational resources of the Grand Old Party Action Committee (GOPAC), his personal political action committee, Gingrich built what became know as "Newtworld." Joe Gaylord, Gingrich's top lieutenant and then head of GOPAC, ran this interlocking structure behind the scenes. Dan Meyer moved from Gingrich's personal office to head the whip's office. Tony Blankley, a veteran of the White House and an active member of various conservative networks during the Reagan years, became the Speaker's spokesman. A GOPAC consultant, John Morgan, who was also an expert at tracking polls, began weekly assessments of how this new operation and its aggressive strategy were working.

The new organization moved the COS's combative style to center stage. There were weekly "themes" for members to focus on. This meant floor speeches backed up by fact sheets and talking points that members could use back in their districts. An "echo chamber" of opposition, linked to conservative grassroots groups, was becoming a machine. Its goal was to topple the Democrats in 1992 or 1994.

The elections of 1992 disappointed some House Republicans who had hoped for more voter outrage over the scandals of the 102nd Congress. The Republicans were left to ponder both their minority status in the House and their having to deal with a Democrat in the White House.

On December 7, 1992, the Republicans met to sort out their leadership in the 103rd Congress. Michel remained a declining figure among the insurgent House Republicans, but his popularity gave him another two years as minority leader. Gingrich would have to run his opposition effort as minority whip. However, Gingrich's strategy of aggressive opposition received another major boost. Representative Richard "Dick" Armey (R-TX) defeated Representative Jerry Lewis (R-CA) for chairman of the Republican Conference. Another moderate non-confrontationalist was defeated and another conservative in favor of total warfare with the House Democrats was elevated to a key leadership position.

Bolstered at the top by Gingrich and Armey, the Gang of Seven, the COS, and the freshman class entered the 103rd Congress churning out ongoing indictments of the Democratic majority. Their one-minute speeches and endless special orders replayed the scandals of the 102nd Congress. Their efforts were boosted by yet another scandal—the House supply store.

THE HOUSE SUPPLY STORE

As the House grew in size, there arose a need for a convenient source for basic office materials. In the late nineteenth century, a simple House office supply store was created under the Clerk of the House. With the explosive growth in staffs, the House store was looking more like a modern-day Staples or Office Depot, offering pens, paper, three-hole punches, and even small calculators. All items were considered for official use and staff could use purchase orders to obtain the needed supplies.

Demands grew for the store to supply accessory items for offices, such as paperweights and bookends bearing the House seal. Such items had the possibility of being used as gifts for constituents. Staff and members also began buying these accessory items as personal gifts to friends and families. This increase in nonofficial purchases led to allowing cash payments instead of official purchase orders so that these personal transactions could occur.

Once cash was flowing, the nonofficial selections expanded rapidly. Entire china sets, crystal vases, luggage, and silver services were now available with the House seal. The office supply store now looked like the bridal section of Bloomingdales. Unfortunately, because the inventory of supplies and "accessory" items were commingled, so were the financial accounts. None of the store employees, who owed their jobs to the patronage of House members, were willing to challenge whether any of these "accessories" were for official or nonofficial use.

During the 103rd Congress, it became clear that this commingling had resulted in major abuses. Taxpayer dollars were financing extensive buying of "accessory items." The first member to come forward to resolve his account was Representative Dan Rostenkowski (D-IL). Already feeling the heat of federal investigators relating to the House post office scandal, Rostenkowski worked out an arrangement with Speaker Foley and Don Anderson, the House clerk, to repay $82,000 in questionable store purchases. These purchases included 60 armchairs with hand-painted pictures of the Capitol, 60 crystal sculptures of the Capitol, 250 pieces of fine china, and 26 pieces of luggage.[24] Word of this leaked to the *Wall Street Journal*. The story broke on February 2, 1994, beginning a new round of editorials about the "imperial Congress."[25]

House leadership, learning from its missteps in the 102nd Congress, immediately agreed to investigate misuse of the House store. In a colloquy on the House floor, Gephardt and Gingrich worked out the details of the probe and pledged a full and open report to House members.[26] The CHA was mandated to review the situation and develop a set of recommended actions.

The report was released in July 1994. On July 20, the CHA announced the immediate closure of the House supply store and that the store's practice of allowing members to reimburse the House for personal purchases would end as of September 1. Now there would only be official expenditures occurring in a stationery store filled only with office supplies. They also approved the creation of a separate gift shop, open to the public, and all accessory and gift items were to be offered only in this new facility.[27]

These new revelations allowed House Republicans to build on their central theme—it was time to end Democratic rule of the House. "Mr. Speaker, the American people can only take so much of this before they decide to throw out the entire institution," thundered freshman Representative Rod Grams (R-MN). "If you were surprised by the dramatic turnover last year, just imagine what will happen if this House ignores the concerns of the American people once again."[28]

On July 22, 1993, Representative Boehner led with a one-minute speech:

> Mr. Speaker, it's one, two, three strikes you're out at the ole ball game. First it was the House restaurant scandal, second it was the House bank scandal, and now the Democrat leadership is facing the third strike with the House post office scandal.
>
> The public's right to know is paramount and should be the overriding reason for the release of all the documents of the post office investigation. With the guilty pleas of eight post office staffers over the past year and a half, including the Postmaster himself, it is obvious that wrongdoing did occur, and House rules were indeed broken.
>
> The American public is sick and tired of the scandals racking this institution. What is the Democrat leadership trying to hide? Why can't we learn from our mistakes? Trying to keep information secret from the

public only ends up exploding in our faces. Mr. Speaker, we are at the plate now and the pitch is on the way. I only hope, for the sake of this institution and the American public, that it is not strike three.[29]

House Republican momentum was building. The early fumbles of the Clinton administration on issues like national health insurance led them to believe that 1994 would be a very different election year. The fallout from the scandals of the 103rd Congress continued. On October 6, 1993, Jack Russ, the former sergeant at arms who oversaw the House bank, pleaded guilty to three felonies. More indictments, possibly against members, were still in the works. The recent supply store scandal had given immediacy to the reform effort; it showed that there was still work to be done. Behind the scenes, John Morgan's demographics were showing that the forty-year dream of a Republican Congress was in shooting distance. One more issue remained for the revolutionaries—would they have Gingrich or Michel as Speaker?

The last hurdle for Gingrich's drive to lead a revolution was resolved on October 9, 1993, when Michel announced he would not seek reelection. A kindly and personable man, Michel had sensed his fraternal approach to a "loyal" opposition was not the wave of the future.

At their February 1994 policy retreat, held in Salisbury, Maryland, the House Republicans were eager to press for a bold strategic agenda for the upcoming elections. In addition to policy issues, the issue of reinventing House operations arose. There was a general sense that revolution needed to happen to the institution. Nussle and the Gang of Seven led this discussion. The experiment of having a bipartisan administrator answering to the CHA had just failed (see chapter 2). A new approach was required to bring an end to the scandals and to change the institution for the better, once and for all. A task group headed by Nussle was formed. Signifying the youthfulness and nontraditional nature of the Republican reformers, staff members were also named: Dan Meyer from the whip's office and Jack Howard from Representative Bob Walker's (R-PA) office.

Their mandate was to fundamentally rethink House operations and develop something based on business approaches. This concept had its roots in pilot experiments (1983–1992) in a handful of individual member's offices, run at the initiative of the members themselves, and the methodological work of the nonpartisan Congressional Management Foundation.

There was little public discussion of the work of this task group until running the House "like a business" became part of the "Contract with America" announced on September 27, 1994. As part of the final push for the 1994 elections, each element of the "contract" was to be amplified on the House floor using the one-minute speeches and special orders that Gingrich and the COS had perfected years before.

On the same day as the "contract" was made public, Representative Joel Hefley (R-CO) took to the House floor. The Democrats, in one final effort to forestall disaster, pressed for a series of administrative reforms. However, the proposal, as drafted by a bipartisan joint committee, was breaking apart. Hefley, not only in the name of the "contract" but also on behalf of salvaging the institution, spoke eloquently:

Mr. Speaker, today I would like to talk about one aspect of the contract, something we do not need a contract for, that we should be doing, and most of us agreed we wanted to do, and that was Congressional reform.

Mr. Speaker, with just a few days to go before the elections, the House is close to losing a golden opportunity to enact true Congressional reform. Instead of voting on the joint committee's broad package of reforms, the Democratic leadership decided to split the reform bill into several pieces.

The last time each chamber debated internal reforms, the effort turned out to be largely unsuccessful. That was 20 years ago. This time, things were supposed to be different. Unfortunately, as the taxpayers know all too well, it is very difficult to bring change to this place.

After the House post office scandal, I thought 1993 might be the year of reform. We had 110 new members, each of them elected to the House on a reform platform. Those new members had campaigned on platforms saying they were going to reform everything from ethics and campaign finance to budgeting. The status quo was no longer going to be tolerated.

So what happened? Politics has found its way into a process that was supposed to be void of partisan wrangling. . . . Congress has an opportunity to alter the public's perception of this institution. On the other hand, failure to enact meaningful reforms will only provide cannon fodder for those who preach hatred for this institution.

Finally, Mr. Speaker, the disdain and distrust the American people have for this institution is not good for our system of government even though it is often deserved. We have an opportunity to restore confidence. This kind of opportunity comes along rarely. We dare not squander it.[30]

THE TRANSITION BEGINS

At 2:00 a.m. on November 9, 1994, as the election returns clearly showed the Republicans becoming the majority party in the House, the Speaker-designate initiated the first transition process for the House since 1954. The transition from one party to another had never been formalized. The modern House, with all its staff and committees, grew under the previous forty years of Democratic Party rule. The thought that one day, a different party would take over had never been taken seriously enough to address. Unlike the executive branch, with its mechanistic rituals for handing over power every four to eight years, the House had no rules or budget for such a fundamental procedure. The task of sorting this out fell to Representative Nussle. His four years as the major force behind the Gang of Seven earned him the leadership of the historic changeover.

Gingrich and his core of supporters went forward in planning the legislative strategy that would make the Contract with America a reality. They also had to quickly sort out leadership posts. This was both to minimize internal battles that could weaken the new majority and to maximize the time used to launch the 104th Congress. On December 5–7, the House Republican Conference met. As expected, Newt Gingrich became the Speaker-designate. Representative Dick Armey (R-TX) was unopposed for majority leader. The major upset was Representative Tom DeLay's (R-TX) 119–80–28 vote victory over Gingrich ally and COS stalwart, Representative Bob Walker (R-PA), for majority whip in a three-way race that included Representative Bill McCollum (R-FL). "Tom proved he was a better vote counter," Walker later mused to me. "I guess that will make him the better whip." Rounding out the top slots was the election of Boehner over Representative Duncan Hunter (R-CA) by 122–102 votes as head of the Republican Conference. The Gang of Seven had come of age.

Another complication during this historic period was the lame-duck session scheduled for November 28–December 1 to resolve the North American Free Trade Agreement (NAFTA). This major international agreement pitted the Clinton administration against Dick Gephardt. It was ironic that such a divisive fight would inaugurate his becoming the titular head of the Democrats in the House in the wake of Foley's reelection defeat. The lame-duck session, in addition to ratifying the far-reaching provisions of NAFTA, was the last official public moment for Foley and Michel. As a symbolic act of friendship, Foley handed over the gavel to Michel so he could preside over the House's consideration of a resolution honoring Foley. An era of old-time camaraderie and old-time politics had come to an end.[31]

Through it all, Nussle and his team methodically threaded their way through the lack of precedents. They were able to establish a transition office in the House "courtyard." This was a maze of modern meeting rooms built in what used to be grassy courtyards tucked between the west front of the Capitol and the west terrace of the Capitol. The subterranean courtyard represented a major victory for preservationists in the 1980s. These forces had fought those who had wanted to balloon out the entire west front of the Capitol to create dozens of new personal "hideaway" offices. The result would have been destroying a historic facade in favor of a neofascist architectural monstrosity. Fortunately, the more rational minds won.

Assisting Nussle with his task was Representative John Linder (R-GA). He was one of the freshmen elected to the 103rd Congress. A wealthy businessman, Linder was close to Gingrich and to GOPAC. Boehner split his time between Gingrich's strategy sessions and helping Nussle with transition duties. Other members who assisted on aspects of the transition were Jennifer Dunn (R-WA), Vern Ehlers (R-MI), Bob Franks (R-NJ), Deborah Pryce (R-OH), Pat Roberts (R-KS), Bill Thomas (R-CA), and C. W. Bill Young (R-FL).

Staff support for Nussle came from his personal office; his chief of staff, Steve Greiner; and his task-group colleagues, Dan Meyer and Jack Howard. Representative Pat Roberts (R-KS), a veteran of the

CHA, lent Jeff Trandahl from his staff. Linda Nave, a staffer who had served both Michel and Gingrich and had been the minority staff director of the CHA during the 1980s, rounded out the initial staff group. Ed Gillespie, who was on loan from the House Republican Conference, coordinated media.

As there were no funds or supplies for the transition, the team became expert "scavengers," borrowing typewriters, computers, telephones, and paper from various offices. Even finding someone to answer the increasing number of telephone calls had to be worked out with "volunteers" from various staffs. The challenge was greater, in that so few Republicans had really believed that they would take the House. Vacation and family plans were turned upside down by the unexpected victory.

As leader of the team, Nussle was determined to model some of the new management culture. He introduced everyone to the works of Stephen Covey. Every day, Nussle required transition staff to prioritize their daily and weekly actions using Covey's "four quadrant" model. This model sorted out what items were urgent versus important. Covey maintains that most organizations expend countless amounts of energy on items that seem very urgent, but that in the long run are not important. This is a variation on the old "the squeaky wheel gets the grease" maxim.

While scavenging for supplies and remembering Covey quadrants framed the days of the transition, the work of the transition was in sorting out the structure of the House for the 104th Congress. Large boards with detailed organizational charts lined the walls. Yellow "stickies," magic markers, and flip charts filled the courtyard rooms. What would go where? What should the new officers of the House be called? How many officers should there be?

Résumés started to arrive. Members' calls swamped the transition offices with requests for "special handling" of their office selection, committee slots, and employee hiring. The old habits of patronage had not yet died. Favorite candidates were pushed. Nussle remained firm; the new officers would be different. Above all, he and his team wanted to select people who would make the House run well, once and for all.

The ghost of General Wishart hung over the courtyard. Every day, the transition team members had to walk past Wishart's old office. It was a constant reminder of what had happened and not happened during the 103rd Congress. Randall Medlock, Wishart's deputy, who was staying on in an acting capacity, now occupied the office suite. "This time it has to work"; painful thoughts resounded over and over again in Nussle's mind. "We can't relive 1993. We can't let another professional go through what happened to Wishart."

★ GENERAL WISHART'S ★
ORDEAL

February 1, 1994

Representative Robert Walker (R-PA) addressed the House:

Mr. Speaker, when the American middle class hears the Democrats talk about reform, they ought to consider the record in the House of Representatives. . . . The leadership of this House of Representatives promised there was going to be reform, that we would have a professional administrator to take care of those kinds of problems in the future. That professional administrator has now resigned. The question is: "Why?" He just resigned because we have not reformed.[1]

Walker was truly angry. It was cold outside and he could not help making a reference to the single-digit temperature: "Mr. Speaker, one of my colleagues said a few minutes ago in coming to the House chamber that we were going to have a momentous occurrence—that the temperature is going to drop below the congressional approval rating. No wonder. The House does not know how to reform."

Cheers went up from the Gang of Seven and the growing band of reformers. Three weeks earlier, on January 10, 1994, General Wishart resigned effective January 21. He had lasted less than fifteen months, but his tenure had become a personal and professional ordeal long before.

On July 23, 1993, just seven months into his term, Wishart wrote in anguish to Speaker Foley: "Mr. Speaker, this situation is destructive of my position and unacceptable. It must be corrected. I urgently request a meeting with you, the minority leader, and the majority leader."[2]

It was not supposed to have been this way.

A HOUSE REFORM BILL PASSES

On April 9, 1992, the House passed House Resolution 423 to reform House operations. The Democrats hailed the measure as an important step in solving the underlying problems that had caused the scandals. The Republicans called the measure cosmetic. The floor debate frequently deteriorated into shouting matches. There were plans for a symbolic walkout by Republicans, but this protest effort fizzled.[3]

The idea of placing the House on a more managerial footing had its roots in the House Commission on Administrative Review (aka the "Obey Commission"), headed by Representative David Obey (D-WI) in 1977. Like the 1992 effort, this initiative was born from scandal. At that time, Representative Wayne Hays (D-OH), as chairman of the Committee on House Administration (CHA), had placed mistresses on his payroll, the most famous being Elizabeth Ray.

The "Obey Commission" was composed of eight sitting members and seven private citizens with senior management experience. The *Final Report of the Joint Committee on the Organization of Congress* (H. Rep.103-413), was a massive two-volume administrative and procedural review of House operations. It found that these operations were "riddled with anomalies"[4] and contended that numerous duplications and lack of coordination led to "wastage."

In 1978, Representative Norman D'Amours (D-NH) sponsored legislation to establish a House administrator, which was recommended by the Obey Commission. It was defeated.

As the years passed, there was a minor change in political patronage. The CHA established the Subcommittee on Personnel and Police to review patronage issues and to serve as the arbiter of patronage slots. This shifted some power away from the long-standing Democratic Patronage Committee that operated within the majority leadership of the House. However, administrative employees still had to be sponsored by a sitting member. Supervisors could hire only through member sponsorship and could fire only by obtaining permission from that same sponsoring member.[5] The Democratic Patronage Committee within the Democratic Caucus remained the place to go for seeking House administrative employment.[6] This was what had become known as the "last plantation." Patronage created a system whereby an elite, which was mostly white and male, held people, mostly minorities, in political and professional bondage. It was, in the words of the *Congressional Quarterly*, "an incubator for corruption."[7]

When the 1991–1992 scandals first surfaced, Ralph Nader, the consumer advocate, surveyed the perks and privileges and declared, "Government officials who require royal treatment have no place in a democracy."[8] Minority Whip Newt Gingrich derided the system and pointedly criticized the majority for its lack of action: "This entire cocaine and theft scandal has been handled by the Democratic leadership as a partisan cover-up of their patronage problems."[9]

The scandals of the 102nd Congress were different. They did not go away. The Gang of Seven, along with investigative journalists, made sure of that. This core of reformers was bolstered by the election of 1992. As 1993 dawned, the reformers were not to be all of one party. The new freshman Democrats also recoiled at what they saw.

"They should have gotten a powerful wake-up call," said Representative Dan Glickman (D-KS), one of the Democratic reformers who began raising his voice. "If they [House leaders] don't read members' mood right, I think they could see serious challenges in the next Congress. . . . The leadership has a special responsibility to protect the institution and to protect the members. And by 'protect' I don't mean cover up—I mean clean up."[10] He expanded on this reform mandate: "This is a powerful earthquake that will cause us to modernize the House. Those of us who are reelected have to lead the House into a new era."

This sea change was predicted by Ronald Elving of the *Congressional Quarterly*. In an early "Perspective" editorial, he likened the scandals to the Titanic: "Just as the Titanic was presumed unsinkable, the contemporary Congress has assumed an aura of permanence."[11]

"The great potential peril in the overdraft scandal is its power to tie individual members to the inherent problems of their institution."

Elving ended with a final tie-in to the Titanic disaster: "Will those who hate Congress in the abstract continue to exempt their own representatives? If they do not, there will not be room enough in the lifeboats."[12]

The effort to design a real reform package began to take shape. On March 13, 1992, the Democratic Caucus approved a plan giving the Speaker more power over House officers. A plan for creating a House administrator was also proposed.[13]

During the week of March 23, 1992, steps were taken toward a reform package. One secret perk of the House, the free use of a taxpayer-funded gym, was eliminated. A fee-for-use system was announced. The gym had been constructed in the Rayburn House Office Building by the architect of the Capitol. Attendants and masseurs were at the ready to serve the members, but none of this appeared in any public report.

This was clearly not enough. "They have allowed themselves to be colored royal purple. Getting rid of free prescriptions, upping gym fees—all of that has a kind of desperate quality to it," said David Cohen, former president of Common Cause. He echoed a growing chorus of media and political leaders who were fed up with the House's inaction.[14]

Speaker Foley proposed a House administrator. He also worked out with Representative Michel that a joint Democratic and Republican "task force" would convene to compose a plan for reorganizing House administrative operations. The task force was announced on March 25. It comprised equal numbers of Republicans and Democrats, a major bipartisan gesture at the time. Significantly, the panel included a number of the "closet reformers" for the Democrats: Representative Obey and Representative Steny Hoyer (D-MD). It also included some members of the Conservative Opportunity Society (COS): Representative Walker and Representative Gerry Solomon (R-NY).[15]

Foley's embrace of the fifteen-year-old idea for a House administrator triggered a series of debates that would rage through the daily meetings of the reform task force.

Issue #1: To Whom Should the Administrator Report? The Democrats wanted to make the administrator accountable directly to the Speaker. This was a move to take power away from Representative Charlie Rose (D-NC) and the CHA. The Democrats also wanted to move all House officers to a direct reporting relationship with the Speaker. Their rationale was that having officers accountable only to the Speaker would reduce the incentive for them to try to curry favor with all 440 members and delegates of the House. This reporting change could also lay the groundwork for finally eliminating patronage politics from the hiring process. Finally, they cited the constitutional issue of the Speaker having the obligation to run the House. Direct reporting would, therefore, provide the Speaker with the tools to do so. "I am insistent that the Speaker's constitutional obligations be protected," asserted Obey.[16]

The Republicans opposed this approach. They felt that direct reporting would only consolidate patronage to the Speaker's office. "The Democratic leadership needs to explain why the Capitol Police need to be under Democratic control," countered Representative Bill Thomas (R-CA), who was the ranking Republican on the CHA.[17]

A related issue to reporting authority was who should select the administrator. The Democrats wanted the Speaker to appoint the administrator after consulting with the Republican minority leader (Michel). The Republicans insisted on a two-thirds vote of the full House.

Issue #2: What Is the Administrator's Mandate and Portfolio? The original Obey plan viewed the administrator in much the same way as a county executive or a town or city manager. Most, if not all, administrative functions would be consolidated into this new office. This would mean running the day-to-day operations of the House in a professional manner with minimal interference from political leadership. Policy guidance and oversight would be provided by someone or some entity, much like the congressional relationship with the executive branch of the federal government. "I think it is useful to have some central responsibility for appropriate administration [of the House's extensive services and vast work force]," recommended Foley.[18]

The new administrator would also have the mandate to address "complaints about the patronage system that has filled most House jobs; the administrator would be charged with professionalizing personnel recruitment and hiring."[19] The Republicans favored this approach.

Issue #3: What Kind of Person Should Be the Administrator? All involved agreed that the administrator should be a professional manager with the appropriate training and experience. "The House of Representatives has recently experienced an intolerable rash of management problems," stated Glickman. "While the specific problems may seem unrelated, they all stem from a lack of professional management at the top."[20]

Several other reform efforts arose in the debate over the administrator position. One was to establish either a "financial comptroller" or "inspector general" to review the finances of the House. One of the initiative's main backers, Representative Tom Ridge (R-PA), said the review mandate must be strong: "We need a pit bull in these halls, not a lap dog."[21] Another initiative, sponsored by Representative Charles Bennett (D-FL), was called an "anti-perk bill." House Resolution 3555 attempted, among other things, to end free plants from the botanic gardens and eliminate free parking at National and Dulles airports. All of these bills died in committee. The defenders of the existing order continued to hold out against the wave of change. The reformers derided the efforts as too little, too late. "It all looks so reactive," said Glickman. "It's window dressing. It's symbolic," said Nussle.[22]

On April 7, the Democrats brought House Resolution 423 to the House Rules Committee. The Rules Committee quickly cleared the resolution for House consideration on a 9–4 party-line vote. This brought the resolution to the House floor just two days later. "In the wake of abuses and management inefficiencies that have arisen in the House restaurant, banking, and postal services, it has become increasingly obvious to all of us that significant improvements in the organization, administration, and supervision of nonlegislative functions were long overdue," announced Majority Leader Gephardt.[23]

However, this legislation was a shadow of what had been promised just two weeks earlier. The new administrator would not be a House officer but a functionary called the director of nonlegislative and financial services (NLFS). This director would answer to a subcommittee of the CHA, not to the Speaker, so the director would have to implement real reforms within the very committee—House Administration—that had built and defended the old order.

Michel felt betrayed: "It is a sham and a charade. The real scandal is the way Congress does its legislative business."[24]

Representative Bill Thomas (R-CA) introduced a substitute, which included changes to general legislative processes. Thomas's broader package was defeated on a party-line vote (159–254). In the process, the Gang of Seven's message of Republican-backed administrative reforms got muddled and the opposition strategy fell apart. The planned symbolic walkout collapsed.[25] Many Republicans voted "present" on final passage as their one act of rebellion. Representative Paul Henry (R-MI) summed up the dilemma facing the House: "We can't sign on to something without substantial reform or our younger members will explode. The Democrats can't sign on to something with substantial reform or their 'Old Guard' will explode."[26]

A DIRECTOR IS FOUND

The search for a director began slowly. The dilemma was to thread through the opposing views of what was required. The House leaders turned to Ron Walker, managing director of Korn/Ferry International. Walker brought to the table the prestige of one of the world's largest executive-search "headhunting" firms. He also brought his own well-honed political skills. Walker had been the head of advance for Nixon and Reagan. He was the master of political organization, running numerous Republican National Conventions. The Democrats saw in Walker a professional insider with impeccable Republican credentials. The search began.

The search ended on October 23, 1992, over six months after the reform resolution was passed. Walker had found Leonard P. Wishart III, a retired lieutenant general. "He's a general—he carries that presence," noted Walker.[27]

Wishart did have an impressive background. He graduated from the Virginia Military Institute (VMI) and West Point. In 1957 he began a thirty-four-year career in the military. He served in Vietnam and returned to West Point to be a tactical officer. Over the course of his career, Wishart became skilled at management. He had a knack and interest in running military bases. He commanded Fort Leavenworth and Fort Riley. In the process, he learned command techniques and gained an understanding of the role of—and a commitment to—training. He rose to be the deputy of the U.S. Army's Training and Doctrine Command.

Wishart retired from the army in 1991. Like many retired military in the Washington, D.C., area, Wishart became a consultant. It was while he was working with Burdeshaw Associates Ltd. that Ron Walker contacted him.

Wishart, fifty-eight, had dealt with medium-sized budgets and personnel. His largest command, Fort Leavenworth, comprised 6,202 employees and a $150 million budget, compared with the House's 14,000 employees and $800 million budget in fiscal year 1993 (October 1, 1992, to September 30, 1993). He had faced enemy fire, and he had been successful in the military. However, he had only recently entered the private sector and had never worked in the congressional environment.

His supporters felt that he would be tough enough for the task ahead. "He'll tell them what they need to hear, not what they want to hear."[28] Walker boasted, "He's had any number of very large commands. He's run great big organizations both in combat and peacetime. I think he has the temperament to deal with those members of Congress and their egos."[29]

There was general agreement that the six-month search had found the right person. However, House Rule VI was exceedingly vague. Representative Walker warned, "The legislation is pretty ill-defined."[30] Wishart joked, "The first thing is to find out what the job entails."[31]

THE COMMITTEE

The arena for sorting out "what the job entails" was to be the CHA. House Rule VI stated that the director was "subject to the policy direction and oversight of the CHA." The rule further stated that "subject to the policy direction and oversight of the CHA, the director shall have operational and financial responsibility for functions assigned by resolution of the House" (referring to the April 9, 1992, resolution).[32]

The stage was set for a series of major conflicts. Central to this process was how a House committee called "administration" and accustomed to controlling the minutest detail of House support operations, would hand over control to a person who was not a House officer and who was technically an entity of the committee.

Complicating the situation further was the fact that the April 9, 1992, resolution was in effect for the 102nd Congress (1991–1992). When Wishart took office in the 103rd Congress, his mandate had evaporated. It was left to a stretching of House Rule X, which authorized the CHA to "provide for transfers," to ensure that Wishart had something to do. This handoff to the CHA generated instant problems. The committee's culture and the agendas of its various members collided with the reform mandate, and with Wishart. The year 1993 was to become a terrible time for everyone.

The culture of intertwining every action of the House with politics was fundamental to the workings of the CHA. This committee had extensive resources to run the House. Fifteen Democrats and nine Republicans sat on the committee. The CHA had seven subcommittees, many of which reflected more an organizational chart for administrative operations than a simple legislative committee. These subcommittees included accounts, procurement and printing, personnel and police, and office systems. A professional staff of fifty-five, in addition to secretaries, receptionists, and interns, supported the CHA's work.

What most people outside Washington would consider basic low-level management issues, such as assigning parking places and issuing permits, repairing furniture, developing film, running cafeterias, and cutting paychecks, were elevated to major political issues by the CHA. The rule book issued by the CHA was a massive five-inch-thick document that outlined in amazing detail how a member could run his or her personal office. Even the member's representational allowance—an account that provided funds for the paying of staff; travel to and from the member's home district; and normal office expenses such as pens, paper, and subscriptions—was divided into accounts with strict limits and step-by-step guidance.

This might all seem contradictory to the image of the freewheeling House of the 102nd Congress. The reason for the contradiction was the way the CHA administered this rule book. First, everyone ignored the book. The rules and guidelines were a cynical fiction. Worse, wherever members required political cover for ignoring the rules, they sought a waiver from the CHA. Although the interaction for a waiver was documented in all the pomp of legal and managerial due diligence, the real discussions surrounding a waiver are lost to the ages. The countless telephone calls between members or between staff, the private discussions on the House floor or in the cloakrooms, in which waiver letters were arranged were never documented.

The truth about these waivers was that many of them were granted in exchange for legislative favors. Need an additional parking spot? Then vote with leadership on final passage of some bill. Want your sofa re-upholstered? Then stay quiet in the next committee hearing. You overspent your allowance and need more funds? Then speak at my next fundraiser and introduce me to your contact at a major political action committee (PAC). Many members of the CHA, Republicans and Democrats alike, went on to major leadership positions in the House.

This culture of political brokerage embedded itself in everything the CHA touched. The waivers, the patronage hiring, the favors—such as moving someone up on the waiting list for processing bulk mail—were all run through the CHA. It was the concept of acquiring and investing "chits" as old as Tammany Hall and the nineteenth-century political machines, as current and unseemly as the scenes in the *Godfather* movies. "What is the Constitution among friends?" said Tammany functionary Tim Campbell nearly a hundred years ago.[33] His words could have been the motto for much that happened within the CHA.

A pivotal member of the CHA during this twilight period of its existence was Representative William M. "Bill" Thomas (R-CA). Thomas began his career as a political science professor. In 1974, at age thirty-three, he successfully ran for the state legislature. He positioned himself as a conservative, pressing for the death penalty among other key issues at the time. Yet in 1976 he supported Ford over Reagan for the Republican presidential nomination during the divisive California primary. Two years later, Thomas ran for a vacant House seat as a moderate. It took seven ballots for Thomas to defeat more conservative-leaning opponents to gain the nomination.[34]

As a freshman, Thomas was named to the House ethics panel and thrust into investigating one of the worst political scandals of the time—

Abscam. This was an FBI "sting" operation that snared numerous House members taking large bribes from bogus Arab businessmen in exchange for votes. "You realize how low members can stoop when you see them scooping up gems and money and stuffing it into their pockets on FBI videotape," Thomas explained to me.

Thomas was a brilliant political partisan. In 1981, he was chosen to oppose the Democrats' outrageously one-sided redistricting of California House districts. Early on, he moved to the House Budget Committee. While on that committee, he became known as a "good detail man." David Stockman, President Reagan's director of the Office of Management and Budget, called Thomas "the official cook of the GOP kitchen," the man who could tell you what little plums—federal projects, appointments—you needed to give away to win wavering Republican votes.[35] In 1985, he led the crusade for a fair recount of an Indiana House race. When the Democrats overruled his effort, he called it "rape" and "an arrogant use of raw power."[36]

For all his political skills, his emotions got the best of him. The *Almanac of American Politics* refers to his "heated temper."[37] *Politics in America* commented, "Thomas's style does not suit all tastes. He can be snide to slower-witted colleagues of either party and quick to anger when he does not get his way."[38] The *Congressional Quarterly* assessed his personal style as one that "sometimes hampers his ability to exercise influence."[39]

This approach brought him at odds with Representative Newt Gingrich (R-GA). In 1980, Gingrich and the fledgling conservative network in the House rallied around Representative Guy Vander Jagt (R-MI) against Representative Bob Michel (R-IL) for Minority leader. Thomas counseled members to remain uncommitted, to hold out for better pledges from the two candidates. This undermined Gingrich, and Michel won.

Gingrich and Thomas were both part of the freshman class of 1979. They roomed together during their first year in Washington. Both served on the CHA during the 1980s. Whatever transpired between these two rising leaders is lost in numerous rumors and speculations. In March 1989, Thomas supported Gingrich in the close minority whip race against the more moderate Representative Madigan. As whip, Gingrich had to give up his seat as ranking Republican on the CHA. The next in line, based on seniority, was Thomas. Gingrich waged a fierce, but ultimately unsuccessful, fight to prevent Thomas from ascending to that position.

This reversal of fortunes led to other frictions between Thomas and Gingrich. In June 1991, CHA chairman Charlie Rose and Bill Thomas attended a meeting reviewing the beginnings of the House post office scandal. Gingrich was never informed by Thomas of that meeting. Gingrich would later say that the Republicans had not been kept informed on a timely basis of the widening scandal, while Foley was able to cite the Rose-Thomas meeting and fire back, "We informed the minority of the problem some time ago."[40]

The scandals of the 102nd Congress did not reflect well on Thomas. He developed a low-key watchdog role on the CHA, needling Rose about the widening scandals. His lower public profile was overshadowed by the pyrotechnics of the Gang of Seven and the Conservative Opportunity Society (COS). When member accounts were finally disclosed, it was found that Thomas had 119 overdrafts totaling $157,000 with the House bank.[41] Unlike fellow Californian Representative Riggs, who had bounced a minimal number of checks, Thomas did not face defeat during the 1992 elections. Thomas's district was strongly Republican, whereas Riggs had the misfortune of being in a marginal district and being a high-profile member of the Gang of Seven.

Gingrich and other key Republicans thought Thomas's mixed ethics record was the reason for his less-than-dynamic efforts as ranking Republican on the CHA. During the Republican Conference of December 1992, Gingrich backed a coalition of reformers and conservatives who tried to remove Thomas. Representative Paul Gillmor (R-OH) fell only twelve votes short of displacing Thomas on the administration panel.[42]

Later, as federal investigators closed in on Rostenkowski for, among other things, his spending abuses, such as spending $82,000 in the House stationery store, Thomas fired a full partisan volley at the Democrats: "Where's my $82,000? That's my first question. And who knew about this? I want to know. . . Here this guy had use of the taxpayers' money for five years . . . used the official office account for personal use and now says, 'I made a mistake and who cares?' Well I do."[43] It was later discovered that Thomas's own office had spent $81,000 during the same period. The investigative records also showed that Rose's office had spent $109,000 during this period.[44] By contrast, the average annual member expenditure for stationery store items was $11,311.[45]

These events in Thomas's political life represented a complex portrait of a powerful political figure. As the 103rd Congress began on January 3, 1993, it would be this complex man who would be at the center of Wishart's struggle with the CHA.

WISHART'S YEAR

The first major problem Wishart faced, as he began taking charge of the Office of Nonlegislative and Financial Services (NLFS), was that CHA Chairman Charlie Rose took a narrow view of what functions should be part of the new operation. When Wishart walked in the door of his modest, windowless office in the House courtyard, he only had the House post office to run. In essence, his only task was to review the work of Mike Shinay, the acting postmaster.

Nearly a month went by before Rose transferred the finance office from the clerk to Wishart.[46] Two months later, on March 31, 1993, three key operations—office furnishings, the supply service (including the stationery store and gift shop), and office-systems management (all office machines)—were approved for transfer by Rose. By April 1, 1993, only five of the twenty-two entities had been transferred to Wishart. The operation he was mandated to run remained an obsolete document discarded after the 102nd Congress.

The spring of 1993 was equally frustrating for Wishart. He found little, if any, documentation in the files regarding position descriptions, wage and position justifications, contracts, or formal operating policies and procedures. While this hunt for operational order was underway, the CHA continued to operate as if Wishart did not exist. Waiver requests flowed directly to the committee. Hiring remained in the hands of members; in fact, the Subcommittee on Personnel and Police was still operating with five members and a support staff. Reasonable requests, such as asking for written guidance from the CHA on who has contracting authority for Wishart's functions, went unanswered.[47]

On June 9, 1993, Wishart began what he thought was a fairly routine procedure to correct some position classifications within those entities that had been transferred to his office. In a letter to Rose and ranking Republican Thomas, Wishart reported on how he had conducted standard classification reviews of all employees transferred to his organization. He wrote: "There have been several instances where an individual assigned to a position was not qualified for the position or was performing the duties of another position."[48]

Wishart proposed some minor adjustments to address these issues, based on his legal obligation to enforce the House Employees Position Classification Act. This modest step to enforce the House's own Classification Act opened a hornet's nest at the CHA. Robert Shea, the Democratic staff director, would have none of it. Wishart persisted in a letter on July 13, 1993:

> You indicated yesterday that the changes effecting the two employees whose compensation would be reduced, would be deferred. . . . To continue to compensate employees at inflated salaries which are inconsistent with their jobs and the work they perform is an acknowledgment of patronage, and that is inconsistent with the charter for the director and specific guidance provided to the director.[49]

Wishart closed with: "This is not an inconsequential issue."

The months of May and June saw five more functions transferred to Wishart. The general felt he needed the ability to act within his growing operation if any form of professionalism and legal compliance was to be achieved. Then another issue erupted. An employee from the Finance Office was caught sending sensitive documents to members who were using them for partisan purposes. Although this was considered normal practice in the pre-scandal days, it was a major breach of trust in the new culture Wishart was trying to build.

Shea remained unmoved by Wishart's request to punish the employee. The combination of months of frustration, of noncommunication, of continued partisan operations all around him, led Wishart to write Speaker Foley, on July 23, 1993, describing a situation that "has undermined my continued service with the House of Representatives."[50] Wishart went on to state: "My credibility among Members, Officers, staff, and employees of the House rests upon my moral authority, my personal integrity, and the retention of an impeccable reputation for absolute candor and nonpartisanship in my dealings on all issues and with all individuals. . . . Mr. Speaker, this situation is destructive of my position and unacceptable. It must be corrected."[51]

Foley hastily called a meeting with Wishart and included both Gephardt and Michel. Wishart told them that he wanted out of the untenable position he faced. The House leaders knew that such an action would further deepen the credibility problems of the House. They had still not selected an inspector general, whose position was also mandated in the April 9, 1992, resolution. That lapse, along with the departure of Wishart, would bring the wrath of members and media down on the House. They promised to discuss the matter with Rose and extracted a promise from Wishart to "give the process time to work."

After the meeting, Michel alerted Thomas to the growing crisis with the director of NLFS and the CHA. Thomas launched his own effort to force adherence to the mandates of the 102nd Congress. He was well positioned to launch a counterattack. He was the ranking Republican on the CHA and a member of the oversight subcommittee that functioned as the primary linkage between the CHA and the director. The oversight subcommittee was organized as a bipartisan operation—two Democrats and two Republicans. Tie votes could be appealed to the full CHA.

At the August 4, 1992, meeting of the CHA's oversight subcommittee, Thomas pressed the point that the director of NLFS should have "the authority, under an approved structure, to take any personnel actions he believes necessary, including selection, appointment, assignment, transfer and termination, without exception." Thomas then offered a motion to approve Wishart's June 9 request. It was defeated on a tie vote. It was referred to the CHA for consideration.

In the wake of the defeat, Thomas negotiated with the Democrats on the CHA. Shea refused to cede any authority to Wishart. Thomas rejected all compromises, "believing them to be blatant interference with the Director's ability to run his shop professionally."[52]

The majority staff continued weekly meetings to review and dictate Wishart's activities, but did not include Republican staff or members.[53]

On November 24, 1993, sensing that the Democrats were shutting out the Republicans and shutting down Wishart, Thomas submitted a blistering indictment of the CHA's actions to Michel and Gingrich. In the letter, Thomas outlined the emptiness of the reforms and the continuing abusive patronage practices of the majority, as guided and implemented by the CHA. He went on to outline a manifesto for true nonpartisan management of House operations:

> As you know, Chairman Rose's signature is required on all official forms of the director . . . payroll changes have languished since June, and the director has a virtual "stack up" of other changes. . . .
>
> At the August 4, 1993, oversight subcommittee meeting, I strongly advocated a policy in which the director would have the authority, under an approved structure, to take any personnel actions he believes necessary, including selection, appointment, assignment, transfer, and termination, without exception. . . .
>
> I have instructed my staff that the intent here is to allow the director to operate outside the patronage, partisan system and to run his operations as much like the private sector as is feasible. . . . These combined efforts by Mr. Rose and Mr. Clay appear to be a throwback to the old practice of members' personal intervention in administrative functions.[54]

The continued undermining of the director and his reform mandate spilled onto the House floor. During the fall of 1993, various Republicans used one-minute speeches, much as the Gang of Seven used to do, to raise the issue that the reforms were not real. On October 13, freshman Representative Jim Istook (R-OK) railed against the Democrats: "The questions raised by the House post office scandal continue to attack this body, but few are willing to take the medicine of truth or responsibility. Perhaps we cannot see the illness, but it is here. Mistrust is like a virus. It grows among the public body until it can overwhelm us. The only cure is for Congress to take its medicine and clean up its act."[55]

Despite the increase in political support, Wishart remained a "bird in an ungilded cage." On January 5, 1994, Wishart wrote one last time to the CHA asking for action. He cited numerous issues arising from the House's own rules should his recommended actions not be taken. The letter went unanswered.[56] Seeing no end to this ordeal, Wishart headed for the exit:

Dear Mr. Speaker:

Over the past five months since we last met and discussed the position of the director, I have become convinced that the situation, which existed then, is not likely to change. The difficulties I encountered last summer have persisted. Further, it appears that some individuals have begun to make the director the issue, thus undermining the credibility of the office. That cannot be helpful to you or to the House. . . . It is my hope that a new director will enjoy greater success and my departure now will achieve a more useful purpose than any short-term benefit my continued service as director might provide.[57]

MEDLOCK

Wishart's letter was released to the media. Its impact was surprisingly minimal. The public had given up on the 103rd Congress. It was now moving toward a major revolution at the voting booths later that year, and nothing the House did could change that outcome.

Wishart left quietly on January 21, just over a year after taking office. His deputy, former military officer Randy Medlock, became the acting director.

Medlock's tour of duty was no more productive than Wishart's. The same personnel issues piled up. The CHA continued to ignore even the most mundane management requests.

In a letter to Rose, Thomas wrote:

Attached is a memo . . . in which he [Medlock] discusses your staff's unilateral decision to second guess the director's employment decisions by refusing to process several merit pay increases. The reasons for this blatant and partisan interference are irrelevant; Republicans were never informed of this action by anyone on your staff.

By unilaterally vetoing employment decisions of the director, your staff has taken another giant leap backwards toward the days of patronage and partisan interference in the nonlegislative services of the House. . . . We demand that corrective action be taken. . . .

If you do not take one of these steps, we will have no alternative but to assume that your stated commitment to the bipartisan structure is no longer valid.[58]

THE HOUSE RESTAURANTS

Since the restaurant scandal of 1991, the House food service had been under increasing pressure to move to service-based operations. The quality and selection of food remained mediocre and the costs of subsidizing food operations ran over a million dollars a year.

In January 1993, the carryout and snack bar in House Annex 2 was noncompetitively contracted out to a firm from Rose's home district. Significantly, this contract was entered into while the CHA delayed the mandated transfer of food operations to Wishart. Once this contract was fully in effect, food services were transferred to Wishart on June 1, 1993.

Other food-service actions by Rose raised more concern. On March 9, 1994, the full CHA met to mark up legislative authorizations. Representative Clay introduced a resolution to mandate the contracting out of all House food services. Tucked away in the resolution was a freeze on all employment in the director's office. The Republicans were taken by surprise as the resolution sailed through with limited discussion on a 12–7 party-line vote.[59] Thomas, who enjoyed good relations with the reporters and editors of *Roll Call*, fired them up on the blatant power play of Rose. In a March 14, 1994, editorial titled "Charlie's Ploy," *Roll Call* wrote:

> Rose was a bully. No advance notice of the transfer [mandate to contract out food service] was given to House administration Republicans. When they objected, they were ruled out of order. The transfer passed on a straight party-line vote. What's worse, Rose bypassed the House director of nonlegislative and financial services, who earlier was told to conduct a yearlong study on the restaurants. . . . Rose's action was a throwback to the bad old days.[60]

Medlock eventually contracted out the House restaurants, but with much of the contract language dictated by CHA staff. These elaborate

CHA-dictated provisions would hinder food service during the 104th Congress.

FINANCIAL AUDIT OF THE HOUSE

Representative Thomas decided to mount his next assault at the fundamental issue of the General Accounting Office's (GAO's) independence. The House's internal fiscal year coincides with the calendar year. The GAO would begin reviewing the House's books as the new year began and release its findings in July. These findings would reflect on the House's financial activities for the previous full calendar year. Therefore, the GAO's review of 1993 was ready for release in July 1994. On July 28, 1994, with the GAO's draft report in hand, Thomas met with Charles Bowsher, the comptroller general.

At the meeting, Thomas criticized the practices of the GAO. Bowsher countered with a letter to Thomas, on August 4, attempting to reassure him about the validity of GAO audit procedures. Thomas followed up with a letter to Bowsher on August 18: "My overall concern is that these audits misrepresent the scope of the GAO's work, therefore their validity and independence is in doubt." [61]

Thomas went on, point by point, to dismantle the assertions of the GAO. He hammered away on the House Finance Office's refusal to grant the GAO access to its computer records and the GAO's willingness to accept looking only at the handwritten financial ledgers of the House. He also was critical of the GAO's not reconciling the hand ledgers with the House's rudimentary computerized financial system then in use:

> Given refusals to the GAO's request for access to the computer systems, and then this year's inability of the GAO to complete any such review due to "problems," I believe we have virtually guaranteed a scenario in which the House Finance Office, in order to avoid having its computer systems reviewed or audited, may never fully automate its books and will retain a duplicate record keeping system.[62]

Thomas also criticized the GAO's review of payroll transactions: "The fact that documents were missing was discovered when finance tried to comply with a subpoena. Further investigation found that several finance office policies had been routinely violated in past years. Now I have discovered that these same issues were raised by the GAO in the 1991 and 1992 'close-out conferences.'"[63]

Thomas completed his indictment of GAO by assaulting its lack of communication with members: "At no time has the GAO or the Finance Office brought the concerns outlined above to the attention of the members of the Committee on House Administration, the committee responsible for oversight of the Finance Office. At least they have not been brought to the attention of Republicans on the committee."[64]

Laying the groundwork for what would become a key element of the "Contract with America," Thomas ended: "Given the GAO's performance to date in this matter, however, I agree that perhaps we should seek expertise elsewhere."[65]

LAINHART

Part of the package of administrative reforms passed on April 12, 1992, included the creation of an Office of Inspector General with very limited scope and powers.[66]

The last straw for Republicans was that the resolution authorized only one additional professional staff member and one clerical staff member for the inspector general's office. Such a limited mandate, combined with only two other employees, made the entire effort an empty gesture toward real accountability in the House.

The resolution passed, despite vehement Republican objections and misgivings. The search for someone willing to take the doomed assignment would take more than eighteen months.

On October 27, 1993, Speaker Foley, with the backing of Representatives Gephardt and Michel, announced the appointment of John W. Lainhart IV as the House's first inspector general. Lainhart, about to turn forty-seven, had just spent the last four years as the assistant inspector general overseeing policy, planning, and technical support at the Department of Transportation (DOT). He began his career as an auditor with Price Waterhouse. In 1980, Lainhart moved to the public sector and began rising in the auditing ranks at the GAO. He then moved to the

DOT's inspector general's office in 1984, as director of the Office of Automatic Data Processing Audits and Technical Support.[67]

As Lainhart was moving into his two-room office in House Annex 2, Wishart was packing up to leave his two-room office in the Capitol basement. By the end of January 1994, Lainhart was staffed and operational. However, Wishart, a strong potential ally for Lainhart's building of system integrity, was gone.

Just as Wishart labored under frustrating conditions, so did Lainhart. On September 15, 1994, Lainhart sent a memorandum to his oversight panel, the CHA, stating that eight more professionals would be needed if he were to fulfill his mandate.[68] Another major appointee of the 103rd Congress was confronting the institutional inertia of the House. In an ironic way, the eighteen-month delay in Lainhart's appointment may have saved him. For just as his frustration levels rose, the Republican era began.

THE MANIFESTO
FOR REVOLUTION

September 27, 1994

As Republican Members of the House of Representatives, and as citizens seeking to join that body, we propose not just to change its policies, but even more important, to restore the bonds of trust between the people and their elected representatives. That is why, in this era of official evasion and posturing, we offer instead a detailed agenda for national renewal, a written commitment with no fine print.[1]

—Newt Gingrich and others, *Contract with America*

The day was sunny. Three hundred members of Congress and candidates for Congress stood on the west front of the U.S. Capitol and smiled for the legions of photographers. It was a bold stroke. It was unlike the national party platforms that are crafted every four years and quickly forgotten. Representative Gingrich and his inner circle had created a true manifesto for change. Both supporters and detractors viewed the document as a manifesto for revolution.

The years of being in the political wilderness were coming to a close. The candidates could feel it as they campaigned in their home districts. John Morgan and the other Republican pollsters and demographers could see it rising in their tracking polls. Many strands of history were converging toward a watershed moment: the legacy of limited government from the Reagan era, the mounting problems surrounding President Clinton relating to his failed national health plan and the Whitewater scandal, the rise of Gingrich and his allies among the reformers and the Conservative Opportunity Society, the deepening of cynicism about the federal government among the electorate, and the compilation of scandals and abuses by government in general and the House in particular.

To prepare for this convergence, a small group of leaders gathered for dinner to discuss what it would mean to be in the majority. Representatives Armey, DeLay, Gingrich, Paxon, and Walker laid out plans for forging a unified strategy for victory and governance. The dinners led to formal planning sessions held every Thursday through 1993 and 1994. Representative John Kasich (R-OH) joined the team to provide his insights into budget issues.[2]

The result of these sessions was the "Contract with America." It was a sweeping manifesto pledging specific actions to address specific issues. It was quite similar to those issued at the beginning of parliamentary campaigns in England, but was quite unprecedented for American politics.

The primary focus of the national media was on the "contract's" ten major policy bills. Gingrich pledged a House vote during the first hundred days of the 104th Congress. Yet the first substantive pledge in the contract was that

the very first day of a Republican House will bring marked change to the business as usual seen in the House of Representatives since 1954.

- Apply all laws to Congress.
- Cut the number of committees and subcommittees and cut committee staffs by a third.
- Limit the terms of committee chairs and ranking members.
- Ban "proxy" (ghost) voting in committee.
- Implement an "honest numbers" budget with a zero baseline.
- Require committee meetings to be open to the public.
- Require three-fifths majority to pass a tax increase.
- Audit the House's books with an independent firm.[3]

The Republican pledge was to enact these major changes on the first day of the Republican era. Only then would the policy agenda be addressed: "After changing the way the House does business, Republicans will change the business the House does."[4]

Republican members, along with a small brigade of staff, began to draft the mechanics of "changing the way the House does business." They drew from three legislative proposals that had formed the foundation for debate on administering the House: the 1977 Obey Commission bill, the House Administrative Reform Resolution from April 1992, and the Michel substitute for the reform resolution. They also had to take into account another approach to running the House that had arisen in the late spring of 1994. It was to be the last battle of the last session of the old plantation culture: the Shays bill.

THE SHAYS BILL

The reform resolution that passed in April 1992 was not the final chapter for the Joint Committee on the Organization of Congress. The committee lived on, with both a Senate and a House component. The set of recommendations reported in November 1993 opened a new round of debate. Many of the old guard in the House and Senate thought that the committee had gone too far, whereas the reformers considered the changes too modest and in some cases, counter to the intent of their mandate.

Two House members emerged as pivotal in this new round of debates over the future administrative and procedural environment of the chamber. Representative David Dreier (R-CA) was swept into office in 1980 as part of the Reagan landslide. As an aggressive and articulate conservative, Dreier tried to press major reforms for the executive branch during Reagan's two terms, only to see them die before the Democratic-controlled committees of the House. Representative Christopher Shays (R-CT) was elected in a special election in 1987 and immediately positioned himself as a maverick against the ways of Washington. One of his most notable early remarks was to Ronald Reagan, telling the president that he could not count on his [Mr. Shays's] vote 100 percent of the time.[5] Shays went on to reach out from his own party to work in bipartisan coalitions, including joining with Representatives Tom Tauke (R-IA) and Tim Penny (D-MN) in a task force to find solutions for balancing the federal budget.[6]

In the spring and summer of 1994, these two members, Dreier with a solidly conservative 100 percent voting record and Shays building a liberal and renegade style with a 24 percent conservative record, became leaders in wanting real change in the way the House operated.

Dreier was well positioned to press for change. He was selected, in the wake of the April 1992 resolution, to be the ranking Republican on the joint committee. When in November 1993 the joint committee issued its report (H. Rep. 103-413), he pressed for the immediate adoption of its recommendations. However, the legislation, House Resolution 3801, got bogged down in its details. Some reformers felt it still did not go far enough, whereas many of the "old guard" raised concerns that any reform might damage the continuity of the institution.

At the same time, the Senate counterpart legislation ran into strong institutional opposition. The Senate lacked an organized reform coalition. This "upper" chamber had not gone through anything like the recent scandals in the House. As a result, the change effort was not a priority, and the reform legislation arrived with no hope of quick or serious action.

Speaker Foley, backed by the House Rules Committee, stopped House Resolution 3801 in June 1994. The only portion of the joint committee's recommendations that would go forward would be those addressing congressional compliance with certain employment and safety regulations.

Traditionally, the Congress had exempted itself from all regulations. Citing the separation-of-powers doctrine, Congress felt that allowing executive branch regulatory agencies to enforce their rules against another branch of government would weaken the Constitution. To many reformers, however, this constitutional argument masked the real reason. To them, the dirty little secret of Washington was that the Congress knew how crippling and nonsensical these regulations really were to businesses, and members did not want to labor under a similar burden.

This hypocritical combination of publicly expressing commitment for regulations while privately undermining attempts at reform culminated in the wholesale exemption of Congress from all federal employment and safety regulations. This holding back of regulatory reality from the Congress was viewed as the most cynical of acts by a new reform caucus founded by Representative Shays. Shays mounted an effort to bring the full weight of private-sector regulation "home to roost" in the Congress. Shays's bill, House Resolution 2739, had bipartisan backing by the compliance reformers. They avoided the separation-of-powers issue by establishing an independent compliance board that would enforce and adjudicate the regulations. Under this legislation, Congress would be subject to many of the most burdensome laws, including the Occupational Safety and Health Act, the Equal Employment Opportunity Act, the Americans with Disabilities Act, and all fair-employment and fair-labor standards.

The legislative struggle occurred on two fronts. Some reformers, headed by Dreier, wanted to keep the entire package together, stating that passage of just Shays's compliance component would allow the Congress to avoid needed overall reform. Shays and his coalition contended that something is better than nothing, and after all, the House Rules Committee had already stopped the comprehensive bill. The traditionalists began to pick apart the Shays bill, attempting to limit its scope and to minimize its impact. These opponents raised concerns over the potential costs of the Shays bill, stating that the act might require major retrofitting of offices and that there might be high overtime payments to staff.[7] The joint committee leader, Representative Lee Hamilton (D-IN), stated, "Everyone is for reform in a general way. It is always the specifics that kill it."[8]

Republican unity behind the Shays bill was restored with an internal agreement to press for all reforms over time. Representative Roscoe Bartlett (R-MD) spoke for many when he called the Shays bill "just a down payment" on a pledge to increase the "integrity of the institution."[9] However, on August 4, 1994, the House Rules Committee, using party-line votes, put forward a weaker bill, House Resolution 4822, and then rejected a series of Republican amendments that would have restored much of the language of the Shays bill.

Representative Dreier, a member of the Rules Committee, was also thwarted in bringing his comprehensive bill up as an amendment. Democrats on the panel felt that further reform should be delayed until the impact of existing reforms could be evaluated. "The House had not had time to assess the extraordinary changes we made at the beginning of this Congress," complained Representative Louise Slaughter (D-NY). Dreier was appalled at this view, "I think they were minor changes. Why the hell did we establish the Joint Committee?"[10]

One of the biggest disappointments was the removal of a provision that would have subjected selected nonlegislative operations of the House to the Freedom of Information Act (FOIA). "If the FOIA had applied to Congress, there would never have been a House bank scandal, never have been a post office scandal or a restaurant scandal," observed Representative Boehner.[11] Representative Solomon, the ranking Republican on the Rules Committee, was appalled: "The new scandal is the way the Democratic leadership is sweeping real reform under the rug."[12]

The highly modified Shays bill passed the House 427–4 on August 10, 1994. The passage of a separate compliance bill "amounted to selling out the larger reform package," according to Dreier. As to Speaker Foley's pledge that other reforms would be considered, Dreier commented that it was a pledge "written in fool's ink."[13]

The House bill quickly ran aground in the Senate. Concerns over interchamber coordination of the compliance board were among the last-minute issues raised to sink the legislation. It remained for the House to try again, with time running out on the last session of the 103rd Congress, to pass some form of the Shays bill. They attempted it as a House rule.

On October 7, 1994, a House rule, House Resolution 578, passed 348–3. The House had something they could take to the voters proving their sincerity for changing the institution. However, the bill was weaker than even the version passed in August. Among other things, House employees still could not take their grievances to the federal courts. Shays protested that it was "a halfway measure that would undermine efforts to do the job right in the 104th Congress next January." Dreier charged that the entire process was "designed to fool the American people into believing we live by the same rules as everyone else."[14]

One month later, on November 8, the reformers' battles with the ruling Democrats were resolved, in their favor, by the voters. By a historic landslide, the Democrats were purged from the House, the Senate, and in state capitols across America. Not one Republican incumbent was defeated at either the federal or state level. It was a resounding mandate for change. The reformers had won their battle with the past. The reformers' battle for the future, much of it waged within their own Republican Party, was set to begin.

THE OPEN HOUSE

Jim Nussle's transition team began working around the clock as soon as they could collect themselves in the transition offices. They were racing the clock. The Republican Conference to select leaders and to adopt rules for the 104th Congress loomed less than a month away. To launch the most sweeping changes since the 1946 Legislative Reorganization Act, and possibly in the 207-year history of the House, Nussle had to have enough of his reforms fleshed out to sell key members. This meant that major themes and directions of the reforms would have to be readied by Thanksgiving.

On November 9, Gingrich fired off a letter to outgoing Speaker Foley warning Democrats not to remove or destroy documents. He had learned from the reports of mass shredding parties in the wake of the Republican Senate takeover in 1980. At that time, incoming Majority Leader Howard Baker cautiously moved against the outgoing Democrats, allowing many Democrats to retain operational control and sit in highly desirable office space through the summer of 1981. Gingrich was not going to make that same mistake.

Gingrich also heeded the advice of legislative scholars to move quickly on his reforms before all the committee assignments were made, to avoid creating a set of Republican chairmen with a vested interest in the status quo.[15] He appointed Representative Dreier to head a revamping of the committees. His hope was to abolish many antiquated forums and to fundamentally realign jurisdictions prior to naming new chairmen. This overhaul would also allow for cutting committee staffs by a third.

In addition to directing Representative Dreier to resurrect his committee and procedural reforms, Gingrich directed Representative Shays to update his compliance legislation, with the promise of its becoming House Resolution 1, the first legislative business of the 104th Congress. These major delegations allowed Nussle to focus, along with the Gang of Seven, on completely rethinking House administrative operations. Nussle pledged, "If we are naive enough to keep running business as usual, we will meet with the same demise that the Democrats met this time."[16]

Nussle was aided primarily by Boehner. Boehner wanted to make the administrative reforms reflect the fact that Republicans could, among other things, cut government spending. He wanted to revisit the legislative branch appropriations for 1995. Earlier he stated, "If we're going to lead by example, this is the place to do it, this is the time to do it."[17]

Gingrich weighed in with his own approach to House reform during his first major speech after the November 8 elections. On November 11, Veterans Day, before the Washington Research Group Symposium, the incoming Speaker of the House outlined his major objectives for the next two years.

He began by outlining his view of leadership. Using a successful model from World War II, he described his own approach:

> Essentially they had a four-layer model, and it's a hierarchy. The top of it was vision, and after you understood your vision of what you're doing, you designed strategies, and once you have your vision and strategies clear, you designed projects which were the building blocks of your strategies, and inside the context of those projects you delegated dramatically an entrepreneurial model in which a project was a definable, delegatable achievement. Eisenhower's job was to invade the continent of Europe, defeat the German army and occupy the German heartland. His actual order from the combined chiefs was two paragraphs; all the rest was detail. That's delegation on a fairly grand scale. At the bottom of the model is tactics, what you do every day.[18]

Reflecting back to his floor speech of April 1991, Gingrich went on to discuss the works of Dr. W. Edwards Deming and recommended that all members study the concepts of quality.[19] He then stated his own mandated priority of bringing the House into the twenty-first century:

> We will change the rules of the House to require that all documents and all conference reports and all committee reports be filed electronically as well as in writing and that they cannot be filed until they are available

to any citizen who wants to pull them up. Thus, information will be available to every citizen in the country at the same moment that it is available to the highest paid Washington lobbyist. Over time, that will change the entire flow of information and the entire quality of knowledge in the country.[20]

Gingrich outlined specific actions that would flow from the "Contract with America." He renewed his commitment to passing the Shays bill on the opening day of the session. He discussed the cuts in committees and committee staffs. He ended with a pledge for real reform and a dire warning: "Let me say one last thing: If this just degenerates, after an historic election, back into the usual baloney of politics in Washington, and pettiness in Washington, then the American people, I believe, will move toward a third party in a massive way. I think they are fed up with Washington, they are fed up with its games."[21]

Critical to making this mandated reform real was sorting out the administration of House operations. Nussle and his team were well aware of the difficulties encountered by Wishart and Medlock. The person they selected had to have real duties, and clear reporting authority. To resolve these issues, they needed to rethink the jurisdiction and powers of the CHA.

On November 30, 1994, Nussle and his team presented Republican leaders with their blueprint for "changing the way the House does business." Nussle declared that the dramatic changes to House operations "were necessary to restore efficiency in its operations and accountability by its officials."[22]

Nussle reviewed the prior problems of the House:

In current House operations, there are vested interests in maintaining power, in perpetuating a political system where individual members call the shots and get the breaks. These problems are largely because political advantage and patronage have become the dominant characteristics of the House's administrative operations. Too many issues have been decided on what they mean for personal fiefdoms, not what they mean for the public good. Decisions have been made in secret, by staff or members of only one party, for reasons unclear to most House members, media, or the public.

The extra services, bloated staffs, and layers of offices have helped the fiefdoms of a few individual members but harmed the functioning of the institution.[23]

Nussle's report continued with a review of the "lessons learned from past scandals and the unsuccessful attempts at institutional reform":

> The "nonpartisan label" has served to hide partisan maneuvering. It is our judgment that openness and party accountability are the best combination in administering House affairs.
>
> Accountability will lead to efficiency and openness. House operations will be open for the first time ever to public examination.
>
> Incrementalism doesn't work: bold, dramatic overhaul is needed. The experiment of the director for nonlegislative and financial services (NLFS) was a makeshift, incremental change, failing under the continued secrecy and inefficiency of the old regime. The old structure must be scrapped completely before any reorganization can make a difference. We need new offices, new distributions of functions, and new lines of authority.[24]

Nussle's proposed new model for House operations would have a new conceptual framework:

- The basic structure would consist of seven entities reporting to the new Speaker, with four of these representing elected Officers of the House (Clerk, Chief Administrative Officer, Sergeant-at-Arms, and Chaplain). General oversight would be provided by the House Oversight Committee and the Inspector General. Oversight of specific employment and other matters would be provided by the new Office of Compliance.
- The mission of the House Oversight Committee would be to provide greater emphasis on developing broad policy recommendations and alternatives to the House rules that govern administrative procedures. It would concentrate its oversight responsibilities on major management issues and limit its involvement in day-to-day administration operations.
- The Inspector General (IG) would be provided with the necessary resources to permit him to carry out the functions assigned to that office.
- Starting in January, the Inspector General would manage the audit of the House financial accounts by private sector auditors.

- The Congressional Compliance Office would be established to ensure the applicability of several federal laws to the House and provide a forum for employee grievances.
- The Clerk of the House would be responsible for all activities involving the administration of the legislative process.
- The Sergeant-at-Arms would continue to be responsible for those House functions relating to the Capitol Police, security, law enforcement, and protocol.
- The administrative functions of the House would be organized and performed under the direction of the new Chief Administrative Officer.[25]

These changes, especially eliminating obsolete positions like the door-keeper, were designed to wrench the House into the late twentieth century with one set of dramatic changes. However, the most significant and controversial change was the role of the CHA. Ever since the Obey Commission's recommendations of 1977, the CHA's role had been under assault. As long as members could minutely direct support actions for members, there would be a potential for abuse. The only solution was to "decouple" the CHA from day-to-day operations.

The original Republican proposals in 1992 went so far as to eliminate the CHA completely. In its place, they proposed a smaller "Administrative Committee" composed of equal numbers of Republicans and Democrats, whose sole responsibility would be to develop annual oversight plans for improving House operations. This left a fully-independent chief financial officer and administrator in charge of administrative functions and financial integrity.[26]

As Nussle finalized his plans, issues arose as to the roles and responsibilities of the CHA. Gingrich wanted full authority to hire and fire the administrator, independently of the CHA, which would consolidate the Speaker's authority and accountability over House operations.

Some form of the CHA would still be needed as the authorizing body for legislative spending and as the arbiter of contested House elections. A committee of jurisdiction for campaign-finance legislation and for the oversight of the Federal Election Commission (FEC) was also required. The House could follow the example of the Senate and assign all of these to the Rules Committee, eliminating the need for a CHA. This option was discussed, as Gingrich wished to further reward Representative Solomon.

The discussion over how to handle the CHA dominated much of November 1994. A "board of directors" providing limited and general policy guidance, but having no daily say in the operations of the House, arose as the possible approach. This aligned well with Gingrich's "Vision, Strategy, Projects, Tactics." It was assumed that Gingrich, and the transition team, would articulate a vision for what the House should become. The new administrator would work with them to develop a strategy that would be formalized by the new Committee on House Oversight (CHO). These approved "projects" would then be implemented by the administrator. The administrator would also carry out the routine daily "tactics" with no political interference. The administrator would be accountable to Gingrich, and Gingrich would be accountable to the House and the American electorate.

However, another issue entered into this power equation. California, with twenty-five Republican members, was the single largest Republican delegation in the new House. Yet despite these numbers, California Republicans could count only one leadership position, that of Representative Christopher Cox (R-CA), chairman of the Republican Policy Committee. Cox's election was still not a sure thing. Representative Ron Packard (R-CA) was in a position to chair an Appropriations subcommittee, and Representative Thomas potentially would chair a Ways and Means subcommittee, but these were subcommittees, not full committees. The Californians were restive.

Under the proposed rules, Gingrich would appoint the members of the new CHO. Representative Nussle had hoped he would be rewarded with the chairmanship, thereby assuring complete alignment between the transition and the implementation. Thomas had been a problematic member, with ethical issues of his own relating to the House bank and gift shop.

Despite all that had transpired in the 102nd and 103rd Congresses, Gingrich announced Thomas as head of the new CHO. Gang of Seven member and new chairman of the Republican Conference, Representative Boehner, would be representing leadership on the panel. Nussle would not be a member of the CHO but would remain active as transition director as long as required.

This stunned many reformers. Nussle felt betrayed. No one understood why Gingrich, the man who tried to prevent Thomas from becoming the ranking member of the CHA in March 1989, would now present him with a chairmanship so central to the management revolution. Their concerns about Thomas's commitment to real revolution were somewhat eased by their own successful efforts to formalize a strong change program during the Republican Conference of December 5–7, including the sale of one House office building and the elimination of twenty-eight taxpayer-supported caucuses.[27]

However, some saw the beginnings of Gingrich's striking a balance between being an insurgent and an institutionalist.[28] Freshman Representative Lindsey Graham (R-SC) raised the need to carefully monitor Gingrich's intellectual consistency and hold the incoming Speaker to the mandate he created: "I trust Newt Gingrich to lead us to the promised land, but the good Lord never let Moses go. We'll do to him what the good Lord did to Moses."[29]

A CHIEF ADMINISTRATIVE OFFICER IS CREATED

The Republican Conference of December 5–7 adopted a draft set of rules to govern the 104th Congress. Embedded in these rules were the means and the mandates for fundamentally changing the way the House operated. They also sowed the seeds for controversy.

Issue #1: To Whom Should the Administrator Report? Rule V of the House established the chief administrative officer (CAO) as an officer of the House. It elevated the old director's position out from under the old CHA. The CAO would still "be subject to the policy direction and oversight of the Speaker and the Committee on House Oversight (CHO)."[30] Under Rule X, the CHO was to have the general responsibility of "providing policy direction for, and oversight of, the clerk, sergeant at arms, chief administrative officer, and inspector general."[31]

It was hoped, by Nussle and Gingrich, that Thomas's defense of the managerial independence of Wishart would remain consistent during the 104th Congress. In addition, Gingrich set up an elaborate system for the CAO to report to the Speaker's staff on a regular basis and for the transition team to remain operational through the 104th Congress. Under these arrangements, Nussle would sit in on weekly operational sessions of the House officers and conduct his own weekly reviews of the transition's progress. The CHO would follow the dictates from the Speaker's office and the transition, serving as a forum to review, in open hearings, and formalize their strategic plans.

Issue #2: What Should the Administrator's Mandate and Portfolio Be? House Rule V immediately transferred all operations previously mandated to the director of nonlegislative and financial services. This made the CAO, on the first day of the 104th Congress, the "city manager" of the House. The CAO's jurisdiction was over all nonlegislative and nonsecurity functions. Under Rule III, the clerk would retain parliamentary support functions, and under Rule IV, the sergeant at arms would become a fully-professionalized security official.[32]

Issue #3: What Kind of Person Should Be the Administrator? The search for a CAO began in earnest in late November 1994. A number of conservative activists were campaigning for the doorkeeper's post, not realizing it had been abolished. Their narrow credentials of being "good conservatives," with only political and government experience, eliminated a number of prominent "movement" candidates. Nussle and Gingrich were adamant that the person should be someone from outside government. They wanted someone who could take a fresh look at House operations without any loyalty to the old order. Gingrich also hoped for someone with a background in quality management.

Nussle and Linder interviewed a dozen candidates and reviewed the résumés of dozens more. Most lacked one key ingredient—they had no record of designing or implementing major management reforms. Most conservatives with management experience from the Reagan era had no substantive achievements in management reform. This could have been the result of either their confronting seemingly invincible institutional barriers to change or their own lack of knowledge or will to make major changes.

The leads from the private sector fell short as well. Most were priced far above the $124,800 that remained the legal limit for paying House officers. Others could not disengage from their business holdings to adhere to the House's complex financial-disclosure and conflict-of-interest regulations. Many businessmen, remembering the horror stories of previous private-sector appointees from the Reagan, Bush, and Clinton administrations, were unwilling to run the Washington gauntlet of probing news media and zealous government investigators. They saw too many careers ruined. Worse, they watched as ultimately-vindicated professionals ran up massive legal bills to clear their names.

It was now early December. The transition team needed not only a CAO-designate but also a person who could bring in a team to make their historic agenda an operational reality. They wanted a person who could and would navigate the treacherous shoals of Congress. They wanted someone who actually wanted what they wanted, a revolution.

In the midst of this search, a proposal for training the transition team in change management and quality principles was circulated. My package, submitted on behalf of the Farragut Management Institute (FMI), had landed on Dan Meyer's desk on November 19. Representative Frank Wolf (R-VA), with a personal note attached, sent a similar copy of the proposal to Nussle on November 27. The proposal had been rejected, as things were moving too fast for training, but now, on the morning of December 7, 1994, Dan Meyer reopened the FMI package.

It all began to make sense. Dan recalled that I had been in the private sector for five years, working with Fortune 500 companies on change management. More importantly, I was a follower of quality guru Philip Crosby, having taught Dan and all of the Gingrich staff back in 1991. I had also been a legislative staffer in the House in the 1970s. In fact, he had been a leader of the parliamentary guerilla fighters, and a friend and colleague of Gingrich allies, Solomon and Walker. Dan reviewed the professional credentials attached to the package. It related to my role in the 1980–1981 presidential transition and his roles in designing and leading change in a number of major agencies through the eight years of the Reagan administration. Dan wondered if it were possible that I, and my FMI team, could become the implementers of the House's management revolution.

Dan Meyer looked over at Jack Howard and handed him the FMI package. "Give Faulkner a call. I think we found our administrator."

★ LIFE'S LESSONS ★

Saturday, July 2, 1994

"On my count of three we cut the ribbon," explained Senator Robert Byrd (D-WV), taking charge of the situation. We all lined up with scissors at the ready. Brad Nash, former mayor of Harpers Ferry, and I were both cochairs of this amazing celebration. The senator and Don Campbell, the park superintendent, stood near the middle. The director of the National Park Service and the director of the National Capital Region completed the lineup of dignitaries.

"One, two, THREE." We each sliced through the long red ribbon. The National Park Service's new exhibit on John Brown was officially open.

The crowd erupted in joyous applause. Earlier, the folk group Magpie's tribute to Harpers Ferry National Historical Park touched everyone. The memorable tune and poignant lyrics had resounded through every event during the celebration week. We had all hoped it would be a memorable "theme song" for the park, and it was.

As the ribbon pieces fell to the ground, we all moved inside to the air-conditioned exhibit. It was a welcome reprieve from the heat outside. It was hot, but sunny, for the grand finale of Harpers Ferry National Historical Park's fiftieth-anniversary celebration. Everything was going like clockwork. Fifteen months of preparation and effort was paying off.

The celebration was a time for me to reflect on Harpers Ferry, its history, and its "essence." Harpers Ferry is a true community. Everyone knows everyone else. There is a fundamental commitment by all who live there to help honor its long history and to make things better for the future. Such a mix is increasingly rare in America. My ability to escape the transitory and false nature of Washington, D.C., and to immerse in this corner of real America, provided a much-needed balance and a "dose of reality" to what I had to cope with working in the nation's capital.

Many in Washington never have such an opportunity. The result is a kind of science-fiction world that politicians, lobbyists, journalists, and bureaucrats enter, and most never leave. The insane laws, the absurd regulations, and the excesses in spending flow from a sensory deprivation of real-world inputs. Those inside the Beltway actually believe that their every word and every deed is more important than anything done by anyone living outside this tiny world. They believe that they are somehow brighter, better, and, therefore, inherently more deserving of trust, tax dollars, and media coverage.

My life's experiences ranged far beyond the narrow world of the Washington Beltway. These experiences shaped what I did in the 104th Congress. There were also many special people from whom I learned fundamental life lessons.

The kind of politics I embraced was a legacy of my mother's lifelong devotion to the Republican Party. Early in my life, she introduced me to books by major philosophers and political thinkers. In the sixth and seventh grades, I was reading the works of Henry David Thoreau and Ralph Waldo Emerson. By eighth grade, I was delving into William F. Buckley and Ayn Rand. In ninth grade, Ayn Rand's *Atlas Shrugged* was a revelation in how destructive government can be if allowed to expand unchecked. As a child, I would help my mother stuff envelopes and put together precinct kits for numerous local New Hampshire candidates that have faded into history. I still remember piles of Nixon-Lodge buttons from 1960. The "This House Sold on Goldwater" yard sign that stood on our front lawn still hangs in my home office.

My father was one of the first wildlife biologists, hired by the U.S. Fish and Wildlife Service. Through his eyes I learned the many dimensions of the environment, from tracking animals to identifying birds from their calls and trees from their leaves. He taught me wilderness survival and how to protect and enhance wildlife habitat. His work on animal behavior led me to a lifelong commitment to the environment.

As I grew up, my father took me on field trips to wildlife refuges and to his research sites. He was a leader in rebuilding populations of many endangered species, including the whooping crane, the black-footed ferret, the Kirkland Warbler, the bald eagle, and the timber wolf. I spent many hours as a teenager walking in wilderness areas, watching bald eagles and listening to wolves. The result of this immersion in wildlife led to my first "political" leadership role as the local organizer, at age sixteen, for the first Earth Day observance in April 1970.

A lifetime of these interactions shaped my being. It is, therefore, insightful to review these key people and the lessons I brought with me to Congress.

Lesson #1: Politics Is Not an End in Itself. Growing up in rural America, I saw how many people live lives and accomplish many things without attachment to a political party or a link to Washington, D.C. Although I would spend much of my life "fighting the good fight" in the political realm, this observation taught me that one could walk away from politics and still have a life. My being able to earn a living and be professionally and personally fulfilled without politics is like a drug addict being able to kick a drug dependency. It is liberating and it is healthy.

Lesson #2: We Are Only a Small Element in the Giant Flow of History. The lesson of history is that something always leads to something else. No one idea or one accomplishment "just happens." There is plenty of preliminary activity that prepares for a key historical moment, and there are many ripple effects that then occur and impact the future. The saying goes, "We stand on the shoulders of giants." Perhaps one day when we have passed from the scene, and if we are lucky to have left a positive legacy, future generations will stand on our shoulders to accomplish things currently beyond our grasp.

This understanding of historical context served me well from a number of perspectives. First, it, like lesson #1, was an ongoing reality check. I have seen too many people in politics think that they are the center of some golden age. The age begins with them and ends with them. They are the first to do something and it is all of their own making. Not remembering that they are but part of a larger flow leads to immense ego and not looking for answers beyond themselves. Second, as is often aptly stated, "Those who forget history are bound to repeat it." We can find answers, insights, and "rules of thumb" for everything we face by looking to similar historical events.

A third dimension of this concept is that our lives are interwoven with many people and many unfolding events. A sage once said, "All politics is local." I would take that concept one step further: "All politics is personal." People who helped each other once will rally to assist years later. Grudges and feuds also resurface years later in different forums, but with the same players or their surrogates. Because the ego-driven culture of Washington, D.C., has such a lack of interest in historical perspectives, most people completely miss the real reasons some things happen and other things do not.

Lesson #3: Always Think Holistically. I attended Lawrence University, a small liberal-arts college on the banks of the Fox River in Appleton, Wisconsin. Lawrence University prides itself on remaining a classic liberal-arts institution. Its Freshman Studies program places a random assortment of freshman with a leading professor for the first semester. The primary purpose of the program is for every freshman, whether a science, music, or government major, to learn how to learn. This immersion in pure intellectual inquiry was a life-changing experience for me. Its lessons of looking at all aspects of an issue, putting it in a broad context, and applying multiple disciplines to it, has served me well.

Lesson #4: Change Is Difficult and Will Always Be Opposed. The single most important book I read in Freshman Studies was Thomas Kuhn's *The Structure of Scientific Revolutions.* At the time, the book seemed insurmountable. Kuhn was a professor at MIT and had become fascinated by the history of science. He wrote this incredible book on how the existing dogma, or paradigm, of the day inevitably felt threatened by new discoveries. This is why Galileo and other early scientists faced banishment or imprisonment for arriving at new facts and new solutions that challenged the established order of things.

Kuhn also outlined how revolutions in basic assumptions and basic understandings of fact occur: "In both political and scientific development, the sense of malfunction that can lead to crisis is a prerequisite to revolution."[1]

As I read the book for the first time, Kuhn's blizzard of scientific detail was daunting. It was only years later, as I became a change agent in various management positions, that his historical insights grew in their influence on me. The book now remains one of the top influential works in my life. Its insights into human and organizational psyche deepen with every life experience.

Lesson #5: Always Have Air Cover. My interest in military history led me to review how battles are fought and won. In modern terms, military victory comes from control of the air. In 1980 Congressman Bob Livingston (R-LA) and I stood on the deteriorating runway at Roberto Alejo Aruz's coffee plantation in Guatemala. It was this runway that supplied the training camp for the Cuban brigade that fought at the Bay of Pigs. Many contend that additional air strikes would have changed the outcome of that fateful day on the Cuban coast in April 1961. Nearly nineteen years later, standing amid the ruins of the brigade's camp, Bob and I spoke about how all the lives lost in Central America and the Caribbean could have been saved had the promised air cover arrived.

In the bureaucratic wars fought during the Reagan administration, it was only those change efforts mounted with overwhelming and consistent "air cover" from the White House or an agency head that succeeded. The cleanup campaign at the General Services Administration (GSA) succeeded because Gerald Carmen, its administrator, had the guts to press aggressively for change and to consistently support those of us who were implementing the changes. He, in turn, knew that direct and unwavering support from President Reagan allowed him to stand firm and provide the necessary "air cover" for his subordinates. This, in turn, demoralized the opposition, as they knew they had no hope of waiting out the change effort or in appealing Carmen's policies to his superior. The result was a methodical and successful implementation of substantive and lasting positive change in that once dysfunctional and corrupt agency.

The opposite scenario occurred at the Department of Education, where seventy-five highly capable and motivated conservatives sallied forth to dismantle federal education programs, only to have the White House back away from legislation to abolish the department. The result allowed Terrell Bell, the then secretary and committed defender of the Department of Education, to purge the department of all these conservative appointees during a yearlong internal siege. As long as the White House remained silent, the conservative casualties mounted. While on temporary loan from the GSA, I had the opportunity to witness this bureaucratic "Bay of Pigs" and its lessons were burned into my mind.

Lesson #6: Always Address the "WIIFM." I rarely use acronyms, but this one sums up a concept so well. I ran across it during my orientation with Philip Crosby Associates (PCA). "WIIFM" stands for "what's in it for me." It is based on the assumption that no one, especially in bureaucratic warfare, does anything unless it is in his or her best interest. As most people in a changing organization avoid conflict and remain uncommitted to either side, WIIFM is the only hope a change manager has to enlist support. The challenge is to identify and use an effective WIIFM with the group you are trying to recruit to your effort.

A good WIIFM can work well with air cover. You can build on the support from above if you also create support "on the ground." There are many variations on this. WIIFM can inspire a superior to become your air cover. WIIFM can reassure a superior and encourage him or her to keep providing air cover. WIIFM can take the place of air cover if a superior's attention is diverted.

If the WIIFM is strong enough, then it can pay an added dividend—creating the "fervor factor." Once members of a group see that it is in their own best interests to embrace and assist the change, they may get so enthused about the effort that they become something very rare in bureaucracies—idealistic. As these converts become fanatics, enough change momentum can be generated to ensure that the change effort prevails over even the most entrenched opposition.

These strategies worked well for me as I helped organizations change. In countless classroom experiences, I saw executives experience moments of near-cosmic revelation as they realized how air cover and WIIFM applied to their own situations.

Lesson #7: People Equal Policy. No matter what is thought, said, written, or enacted, operational reality occurs only through the actions of individuals. The concept of people, and their interconnectivity, being the most important element in governance was first taught to me by Gene Hedberg, a gracious and intelligent Washington insider who had "seen it all" in the upper policy and intelligence circles of the federal government since World War II. Gene and I shared an office in the Reagan headquarters in 1980. Born in 1916, Gene had an incredible talent for remembering decades of names and events. During our countless hours together, he began a fourteen-year tutorial, educating me on who was who through three generations of Washington policymaking. I learned of networks driven by blood and marriage ties, of common schooling and state affiliations, of religious and club connections.

Gene's teachings were borne out in the thousands of résumés I reviewed during the Reagan years. They were proved many times over during the hundreds of background checks I either conducted or helped the FBI and the Office of Personnel Management conduct. These linkages proved invaluable as I pieced together why certain things happened or didn't happen. Over many fine dinners, Gene led me through the maze of interconnections to see the history that historians and policy analysts rarely see.

In 1987, as I began my community activism in West Virginia, Brad Nash furthered my education on interconnectivity. During innumerable hours in his home overlooking the Harpers Ferry Gap, he took me back through the players and intrigues of the Coolidge, Hoover, Roosevelt, Truman, and Eisenhower administrations. He helped me apply these insights to present-day Washington. He also walked me through the family and political ties that made the State of West Virginia work. These insights provided the knowledge for me to prevail in local political battles in West Virginia.

I was lucky enough to put "people equals policy" into practice several times before arriving in the 104th Congress. These experiences refined my approach to management and to politics.

On September 12, 1979, around a table filled with Italian food on the upper floor of Toscanni's Restaurant, one of my mentors, Stan Evans, helped me launch the Chesapeake Society. This group of conservative House legislative staff was organized to devise and implement guerrilla tactics on the floor of the House. Through pooling research and parliamentary knowledge, the goal was to kill or delay liberal legislation. The rationale was to prepare the House for Reagan. Every liberal bill not passed was one less law that would have to be reversed once Reagan arrived. Every liberal law delayed was one less day that it would be in effect once Reagan arrived. "Litmus test" votes were devised to help identify the "true believers," smoke out liberal Republicans, and identify those who would become the conservative Democrat "boll weevils" of the 1980s so that the Reagan administration would know whom they could count on when that era began.

By the summer of 1980, the Chesapeake Society activities were being reported as a factor in the rise of an effective Republican opposition in the House. My own encyclopedic knowledge of the House rules and the society's track record of legislative success led to my becoming an advisor to numerous House members and staffs. On a daily basis, my telephone lines lit up with members requesting legislative advice. My "ghostwritten" amendments and floor speeches not only filled the *Congressional Record* under Ashbrook's name, but for a dozen other members as well. "You are the only daily columnist the Record has ever had," mused one Chesapeake member.

My coordination of opposition operations of the House led to another skill, the placement of key people in key places. Chesapeake supplemented the job banks operated by the House Republican Study Committee and the Senate Republican Policy Committee. By the time of the Republican National Convention in Detroit in July 1980, the need for legions of committed and capable professionals to staff the Reagan administration was actively being discussed. Only a few of us in Washington had the card files, boxes of résumés, and Rolodexes to meet this need.

On Wednesday night, while the convention hall awaited the arrival of Ronald Reagan to name George H. W. Bush as his running mate, the issue of recruiting the right people for the general election campaign weighed on the minds of many Reagan operatives. Lee Atwater, one of Reagan's regional political directors and a friend of mine since 1978, approached me outside Congressman Guy Vander Jagt's (R-MI) executive suite. "Can you find nine hundred people for us in the next forty days?" he asked. "I sure can," I said with youthful certainty.

That was the beginning of a once-in-a-lifetime adventure. On August 1, 1980, I became the youngest director of personnel for a presidential campaign in the twentieth century. In the promised forty days, I hired nine hundred people to help the Reagan-Bush ticket crush President Jimmy Carter. In early September 1980, Dick Wirthlin's tracking polls began to show the victory that was to come. John Morgan, the main "number cruncher" for Wirthlin, dropped by Hedberg's and my office to show us the results. Gene Hedberg, a longtime friend of Morgan, looked over the projections with rising enthusiasm. "You had better start thinking about the transition, Scot," mused Gene.

Quietly, very quietly, the resources of the Chesapeake Society began to turn toward staffing the Reagan administration. It was no longer the dream, but a reality racing the electoral clock. In December, we were awash with 90,000 résumés. However, there was a threat that many conservatives could be edged out by more mainstream Republicans for key administration jobs. The transition witnessed major factional battles waged between the forces of the Reagan's "kitchen cabinet" and the "Bushies" under Jim Baker.

Stan Evans gathered another group together in his offices above the Hawk & Dove Pub to discuss this situation. The twenty activists knew that "people equal policy" (a truism jointly created by Evans, Morton Blackwell, and myself) and that whoever became part of the Reagan administration would define Reagan's policy legacy. We discussed how to build an "affirmative action" program for conservatives to obtain key positions around Reagan and within the agencies. "It's like we are already fighting behind enemy lines," said an exasperated Jeff Hollingsworth. "It is the Inchon landing all over again," I mused, thinking of General Douglas MacArthur's famous invasion behind enemy lines during the Korean War. The name stuck. "Inchon," the ultimate underground personnel network, had begun.

Over the next few months, hundreds of conservatives found jobs in the Reagan administration thanks to the daily "Inchon" strategy sessions held in the Old Executive Office Building. "Inchon" was led by a consortium of Reagan "kitchen cabinet" members, including Bill Wilson and Joe Coors and the Reagan regional political directors, including Lee Atwater, Frank Whetstone, and Mike Masson, and by Lyn Nofziger, Stan Evans, Morton Blackwell, Willa Johnson (who contributed her extensive résumé files from the Heritage Foundation to the effort), and myself.

Throughout the Reagan years, "Inchon" met in various forms to foster the appointment of conservatives and hinder liberals. A social group, the Coolidge Society, was founded by Kathy Royce, a top National Rifle Association lobbyist, and myself to add a yearly round of gatherings to supplement the annual July 4 soiree run by Morton Blackwell and Stan Evans. The intent of the Coolidge Society was to build a social and professional support network for all the conservatives who were new to Washington. Coolidge was Reagan's favorite president.

The Coolidge Society acted as a morale builder for Reagan administration appointees and Washington-area conservatives. It also served as a method of obtaining names and résumés of conservatives and certifying their ideological commitment prior to providing them with job-search assistance.

Eventually, the Coolidge Society invitation list grew to 12,000 names. This list filtered résumés through "Inchon" and into the administration. Thousands of conservatives owed their tenure in the Reagan administration, and placement in key congressional and "movement positions," to this secret network. During the second Reagan term, Admiral James Carey continued the work of the Coolidge Society and "Inchon" through the Conservative Network (TCN) and a variety of other support groups he sponsored. He transferred the thousands of names and professional credentials into a massive database used for countless national and local conservative projects.

The Bush era began with massive purges of Reagan loyalists. TCN became the focus of the "Reagan diaspora" as former appointees retreated into law firms, associations, and lobby groups. These activists kept their political edge and looked to future opportunities to rise up and staff future revolutions. While most thought this opportunity would come with a future president, the elections of 1994 thrust Congress into their path. Gingrich's revolution would bring many, including me, back to our roots.

★

I have always considered Congress's culture dysfunctional. Think of the House of Representatives as a huge freshman dorm on a college campus. Everyone is adjusting to living away from home for the first time. Just like college freshmen, they screw around all term and then pull all-nighters to get the most minimal of work done. Occasionally, they even ask for extensions. Look at the end of any congressional session. After numerous recesses, House members will stay in around the clock to complete their work, and then pass a continuing resolution to put off approving a real budget.[2]

Just like a freshman dorm, the House is a mix of people: party animals, druggies, slackers, social-climbing preppies, jocks, idealists, activists, and scholars. During my years in the House, I encountered close to 50 percent of members and staff displaying some form of addictive behavior. The addictions include ego, power, greed, sex, drugs, and alcohol. A freshman member, and almost all staff, can get away with anything, and does. The national media has no interest in the addictions of these small fry. They therefore develop an air of invincibility and unaccountability that carries them through their entire careers. Their lifestyle choices catch up with them only if they aspire to a major policy position.

During hamburger and beer sessions at the Hawk & Dove and other Hill haunts, my fellow House staffers would relate countless stories of adultery and alcoholism. They would talk about tantrums by members, which sometimes resulted in physical assaults or mass firings of their staffs. Our running joke was that the House of Representatives was America's largest adult day care facility.

As the Reagan era drew closer, one group of Republican House members were different. They wanted to do the right things and eagerly watched and learned from the three masters of the craft of parliamentary opposition: Representatives John Ashbrook (R-OH), Robert Bauman (R-MD), and John Rousselot (R-CA).[3] As the senior legislative assistant to Ashbrook, I would meet regularly with these up-and-coming members, usually late at night at the Capitol Hill Club. Representatives Tom Kindness (R-OH), Robert Walker (R-PA), Gerry Solomon (R-NY), Larry Hopkins (R-KY), and I would gather around a table to discuss strategies and dream of the days when Reagan would ride into Washington and put an end to big government.

While talking revolution, we would watch the darker side of Washington unfold around us—members getting drunk to the point of falling off bar stools, married members hitting on and picking up young female staffers and interns, lobbyists bringing attractive female "associates" with them to draw members to their tables. It was stomach turning. We could only shake our heads in amazement and shame. We pledged to rid the House of this culture of moral abandon if we ever got control of the chamber.

On November 9, 1994, while the rest of Washington was buzzing about the congressional elections, my fiancée, Vicki Hunter, and I prepared for the annual meeting of Independent Insurance Agents of America's Maryland affiliate. Maryland was the first state to implement the Farragut Management Institute's (FMI's) new national customer-service workbook.

Vicki was the niece of Texas governor William Clements. Her first husband had been murdered during a mugging in 1972, and she was a single parent raising a son. Her career was varied. She had modeled and acted on the television show *Dallas*. Several national television commercials followed, but her interest lay more in management than in acting. She soon rose in the business networks of Robert Strauss, the former Democratic National Committee chairman. She had a knack for commercial property management and ended up overseeing thousands of condominium and rental units in the Dallas area.

When the Republicans selected Dallas as the site for their 1984 National Convention, Vicki was contacted to be on their management team. Her success at the convention led to a job working for Lee Atwater and Ed Rollins at the Reagan-Bush national reelection headquarters. Her knowledge of housing and labor issues led her to the Department of Housing and Urban Development (HUD), where she became deputy for labor policy under Justin Logsdon, one of my closest friends.

Justin introduced us at a Reagan executive forum, and we became part of the same social and professional circle. She got to know my first wife and we all remained friends until my marriage crashed and burned and I began a new life. We soon became close soul mates and were now contemplating the best time to "tie the knot."

The next morning, November 10, Vicki and I were joined by three of my FMI colleagues: Bill Sturdevant, Don Mutersbaugh, and Paul Sweetland. They were there to learn how to present the customer-service workbook and to help me "work the crowd."

Bill and Paul were both lifelong Democrats. Sturdevant's father, William L. Sturdevant, had been the communications director for Hubert Humphrey's 1960 presidential campaign and for Estes Kefauver's 1956 vice presidential campaign.[4] "Well, what do you make of the election?" Bill asked.

"I don't know," I began, "I'm thrilled, but we will have to see if the GOP will actually make a difference."

"Do you think we can help them?" queried Don. "Will they want any consulting to help with the transition?"

"I was thinking of putting a letter into the transition team," I responded. "I did some Crosby stuff for Newt's staff in 1991. Maybe they will dust off that proposal."

On November 17, I sent a letter to the transition team pitching consulting and training services. I also sent a copy to my longtime friend, Representative Frank Wolf (R-VA), knowing he would make sure the letter landed on the right desk.

The letter was a long shot. I assumed that the House transition team would have more important things to worry about. I also wondered, harkening back to my 1991 discussion with Joe Gaylord, whether any of the lessons from the Reagan era relating to transition and governance would be applied.

Those questions were answered at 10:00 a.m. on December 7, 1994. I was working in my home office in Harpers Ferry and the telephone rang.

"Hello, Scot? This is Jack Howard with the House transition team. How would you like to come up here and run the place?"

★ PASSAGES AND ★
PRECEDENTS

December 8, 1994

"Do you really want a revolution?"

"Absolutely, it is what the 1994 election was all about."

"Do you understand that changing the House of Representatives will be painful, will result in major upheaval, and will lead many to call us crazy until everything falls into place?"

"I have been called crazy before, that will be nothing new."

"You realize that many Republicans will oppose us. Many in our own party hope we will just take a few superficial acts and leave the current system intact so they can wallow in the perks like the Democrats have for the last forty years."

"I have thought of that, and I can guarantee that leadership and a majority of the Republicans will not let that happen. We haven't come this far just to leave the status quo."

It was the second day of interviews. The setting was the Senate members' dining room. Representative Jim Nussle sat across the table from me. It was just the two of us, establishing the early personal, professional, and political bonding that would lay the foundation for our working together. It had become my turn to interview him on how serious he and the incoming Republicans were about changing House operations. He was trying to show me that this time the willingness for fundamental reform might be for real.

It would be twenty-seven days to the hour between my Senate lunch with Representative Nussle and the moment I stood on the floor of the House and was sworn in as the first chief administrative officer (CAO) of the House of Representatives. During that period, every action, every message, established a series of passages from being an obscure private citizen to becoming a public official. At the same time, each briefing and meeting provided an array of insights that shaped my role in and approach to the management revolution that was to come. Each passage was also an opportunity to establish precedents. Since no office like the CAO had ever existed, how I conducted myself would create precedents that would help or hurt me during my tenure. Therefore, some detail on what happened during this period provides insights.

THE NUSSLE LUNCHEON

This phase of the discussion was important. I had seen too often that Washington is a town where management by press release was the rule, not the exception. Too many times I had witnessed public officials announce an initiative to address a serious problem, only to have that announcement be the end of the effort. This was governance by press release. As long as the headline appeared, and they received credit, the matter was considered resolved. Washington politicians bank on the fact that the attention span of American citizens is extremely short.

"There is another important issue," I continued with Nussle. "There can be no 'must-hires' and no 'must-fires.' If I am going to build a business-based organization, I have to maintain my 'virginity.' Patronage politics will be the end of our credibility."

"You have my word and that of the Speaker that you will have a free hand in hiring. We want you to drive this revolution. You will be the city manager of Capitol Hill. Newt will be the mayor. You must manage your operation in a professional manner without outside interference."

November 7 had been a blur of activities. It was like a galactic "wormhole" had opened in space, where, only seconds before, there had only been a void.

The thought of a real revolution was a dream come true. In a flood of recollections, I remembered over twenty-four years of meetings where my colleagues and I had pledged that if the House ever went Republican, we would mount a revolution the likes of which Washington had never seen. If this was to be that moment, then nothing else mattered but total lasting victory.

During the walk from the Cannon House Office Building to the transition offices in the House courtyard, Jack Howard briefly outlined the events that led to his telephone call. He gave me a thumbnail sketch of Representatives Nussle, Boehner, and Linder, the CAO selection team that would interview me.

Nussle led the interview. Linder asked a few questions, and Boehner dropped in for a few moments to say hello. The questions covered a typical litany of what I had done in my life and why I had made career moves from the House to the Reagan administration to Philip Crosby Associates and the Farragut Management Institute (FMI). My ability to shape and implement aggressive change management was a common theme as the interview went into its second hour. We reviewed my change efforts at the General Services Administration (GSA), at the Peace Corps, and for my Crosby clients.

Nussle then walked me into another transition room filled with large organizational charts. They included charts of the existing and future administrative structures. The largest and most complex chart was labeled "Chief Administrative Officer" in bold lettering.[1]

"Can you run it?" asked Nussle as he watched me peer over the charts.

"Absolutely," I remarked. We continued our dialogue over lunch on Thursday. He asked me another series of questions regarding my approach to management and what kind of team I might put together. I told him that if I got the job, I would dismantle FMI and would undoubtedly draw some of my team from among my associates.

Our discussion continued, broadening and deepening our knowledge of each other and the way we would work together to make this once-in-a-lifetime opportunity work for each of us.

"Can you think of anything that you have done that might embarrass us or prevent you from becoming the CAO?" asked Nussle, shifting tone and facial expression and looking me in the eye with the seriousness of the prosecutor he once was.

"My change efforts have netted me numerous friends, but also a number of enemies in this town." I immediately responded.

"That just means you did the right things," rejoined Nussle. "Anything else?"

"I went through a messy divorce in 1992 and 1993." I began to outline just how bad it was. What started as a mutually agreeable ending to a failed marriage took a bizarre turn when I discovered my wife had remarried prior to our divorce being finalized. Her original assertions that there was no one else fell apart as evidence of a ten-month affair flowed in from canceled checks, credit card stubs, and reports from friends in England and Africa. My attorneys had me arrange my personal finances to declare Chapter 13 bankruptcy. By suspending my financial obligations, I forced my former wife to return to the United States and settle for a sum less than originally agreed upon or face bigamy charges.

"I don't need to know any more details," interrupted a very empathetic Nussle. "Nothing in your personal life has anything to do with your management skills."

The next twenty-four hours had my mind in overdrive. If this job became a reality, my world would instantly change. I threw myself into two intense work tracks. One track was to clear the decks of contractual commitments to FMI's clients. The other track was to begin thinking of whom I wanted to bring into the House to be part of the revolution to come.

The telephone rang. It was Dan Meyer.

"Congratulations, Scot! You are going to become the first chief administrative officer of the House!" beamed Dan. He went on to provide details of my schedule for the next few days. "See you in the morning!" He rang off.

I hung up with a great sigh of relief. They had selected me. More importantly, they had acted quickly. This kind of decisiveness would be key to the aggressive change approach I was planning to use. Had they dithered on this decision through the holidays, much critical planning time would have been lost. In my mind, speed equaled success; dithering would spell disaster. This revolution may be real after all!

SIMON AND GARBETT

"You've got me starting now!" affirmed Tom Simon. It was ten o'clock Friday night. I told him that I had to clear the arrangements for staff with the transition.

"Not a problem," said Tom, the enthusiasm mounting in his voice. "You can depend on me! Good luck! Keep me posted over the weekend!" Tom rang off.

Tom Simon had been my boss twice. The first time was at the GSA, where I was his deputy. The second time, I was his consultant when he was the chairman of the Railroad Retirement Board (RRB). In both cases we successfully launched major management reforms. At the GSA these reforms revolutionized the way the agency's finances were managed and tracked. Tom had more than twenty-five years in management and executive-level positions. As an executive with Warren King & Associates, he directed reform efforts for the governors of Massachusetts, Illinois, Michigan, Pennsylvania, and West Virginia.

Through our eleven years of working together, we had become good friends and had jointly accomplished major changes in the way the federal government managed its assets. Tom had spent countless hours helping me refine my skills in reviewing and managing the $42 billion in assets at the GSA. We had created the first-ever business-based financial reports in the federal government; we had also developed tracking and control systems that prevented $2 billion in waste annually. During his tenure at the RRB, he hired me to develop change-management approaches and a communication strategy to diffuse the burgeoning deficit in the agency's retirement obligations.

Tom had tutored me well. In 1990, when Philip Crosby was looking for a vice president for Washington, D.C., I found myself a finalist against one other candidate, Tom Simon. Tom's propensity to lecture instead of discuss and to sometimes use heavily technical jargon to make his points gave me the edge. We weathered that moment and continued to be close professionally and personally. We had supported each other during the collapse of my marriage and a trial separation within his.

"Wow! You bet!" John Garbett reacted, when I called him to join the team. "Scot . . . you amaze me," John said, laughing.

John and I had been friends since eighth grade at Wayzata Junior High School. When I became part of the Reagan transition in 1980, he was a Presidential Management Intern at the Department of Labor. He saw me being interviewed on the *CBS Evening News* and called me. I arranged for him to be detailed to the transition as my deputy, and we renewed our close bonds. We also had a great time reinventing the way orientation was conducted for presidential appointments and their senior support staff. Our "welcome wagon" provided a wide range of personnel compliance "helpful hints" that prevented countless management problems in the first year of the Reagan administration. John, with a double master's in business administration and in fine arts management, had a flair for identifying management issues long before they erupted. His level head, irreverent worldview, and sense of humor always provided a sea of calm when all around was mayhem. I figured this would be an important attribute in the months ahead. He also was the one person who knew me better than anyone except my parents. His presence always served as a revitalizing influence on me.

Since we had last worked together, John had entered the world of Hollywood. He had built a solid reputation as a logistics specialist for movie production and had risen to become a supervising producer for Touchstone Films. When Michael Eisner took over Disney, he brought John over from Paramount to help reorganize Disney's back-lot operations. Fortunately, John was between films and could give me his time, starting immediately.

SATURDAY, DECEMBER 10

The first meeting was scheduled for 9:10 a.m. I was to "check in" in room HC-7, the transition reception room. It was locked, with the lights out. HC-6 was open just across the hall. There I met my fellow House officer-designates for the first time. They had also arrived early. We were all relieved that at least we were on time and seemed to be in the right place. Bill Livingood was to be the new sergeant at arms. He was very cordial. I learned that his background included a career in the Secret Service. In fact, he was the last active agent who had been with the service at the time of Kennedy's assassination.

Robin Carle, the new clerk, was more reserved. She was pleasant, but fairly vague and guarded about her background. I learned over time that she was the one true partisan of the three of us, having spent her life with the Colorado Republican Party and at the Republican National Congressional Campaign Committee. She had had a short tenure as a Bush appointee at the Department of Health and Human Services. "What's with her?" I thought as I watched her interact with Bill and me.

Dan Meyer and Jack Howard entered with Jim Nussle. A moment later two new people, Stacy Carlson and Sue Wadel, arrived. Introductions went around the room. Jack opened up HC-7. It was so quiet in the hall. No one else was around.

Additional introductions occurred. We learned that Stacy was the minority staff director for the CHA, and Sue was the incoming legal advisor to the Speaker, having spent the last several years working in the Michigan legislature.

We walked across the hall to HC-9. It had a series of folding banquet tables displaying clusters of briefing books, each marked for a different House officer. The clerk and the inspector general each had one briefing book. The sergeant at arms had two books. On a separate table were fifteen binders with one large label marked "CAO." Later I would measure the entire CAO stack at thirty inches.

"I will discuss your 'homework' later," Nussle joked.

Nussle welcomed everyone and began to explain how important and sensitive the next few days would be. He walked us through the Saturday schedule and the key events for Monday, the day our appointments would be made public.

"There are a number of key issues we need to keep in mind," began Nussle. "These are . . . one, transition reports. Please document everything you do. We have been asked to submit a detailed report on the transition when this is all over. We had nothing to guide us when we began. I want to make sure that does not happen for the next transition team. I will talk with each of you in detail on what this report will look like later.

"Two. We need to identify and diffuse any ticking bombs. This will be the first time any of us have run the House. We need to make sure the wheels don't fly off as we take control." Nussle turned to me. "Scot, you are going to have to pay special attention to the payroll. We need to make sure everyone gets paid." There was a titter of laughter as I nodded and continued to transcribe Nussle's remarks. "The downsizing of the committees and the office moves will also be critical. With so many people coming and going, property control will also be a key issue. Finally, we will be mandating full compliance with all employment laws; we will need to make sure everyone is familiar with them from day one.

"Three. We need a method of prioritizing our actions for the rest of the transition and for the first 100 days of the new session. I want everyone to use the Covey prioritizing method of four quadrants. Does everyone know them?"

I nodded enthusiastically, thinking, "This is great! They are actually practicing what they preach!" Carle, Wadel, and Livingood were unfamiliar with Covey. Nussle handed out the four-quadrant model and briefly reviewed it.[2]

Nussle continued, "I would like each of you to report on your 'quadrant 1,' those issues that are 'urgent and important,' every morning during our staff meeting.

"Four. We will work on defining the reporting relationships. At this point you will work directly with me, and I will be available to all of you, including being down here in the transition offices as much as possible.

"Five. We will need to work out policies on several key issues. These include the granting of favors to members—there will be no favors or expediting. We are going to run the House as a business; we are going to end the old ways. The single most important way to communicate this is to treat everyone equally and enforce House policies fairly.

"Another issue is the media. You are all about to become very famous. The media will want to know your every move. Let Ed Gillespie on Newt's media staff handle all inquiries for now. You should focus on your jobs.

"Finally, and I am sure this list will continue to grow, we need to resolve authorities. We need to work together to identify strategic thresholds for making decisions and sharing information. You are all professionals and need independence to act. You are also officers of the House and are accountable to the House. We need to make sure there is a balance so that you are not micromanaged, but also that there is political support when you need it."[3]

Nussle went on to discuss housekeeping issues such as temporary identification badges, parking permits, and clearances to access files and rooms under our jurisdiction. He looked up as Jack Howard stood by the doorway.

"I think Newt is ready to see us. Shall we go?"

FIRST MEETING WITH GINGRICH

We walked through the basement maze to elevators that took us up to Gingrich's minority whip office. This was the same office I visited back in the summer of 1991. Newt came out of his inner office and greeted us all. He was effervescent with enthusiasm. We sat down around the coffee table in his reception area.

"This is going to be a historic two years for us all," the Speaker-designate began. "Your role will be key to our redefining how the House operates. I want to completely modernize and rationalize the current system. You should all develop a culture of customer service for all. The days of special favors are over."

Livingood leaned forward. "Remember, I have not heard from the Secret Service on their releasing me from duty for my appointment."

Gingrich looked at Nussle. "I understand that is still an issue. I hope we can have it sorted out before Monday."

He then continued: "I expect each of you to downsize your operations as you professionalize them. I want creative ideas on how we can do things better than before. I am hoping for rational, informed radicalism. I want each of you to work closely with the transition team in quickly implementing their recommendations.

"You are officers of the House. You are appointed by me and will answer to me. Your main points of contact will be Sue Wadel, my new legal advisor, and Dan Meyer, my chief of staff. They are here to make sure you have everything you need to make things happen.

"There will also be an Oversight Committee, made up of seven Republicans and five Democrats. They will act as a political buffer. Any major changes will need to be run through the committee. Once approved, you will have full authority to act.

"I hope we can all work as a team. As Jim has probably mentioned, I am hoping for daily meetings so we can learn from each other. I also want each of you to spend some time with Bill Thomas and Pat Roberts. They have extensive institutional memory on how things have run and may have ideas on how best to direct your efforts. Another person you should all meet is Vern Ehlers. He has been heading a study on bringing the House into the information age. I want all of you to know that a major priority for me will be making this the cyber-Congress. It is my intention to have everything we do online. We will be launching a new website through the Library of Congress when the session begins. This system will feature many House documents and the *Congressional Record*. I then want each of you to find ways to bring everything else onto this new system as the session progresses. Our goal is total 'transparency' of House operations for the public. They should see everything as close to real time as possible. There should be no secrets from the public.

"I wish you all well."[4]

The meeting ended.

"This revolution is for real!" I thought to myself as we left the room and returned to the transition offices. Nussle had each of us write down the numbers where we could be reached. He also called Ed Gillespie into the room and introduced him. Ed requested that each of us provide a one-page biographical sketch by Monday morning for the media kits. Nussle then turned to outlining the schedule for Monday and told us to take as much time as possible to review the transition materials placed on the tables in HC-9. The meeting ended.

At that point I took Jim aside to go over some additional issues.

Bringing In My Team. I mentioned that, for the reform effort to move swiftly, I would need my team on board as soon as possible. Nussle said that the Committee on Standards of Official Conduct (the ethics committee) had made a ruling authorizing the use of outside experts. He reminded me that everything the transition was doing was being invented from scratch, as no one had documented anything from previous transitions. He pledged to work with the ethics committee to clarify how my team could come on board prior to January 3, 1995.

The Role of House Oversight. "Jim, I thought you were going to be running things. What is this Oversight Committee all about?" I quietly asked.

"I don't always understand Newt's motives. All I can say is that you report to the Speaker, and you will report to me. The Oversight Committee will have a role in making sure we have the political support to make the reforms happen. Don't worry, you are here to make the changes happen. We are here to make sure they happen."

I called all my FMI associates. In addition to the ones I was planning to designate as the "first wave," I told others, like Wendy Younk and Carole Kordich, that they would be part of the reforms once I had additional slots identified.

The balance of the weekend was spent reading transition books. The overview binder was an executive summary for the CAO. The first section was the November 30, 1994, transition report with Nussle's announcement of the "Open House" reforms. There was then a section chronicling the last four years of scandal that built the mandate for the "Open House." For the first time, I read documents relating to the anguish suffered by General Wishart during his short tenure as director of nonlegislative and financial services. The final sections had an array of organizational charts and a set of résumés for the executives currently serving in what was to become the CAO offices. I noted that only three had college degrees, and that nearly all had Democratic Party activities listed as their first job. Most résumés also showed that, after the Democratic Party, they had spent their entire lives in the House patronage system. Not one of these "holdovers" had any private-sector experience, yet they were responsible for managing $800 million and serving 13,000 employees. "No wonder the place was falling apart," I thought.

MONDAY, DECEMBER 12

The first sign that things were different was the way the Capitol police officers all immediately stood at attention and saluted as I walked past the guard station and onto the Capitol plaza, and again as I entered the

Senate ground-floor door of the Capitol. "Good morning sir," said the two policemen in unison. This was a little unnerving.

"Why are you saluting me?" I queried.

"Sir, you are now the big boss of the place, sir" said one of the officers.

I walked past the news media, who, with piles of camera equipment, were arrayed at the bottom of the stairs leading into the transition area. HC-7 was already bustling with activity, quite a contrast to Saturday. That already seemed a distant past.

Nussle greeted Robin, Bill, Stacy, and me and handed us a typed schedule for the day featuring a 2:30 p.m. news conference to announce our appointments. "Our quadrant 1 issue for today is to avoid giving the media anything to shoot at," Nussle announced. "We need to make sure that no one talks in future tense. There will plenty of time to announce our plans later."

This made sense. I always subscribed to the old Russian proverb: "Boast when coming from battle, not going to it." If we were to make major changes, we would need to keep the opposition in the dark as long as possible. The Democrats would run the House until noon on January 4, and much could be done to "spike the guns" if they knew what was in store.

The morning was to be spent conducting "protocol" meetings with the outgoing House officers to pave the way for our having access to files and to arrange for the handover.

FIRST MEETING WITH MEDLOCK

Nussle dropped me at HC-2, Medlock's tiny windowless suite. "I'm honored to meet you," I began. "I read how you and General Wishart tried to do the right things, but were stopped. It is a shame how shabby they treated you."

Medlock was taken off guard. I do not think he expected the incoming occupation forces to be solicitous.

"My hope is to work with you for a seamless transition and to continue the reform work you began," I continued.

We commenced a highly cordial discussion of his duties. "Mostly I sign paper already reviewed and approved by the Committee on House

Administration (CHA)," he said. We worked out a schedule to review administrative issues. Part of these sessions would be to go through his daily in-box so that I could learn the forms and flows of the paperwork. We also worked out a general "get acquainted" meeting with Medlock's executives.

The 11:15 a.m. meeting with James Malloy was a joy. His "doorkeeper" position was to be abolished as part of the transition recommendations. He was naturally affable, but, with no successor to transition with, he was determined to enjoy his last weeks. Malloy effusively welcomed us. We were ushered into his small office that overlooked the Mall. He then began to regale us with humorous stories of his many years in Congress.

"We've got a problem," Ed Gillespie greeted me after lunch. He ushered me into HC-7, away from the others. "*Roll Call* says you were fired from Ashbrook's office and that you were under investigation in Reagan's Debategate."[5]

"No honeymoon for me," I thought to myself as I began to give Ed some sound bites. "First, I left Ashbrook to work for Reagan in August 1980; Ashbrook then put me back on his staff to supplement my pay during the transition." Ed smiled.

"My pay record is in the 1980 Clerk of the House Report. They can look up the rehiring." Ed smiled more broadly, remarking, "That is hardly the act of a boss who fired you."

I continued, "The FBI worked with me on Debategate. I was the director of personnel for Reagan's national campaign. My files and organizational charts were the FBI's road map for their entire investigation. They even commended me for my cooperation."

"This is good. This is very good." Ed handed the telephone to me to relate these facts to the *Roll Call* reporter. I then returned to HC-6 to meet the other "career" officers of the House whose reappointments would also be announced at the news conference—the chaplain, the parliamentarian, and John Lainhart, the inspector general. "We have a lot to talk about," Lainhart said as we greeted each other.

The news conference itself was in HC-5, a large room we entered via a small room with a large ice machine. About forty reporters, three camera crews, and ten photographers were waiting. Nussle kicked things off by explaining the criteria used to select the new officers and making some general comments about each of our backgrounds.

Each of the three new officers went to the microphones to make a few remarks. Robin made a general comment about what an honor it was to be the first woman House officer. Bill committed a blunder. True to his Secret Service training, he announced that he would conduct a security audit and risk assessment for the Speaker, stating: "Mr. Gingrich is very visible and he's somewhat controversial." This was the first "future tense" morsel offered to the public, and the media pounced on it. "Are there existing threats to the Speaker?" "Is Mr. Gingrich in danger?" The questions poured forth. Bill recovered from the onslaught and backpedaled, stating that this is standard procedure for any new assignment. The media questions died down, but they had their story. The next day, "Gingrich's life threatened" dominated the announcement of House officers. "Welcome to the asylum," I mused to Bill.

As the appointee to newest officer position, I came last. "I look forward to serving all members and staff in the House. I see my role as bringing modern business practices, quality management, and world-class customer service to House operations."

"What will you use as a measure of success in this position?" asked one reporter.

"My reality check in how I do in this role is that a year from now a Pat Schroeder or a Barney Frank can stand up at these microphones and say things are better now than they were a year ago. I really want to be even-handed. Everyone is elected to come up here and represent their districts and their constituents. They all deserve phones that work and computers that are compatible. I want everyone, Republican and Democrat alike, to know we are providing the most efficient and professional administrative service we can to support this institution."

The questions turned back to Nussle. He had to defend hiring only white people and hiring only Republicans. "I don't know Mr. Livingood's party affiliation," he responded. Nussle also had to counter the issue of how General Wishart was hired through a "nonpartisan" procedure that included extensive consultation with the leadership of both parties. The reporters fired questions: "Didn't the Republicans insist on a nonpartisan administrator when they were in the minority and are now forcing through a partisan appointment now that they are in the majority? Isn't this hypocrisy?"

Nussle reminded the reporters of what a sham the process was under the Democrats and that Wishart had no real power, as the CHA never relinquished their partisan control over House operations. "This time it will be different. We have an independent administrator with a direct reporting line to the Speaker. We selected a professional, and he will have the authority to act as a professional."

The next day, Representative Dick Gephardt (D-MO) held a press conference in which he denounced me as a partisan appointment and asserted that the new Republican leadership had reversed its commitment to their so-called Open House: "I am absolutely stunned, and it's hypocrisy at its worst."[6] Of the three new House officers, only Robin Carle had an exclusively partisan background, yet she was hailed in the media as the first woman appointment. Livingood would spend the next few days through the Sunday talk shows having to clarify that there were no impending death threats against Gingrich. Our first exposure to the surreal world we had all entered was over.

WEDNESDAY, DECEMBER 14

The 8:30 a.m. transition meeting began with a new set of people joining the transition. Nussle introduced an assistant for each incoming officer. Linda Nave, a longtime House staffer, was to help Robin Carle with appointments and teach her "the ropes." Jim Varney, a "career" member of the sergeant at arms staff was to help Bill Livingood. Jeff Trandahl, a young staffer from Representative Pat Roberts's (R-KS) office, was assigned to me.

Jeff had worked with the minority staff of the CHA. His father, like mine, had been a career employee at the U.S. Fish and Wildlife Service in the Department of the Interior. Nussle explained that Jeff would serve as an "aide-de-camp," setting up appointments, helping maintain the files, and tutoring me about House operations.

Nussle's morning transition meeting was interrupted by a request for all of us to meet with the Republican House leaders in HC-8. We walked into the room. Grouped around a table at the other end of the room were Gingrich, DeLay, Armey, Boehner, and all the incoming committee chairmen. I looked around the room and saw many familiar faces. Solomon, James Sensenbrenner, Livingston, Walker, and Young had all known me for sixteen or more years. They each smiled. Solomon gave me a thumbs-up.

"Why don't each of you introduce yourself and tell us a little about yourself," started Gingrich. Nussle waved Carle to the front. She gave her name and mentioned how happy she was to be a part of the new Congress. She said nothing about her past. Livingood then took a moment to explain his background with the Secret Service. Nussle waved me forward.

"Many of you already know me from my previous times on the Hill. You know that I have been a lifelong conservative Republican. You know that I share your commitment to remaking the House into an honest and efficient place to do business. I can assure you that my years of making change happen for Ronald Reagan and working with quality management in the private sector will be used to make the Open House a reality in this Congress."

"Right on Scotty!" cheered Solomon. The other members joined in a round of applause.

"You can see we have a management team that we can all be proud of," Gingrich offered. "I am sure each of you will be talking with Robin, Scot, and Bill as we all plan the next months. I urge each of you to get to know them better."

"We all know Scot," Walker began, a chuckle rippling through the room. "There will definitely be a revolution up here." Another chuckle arose with hearty winks and nods among many of those assembled.

"Thank you all." Gingrich smiled and looked at Nussle to shepherd us out of the room.

In only day three of our tenure, it was becoming standard procedure to have our daily schedule shifted around as the legislative transition intensified. My first meeting with Representative Bill Thomas (R-CA) was moved up, and the ethics briefing was moved back.

"Be careful with what you say to Bill." Nussle took me aside. "We don't fully trust him."

"If that is the case, why is he anywhere near the management reform effort?"

"We will have John [Boehner] and Jennifer [Dunn] on Oversight. They will keep an eye on Bill and be our advocates. Besides, I am assuming that Oversight will only be there to run the political traps if we need them. The real work will be done through the transition and the Speaker's office," offered Nussle. "So don't worry. You will have a lot of help. None of us are walking away from this." With that Nussle walked me into the bustling transition room (HC-7). A moment later Representative Bill Thomas (R-CA) and Stacy Carlson came in.

FIRST MEETING WITH THOMAS

He looked around for some empty chairs and we all took seats. Thomas hunched forward and looked me in the eye. "Listen, I just wanted to briefly get together to let you know what my priorities are. We have a lot to do, and we will have more time a little later to go into details. First, I am going to need your help to consolidate all member accounts. The most important thing will be to give each member a true picture of what they have to spend. I am hoping to create a member's representational allowance and get rid of all these small allotments that will end the [Charlie] Rose era once and for all. You might look at charging a consolidated fee for members who use the physician, the parking garage, and the gym.

"I want your assurance that the trains will run on time starting January 4. We could all have egg on our face if the trash piles up and the checks don't get issued. You better have a good facilities man in mind to work with the architect's people. I expect that we may not get much help in making things run.

"The other big issue will be this new compliance bill. You will need to work closely with my staff to audit all the requirements. We need to make sure this goes well.

"Finally, I hope you are working on a plan of attack for the management reforms. I want the Oversight Committee to be able to review what you plan to do fairly soon into the new Congress. I will need to see how you plan to structure your operations."

I nodded and wrote down everything he said. Stacy leaned forward to see what I was writing. "You have my assurance that nothing will fall through the cracks. I have been through other transitions and know what can happen when the other side doesn't cooperate," I said.

"Good, that's what I wanted to hear. If you need anything, work through Stacy." Thomas stood up. "I am sorry this was so brief. We will get together again soon." He shook my hand and headed out the door.

I returned to my cubicle in HC-6. Nussle was finishing a discussion with Livingood. He looked up and came over, asking how my meeting went. I reported that things went well and that I was careful only to pledge to work with Thomas.

"Good. Don't commit to anything major until we talk." Nussle began looking at my personnel notations that covered the CAO organizational chart. "The ethics folks have worked up some guidance on bringing people in prior to the next Congress. They should be able to help you." Nussle then began to ask about some of the proposed changes on my chart, such as the downgrading of the postmaster. He liked all the ideas.

"You should take this picture as inspiration." Nussle gestured toward the large lithograph of Christopher Columbus on the wall to the right of my desk. "Like him, we are all exploring uncharted territory. It is a new world, and many hazards lie ahead."

The ethics committee is tucked away in the House terrace. The basement hallway was rarely traversed by visitors, making it an ideal place for members and staff to go for conferring about highly sensitive personal and political matters. The standard practice is that any member or staff can come to the committee for confidential guidance. This is important because the committee is one of the few places in Washington where prevention is a priority. The more issues privately raised by a member, the more likely ethical dilemmas will be resolved prior to becoming a public scandal.

The committee staff provided a general overview on financial disclosure and their procedures to the three incoming officers. Afterward, they had good news for me. My team could arrive prior to January 4. All their transition activities were "orientation," as each would serve in the new Congress. The beachhead for reform could be established.

Several rituals filled the afternoon. All the officers and their new aides-de-camp were taken on a VIP tour of the Capitol. We were to have done this on Monday, but schedules remained chaotic.

I had not been on the floor of the House since my days with Ashbrook. This tour included countless facts that I had long ago forgotten. The other officers and I were told that the side of the chamber to the left of the Speaker's rostrum (from the vantage of being in the Speaker's chair and looking out to the chamber) was always the Republican side. The Democrats were always seated to the right. This was a useful insight, as many had speculated that the room was divided majority-minority and that the Republicans would, therefore, trade sides in the coming Congress (as the parties do in the British House of Commons). We were shown the bullet holes in the Republican leadership table from that fateful day in March 1954, when Puerto Rican nationalists fired into the chamber, wounding eight members.[7] It was considered good luck to place your little finger in the bullet hole in the leadership drawer. We all wiggled our fingers in the hole, seeking all the luck we could get for the coming months. I spent the remainder of the day finally addressing the mountain of telephone messages.

"How did you get that job?" was the refrain from the dozens of people I called that afternoon. Only a few began with congratulations or any form of well-wishing. For the most part, my colleagues in what now passed for the "conservative movement" were more like stunned party-goers wondering, "Who invited him?" I was taken aback by the almost shrill and accusatory probing that met my returned calls.

Over the next few weeks, letters flooded in to both the transition office and my home. In writing, people were more celebratory and upbeat. However, the most effusive congratulations came from some of the very people who had tried to hamper my career. Only in Washington can people who had tried to stop my appointments during the Reagan years, or hired competitors when I was marketing consulting services, write, "We always knew you would succeed" and "Please let me know how I can help you." One who had tried to stop me several times in the past was already busy spreading the news that he got me the CAO job.

THE LIST

Thursday, December 15 began with the Capitol police officers snapping salutes as they waved me past the metal detectors. "Please stop saluting," I said smiling. "I am just the hired help."

"If that is what you wish, sir." They finally stopped by the next Monday. It was a minor step toward ending some of the elitism of the old regime.

Tom Simon was waiting for me in HC-6. I introduced him at the morning transition meeting. The key "urgent and important" issue for Tom and me was to meet with all of Medlock's executives. Nussle had just announced that there would be a working session that evening, when Stacy, Jeff, and Linda would finalize what support staff would be fired. I insisted on meeting all the key managers prior to this action. If there was going to be a purge, then it was to be a purge based on performance, not just partisanship.

After the morning transition meeting ended, I left Tom to review the growing reference library of transition documents while I had my morning meeting with Medlock. He had prepared his own list of concerns that he and Wishart had not been able to address during their tenures. He shared it with me as his "farewell" gift. This memo, along with the daily insights provided to me by Medlock during the transition, ensured that Wishart's ordeal would not have been in vain.

Tom and I then prepared to meet with Medlock's top executives. An important part of recent House history was to understand who had driven the House into its current dysfunctional condition. Were they helpless professionals at the mercy of the old CHA, or were they a contributing factor? I had to know before the list was finalized.

Medlock ushered us into HC-4. Around the table sat the executives who ran the remnants of the Wishart experiment. Tom and I conducted the meeting as if we were management consultants entering a new engagement. We asked straightforward questions about the current state of operations and the challenges that lay ahead. In this way we hoped to see if anyone around the table was sincere about helping change the system.

It did not take long to write off the entire group.

To the basic question, "What issues are you currently facing?" every one of Medlock's executive team stated that they needed more money and more people. When asked, "Are there any ticking bombs or impending problems we need to know about?" the answer was a resounding no. Several informational items were offered, including the building of new elevators in the Longworth Building that would disrupt food service in the House's largest cafeteria. Their responses were all delivered with a tinge of smugness and self-importance. It was as if they assumed that, even as patronage appointments, they were going to weather the change and remain forces defending a long-obsolete status quo.

The meeting ended with Nancy Glorius and Mary Ann Wise offering to take us on a tour of the stationery and gift shops along with the equipment rooms. As we rounded the corner in the cluttered and dirty basement of the Cannon Building, Tom and I viewed a hallway filled with photocopiers in various stages of disassembly. Just off the corridor were rooms overflowing with obsolete equipment. In some cases, computers were stacked up to the ceiling, with the lower ones dented and crushed under the weight. In another room, filled with typewriters, we met the House Selectric typewriter repairman. "Some weeks I have two or three machines to work on," he proudly announced. We asked if he repaired anything else. "No, I only know IBM Selectrics." Glorius quickly added that the in-house repair of typewriters had been downsized from three people and that there were plans for outsourcing the remaining activity.

The evening hours were devoted to the "list." I rejoined Simon and the two of us entered HC-7, where Stacy, Jeff, and Linda were already arrayed around a computer compiling the firing lists. Jeff was at the keyboard. Stacy had him scroll through the form they were creating, explaining each column as they went. "We need any names you have of people you want to bring on board so we can slot them into the vacancies we are creating."

I began to list the eighteen people whom I hoped would become my first wave of reformers. Stacy reviewed Jeff's work and began to point to the screen, identifying positions for each of my prospective team members. About thirty minutes later, Nussle arrived, merrily humming the Christmas standard, "Santa Claus Is Coming to Town," and repeating the section, "He's making a list and checking it twice, gonna find out who's naughty or nice." We all laughed.

"How is it coming?" inquired Nussle.

"Great!" said Jeff. "We even nailed Rose's mistress! We're getting everybody!"

"Yeah, they're going to shit!" commented Stacy.

Nussle turned to me. "Anyone you want to save?"

"No. They are definitely part of the problem, not the solution," I reported.

We all returned to our list duties. Linda Nave reviewed the House telephone book, going over each name and position, methodically asking if they had considered each person listed. Jeff continued to enter names and positions on the computer, occasionally stopping to relate a story about how the person had obtained his or her position and what a screwup that person was. He had an encyclopedic knowledge of who was whose boyfriend, girlfriend, relative, and former campaign worker. Stacy reviewed the work, cheering on the effort by repeatedly saying, "This is great!"

Simon and I discussed the next personnel steps with Nussle. I offered the services of Simon and the legal professionals I planned to have on board by Monday to draft the appropriate letters and procedures that would implement the firings. "I hope that we can make these first official acts rock solid, legally," Nussle said, heartily agreeing with my suggestion. Every now and then Stacy interrupted our discussion with questions about the positions and salary levels needed for my reform team.

Nussle took me aside for some final thoughts on the days to come. "Tomorrow will be an important one for you. You will address the Republican Conference on the House floor at one o'clock."

"The whole conference?" I responded, a bit nonplussed.

"Oh yes. I will introduce you and the other House officers. You will all be able to say a few words. In your case, I would want to prepare something because there is a lot of interest in these reforms and what you and your office are all about. You give them something to feel comfortable about. Tell them you understand the mission and have done this kind of stuff before. Remember, you are about to become one of the only private citizens ever to speak on the House floor. The last one was Václav Havel, before he became head of Czechoslovakia!"

FIRST MEETING WITH THE
DEMOCRATIC HOUSE LEADERSHIP

I thought about the speech, penning a rough draft that night. Another draft was completed on the train ride into Washington the next morning. Garbett arrived a little bleary-eyed from the red-eye from California. I was so glad to have him as part of this incredible adventure. I introduced him to the transition team, then left him to get his bearings as Nussle steered the officers into another important first meeting.

Representatives Gephardt and Vic Fazio (D-CA) welcomed us into HC-8. Representatives Gingrich and Thomas had also arrived. Gingrich introduced everyone, then had them array themselves around the table in the center of the room. He asked me to sit next to him.

There were further pleasantries, including some light jesting between Fazio and Thomas about their days in the California legislature and how this would be like "old times," with them both handling House operations. The discussion settled down to focus on the first hundred days of the 104th Congress. Gingrich rattled off a blizzard of information about the schedule he planned, the legislation that would be considered, and the new procedures he was to install. One of the key assertions he made was that every one of the "Contract with America" bills would come to a final vote prior to the end of the first hundred days.

"Just remember, there will be no delays. We will simply work around the clock and seven days a week. So, if I were you, I would let us have our votes, and we can have a somewhat normal work schedule this spring. I do not mind substantive debate and amendments, but I will not tolerate stall tactics," Gingrich stated matter-of-factly.

He went on to outline unprecedented openness for the legislative process. The sharing of information and the lead time granted the soon-to-be minority was stunningly generous. I listened in total amazement, remembering my efforts with the Chesapeake Society to overcome the "mushroom management" used by the Democrats during Tip O'Neill's

Speakership to undermine and stop any opposition. What a different world this was going to be!

Gingrich outlined the Open House reforms and his goal of having a "cyber-Congress."

"So, you plan all the contract votes prior to the Easter recess?" queried Gephardt.

There was a stunned silence. I looked over at the minority-leader-to-be. It was like the wheels of his brain had locked up ten minutes ago. There was a blank expression.

Gingrich backed up and reviewed the key points, taking on a "helpful teacher" tone to his speech and body language. Gephardt was struggling. His thought processes were engineered for old-style partisan warfare, not facilitative leadership. I looked over at Fazio. He seemed to grasp both everything Gingrich was saying and how this was clearly short-circuiting the brain of his colleague. He offered a series of helpful observations that moved the discussion along.

Gingrich, with the help of Fazio, got Gephardt through the framework for how the 104th was to operate. He then turned to trying to develop a more "family friendly" House. He talked about the scheduling of votes to allow for travel from the West Coast (Thomas and Fazio cheered at this). He also discussed the role of Representative Frank Wolf (R-VA) in taking the lead in looking at other ways to be family friendly, including family events for the swearing in of the new Congress.

Gephardt's mind locked up again as Gingrich launched into a light-hearted discussion on how much his family was looking forward to meeting the Power Rangers, stars of a highly popular children's action show. Once again it was Fazio to the rescue, explaining who the Power Rangers were. We then watched as the two most powerful men in Congress, Gingrich and Gephardt, discussed the refreshments and decorations for the family party. They could have been planning a local PTA picnic instead of the beginning of the 104th Congress.

THE FLOOR SPEECH

"I hope you gave your remarks some thought." Nussle ushered us onto the House floor. Representative Boehner was in the Speaker's chair, reading off of index cards. Representative Solomon was by the leadership table, also reading off of cards. They, along with a dozen other members, were rehearsing the first day of the session, making sure that everyone knew the right motion to make. About another hundred or more members sat about the chamber, watching the dress rehearsal with great interest. After all, this was the first time in most of their lifetimes that the Republicans had the responsibility for running the House.

After a few minutes, there was a logical break in the action. Nussle waved at Boehner, who then waved him to the Republican microphone in the "well" of the House chamber.

"I want to take a few minutes from your proceedings to have the new House officers introduce themselves to you," began Nussle, motioning for Carle and then Livingood to come to the microphone.

Nussle then waved me to the podium. I surveyed the House members and began: "All of us here today have followed unique pathways to bring us to this pivotal moment in history." I briefly reviewed how my years in Congress, the executive branch, and the private sector had prepared me for the challenges that lay ahead. I contrasted my path with those of various friends who were now members, concluding, "So now our paths merge and your journey becomes my journey, as we all work to implement the 'Contract with America.' In the next two years, my victories will be different from your victories. Mine will relate to such things as making computer systems compatible and making sure your paychecks arrive on time. However, the sum total of these administrative victories will be to show America that Republicans can reduce costs, eliminate waste, and be open and accountable to all the people.

"Together, we will achieve the dream of a limited, responsible, government. I look forward to serving you and working with you. Thank you and good luck to you all."[8]

There was sustained and enthusiastic applause as I ended my remarks. Several members stood and cheered. Representative Solomon smiled and gave me the thumbs-up. "Right on!" yelled several of the incoming freshmen. Nussle was beaming. "That's just what they needed to hear."

★ THE A RING ★

December 19, 1994

"'Inchon' won after all!" exclaimed Tony Blankley, winking, as he moved past me in the corridor, followed by a half-dozen reporters. It was a recognition of the pledge we had made to each other back in December 1980 that we would not rest until the "Inchon" group ran the cabinet. Instead, fourteen years later, the familiar faces of those early days in the Reagan revolution were now preparing to run the House.

It had already been a busy day. Eleven people were now part of the CAO reform team. The morning was spent introducing them to each other and to the transition process. Thanks to the already invaluable support from Jane Bennett, all the team members had their own copies of the briefing books, had access to an extensive library of source documents, and were moving through a full day of briefings by the ethics office and tours of the Capitol. The House revolution was moving to full speed and was running like clockwork.

"You are better than your interview!" Nussle praised me in the hallway after meeting the team. "I could not have asked for a faster start-up and with such heavy hitters!"

I thanked him for his vote of confidence. Much work had been done, but more lay ahead.

Most accounts of political administrations completely skip over the personnel transition process. The book *RN*, President Richard Nixon's 1,090-page account of his tenure, has only five paragraphs devoted to arguably the best-planned presidential transition in recent history.[1] The published accounts by President Ronald Reagan, and by his inner circle, fast-forward from election night to inauguration day. Yet it is in the building of the first team that key decisions about priorities and processes are made. It is like a huge card game. The transition shuffles and deals the cards. The administration is the playing out of the hand. A skilled leader can make the most of any hand dealt, but it is much easier if it is a good hand to begin with. As coined early on in the days of the Chesapeake Society and "Inchon," "People equal policy."

Starting on the afternoon of Saturday, December 10, I turned my attention to creating a team that would become known as the "A Ring." The focus of my thoughts was the large CAO organizational chart now propped up on my desk. Armed with some Post-its, which I generically call "yellow stickies," I took the first steps to creating a new organization.

It had been my experience that most change efforts failed because the leader never won the hearts and minds of his or her own inner circle. The leader's message of change collapsed as it was filtered through people who did not believe in what was happening. The organization then received conflicting information and direction from the very people who were viewed as the leader's most trusted lieutenants. My goal was to avoid this fundamental failure by bringing in professionals I had already worked with and who shared my goals of revolutionary reform.

It was also clear to me that the sheer volume of information to be analyzed and actions to be taken required a team of capable "change managers" working with me as soon as possible. Having worked in the House and followed the need for reform for nearly twenty years, I thought that identifying the team should come first; understanding the transition findings in detail could wait a few days. In addition, my change team needed to be composed of subject-matter experts in finance, legal, procurement, human resources, information resources, and customer service to better assess the required actions arising from the fifteen transition books. I viewed my coming CAO role as the facilitator and coordinator of expert resources, not being an expert in all fields.

I wrote down names on individual yellow stickies—names that I had pored over in my mind since Thursday, from the thousands of people I had worked with, and from among my colleagues, my clients, and my mentors. One by one, I tapped them into place on the large board.

Tom Simon's yellow sticky went up by "internal controls," as I saw this as the single most critical position on the chart. From that position he would be free to roam the organization, reviewing all operations.

John Garbett's name went by "support services," which was a grab bag of food, supplies, equipment, catering, and all media. It was the closest thing to the House's "back lot." I also liked the idea of having him handle the extensive media and recording-studio operations. "He will have all the cameras and studios he needs to prevent being homesick for Hollywood," I mused to myself.

Facilities management was the place for Paul Sweetland. This operation oversaw furnishings, parking, and warehouse management and would handle the critical liaison work with the architect of the Capitol on maintaining the House buildings.

Paul had more than thirty-four years of management experience. He was the first director of the Federal Quality Institute (FQI). The FQI was the office coordinating and training staff in quality management for the federal government. I had met Paul when I was with Philip Crosby. At that time, he had just completed his detail for the FQI and had returned to heading quality initiatives for the U.S. Forest Service. He had been in facilities and operations management with the Forest Service since 1960. He was a towering man with a gift for presentation and intellectual discourse.

Procurement and purchasing was going to be key to properly outsourcing House services and bringing integrity to the troublesome and patronage-laden area of service contracts. The logical choice was Phil Kiko. I had known Phil since 1978, when he was the legislative assistant for Representative F. James Sensenbrenner (R-WI). He had been one of the most productive members of the Chesapeake Society and had been a key liaison at the Department of the Interior for "Inchon." More importantly for the reform effort that lay ahead, he was currently serving as deputy director of the Office of Hearings & Appeals at the Department of the Interior. This was the unit that resolved all contract and procurement disputes for this cabinet department. Phil combined extensive management experience and knowledge of the complexities of government procurement issues with a highly detail-oriented legal mind.

I looked at the chart and saw a large separate organizational box for "postal operations." This had been the domain of Robert Rota (House postmaster), the place where things had begun to unravel for the Democrats and the old order. My instincts told me that the best action to take would be to abolish this as a separate fiefdom, fold it under the umbrella of "information resources," and consider it as part of the larger flow of data and documents in the House. I would also downgrade this position (it had a car and driver and was listed as one of the most important administrative positions in House directories). This would be the first major signal that the old order of things was being destroyed.

The "information resources" unit would be the pathway to the future. The mandate for a "cyber-Congress" had already been laid out by Gingrich himself. The force of history also led to an aggressive and revolutionary rethinking of how congressional information was acquired, processed, and disseminated.

I looked to Don Mutersbaugh, who had been a senior executive in charge of online financial processing at Blue Cross and Blue Shield of the National Capital Area. Don had become part of FMI, and displayed a gift for seeing strategic impacts, whether they related to change-management issues or information resources.

To work with Don, I had a highly successful senior "techie" in mind. Rick Endres served in the Commerce Department during the Reagan administration as director of space commerce and as deputy assistant secretary for technology policy. He was currently in the private sector running his own information-management consulting company.

Three other senior positions had to be addressed, and they were critical. The original transition chart had a separate executive overseeing both human resources and finance. I felt that this was already one more layer of bureaucracy than would be required. I eliminated this position, leaving the two functions directly reporting to me. My bias had always been toward eliminating positions and layers wherever possible. By eliminating the postmaster and this "resource management" executive,

I could upgrade the human-resources and finance positions to the level of seniority they merited.

With massive downsizing and outsourcing being contemplated, human resources would be a lightning rod for criticism and second-guessing by the members and the media alike. If the sensitive work of rearranging people and positions was not conducted professionally, then we could all end up in court the rest of our lives. In addition, I had read about the inevitability of making the House comply with all federal employment and labor laws. This could be the center of major controversy if the wrong person was in charge.

There were only a handful of people I could trust with such a pivotal assignment. I approached Kay Ford, a senior human-resources professional who had played a significant role in staffing the Reagan administration. She had started the personnel operation for the Reagan campaign in 1979. It was this operation that I took over in August 1980. Kay went on to run campaign operations in California. We worked closely during the transition, with her running personnel for the presidential inaugural. She was an early member of "Inchon" and had gone on to distinguish herself at the Departments of Energy, Labor, and Transportation and in the Intergovernmental Affairs office at the White House. As important, she had knowledge of thousands of skilled professionals whom she could recruit for the multitude of positions we would have to staff in the coming years.

Finance was another key position. Every House scandal had money at its roots. Gaining control of the money and building systems that would ensure sustainable integrity in one of the most corrupt public-finance systems would require stamina as well as intelligence. I turned to Tom Simon for ideas, as he had spent his life in accounting circles. One name came immediately to his lips, Tom Anfinson. It would become Simon's greatest contribution to the House revolution.

Anfinson had more than thirty years' experience as a certified public accountant (CPA) and executive accountant. Tom had started as a CPA with Price Waterhouse. He rose to serve as the deputy chief financial officer for Toyota Motors USA. During the Reagan administration, he was the chief financial officer for the Department of Education and the executive director of the U.S. Savings Bond program. His mind was capable of tracking and analyzing vast arrays of figures. He would become my best ally in finding ways to cut costs and also in finding resources at critical moments.

In the world of Washington, and most certainly in the world of Congress, all roads led to legal issues. I had learned long ago that the competency and creativity of your senior attorney could make or break an organization. The minefields that lay ahead in reforming the House would require a master at the art of strategic legal reasoning and positioning. The person who came to mind was Mike Dorsey.

Dorsey had more than twenty-six years' experience as a senior attorney, including serving as assistant attorney general for the State of Missouri and as general counsel for the U.S. Department of Housing and Urban Development (HUD). He had been a partner with McDowell, Rice & Smith and with Stinson, Mag & Fizzell. He would become a major factor in the reforms to come, both as my administrative counsel and as the de facto legal advisor to the House.

Assuming that the legal issues we were about to face would be daunting for just one lawyer, I turned to another trusted colleague from the Chesapeake Society and "Inchon," Bill Norton. Bill had an excellent combination of experience in legal, procurement, and human-resources issues within the federal government, and he had worked in the House.

The management revolution in the House would start as a destructive act. We would have to quickly and completely obliterate the old order. My experience in change management had taught me that the ultimate success of such an action is in the culture you build to take its place. For this I would need people who I knew understood the challenge in rebuilding trust and enthusiasm among the "survivors" once a reengineering effort had begun.

Bill Sturdevant would not only serve as Simon's deputy but also become the nucleus for the new quality-management-based culture. I had met Bill when he was director of corporate quality for Blue Cross and Blue Shield of the National Capital Area. His long career with Blue

Cross gave him extensive insights into how to achieve excellence in a service environment.

The other member of this cultural nucleus would be Gloria Wright-Simmonds. Gloria had been one of the earliest members of Philip Crosby's team and had the unique skill of being able to accurately plan and track operations and to anticipate implementation problems before they arose. She became my most trusted colleague in the firm's Northeast region. I understood that the chief administrative officer of the House was a new position. Every action I took would potentially establish lasting precedents regarding the office's role in the House and in the position's relationship to congressional and Washington protocol. Gloria, like Simon and Garbett, was also one of the few people who had no reticence in telling me if I was doing something crazy. Such a reality check was critical for anyone taking on a major governing position. It was a trait I would try to nurture in all members of my inner circle.

This first wave of people was identified initially by a set of yellow stickies on the organizational chart in my cubicle. They were further developed through Saturday and Sunday as each person was called and the opportunity explained. I wanted to make clear to potential team members the intensive, difficult, and historic nature of what I was asking them to do. In each case the conversation went something like this. I would start with pleasantries and try to learn what they were up to, in part to assess availability. "I wanted to see if you would like to become part of a major management revolution . . ." They inevitably asked where. "I am about to be named the first chief administrative officer of the House."

"Wow!" would be the first response along with congratulations.

"This position gives us a historic opportunity to make change happen. We can clean up the Congress and introduce modern practices to 'the final frontier' of management."

"Count me in! What can I do to help?" was the answer from those who became the "A Ring." Each conversation ended with my explaining the pending ethics ruling on when they could come on board. I then told them to start clearing their "decks" because they would be needed as soon as clearance was given.

"You've made my Christmas! There is a Santa Claus!" said a delighted Kay Ford. "I am speechless, thank you for thinking of me," said Norton. "This is the only thing that could take me out of a career position," observed Kiko. "This is an opportunity of a lifetime; I hope I can live up to your expectations," said Mutersbaugh.

Other senior members took longer to recruit. I wanted to make sure key deputies to my associate administrators were compatible with them and with me. Therefore, I conferred with Garbett about the two key people who would oversee major elements of his domain, media services and support services. I also conferred with Mutersbaugh about the person who would run the postal, printing, and folding services, the most antiquated and corrupt parts of the CAO's office.

The next day, Jack Howard dropped by my office. He had been following my recruitment efforts and knew I still needed someone who understood both media production and media relations, a unique set of skills. "I would like you to talk to James Davison. He may have the background you need."

Davison was indeed what we needed. Jim had recently been a producer and director for the media office at Purdue University. He had an encyclopedic knowledge of production technology and the creative mind to apply it to crisis situations. He had also served as the news producer at KSLA-TV in Shreveport, Louisiana, and was a member of CBS News, working on international assignments for six years.

For the other senior member of Garbett's team, I introduced him to Carole Kordich. In the years I had known Carole, I had grown to respect her dual abilities of quick and accurate analysis of complex situations, and her ability to facilitate groups. She had been the national director of training for NHP Property Management. Another key element was her experience as an executive handling customer service for United Airlines, critical for the reinvention of frontline service that I had in mind. Garbett was very impressed with Carole and recruited her on the spot.

Bill Sturdevant recruited the final senior member of the A Ring, one of his longtime friends and a coworker from Blue Cross, Benjamin Lusby. Don Mutersbaugh had also been at Blue Cross and enthusiastically endorsed him as a tireless worker with incredible perseverance.

Ben had served twenty-four years as an executive with Blue Cross and Blue Shield, rising in the ranks to oversee all their communications support operations: mail, printing, and distribution. This was a perfect background for the task ahead. After leaving Blue Cross, he had become the district service manager for Pitney Bowes, the world's leading mail-support company, in the Baltimore-Washington area. Unfortunately, he had to give two weeks' notice and would not be on board until just before the new Congress had begun.

I next turned to administrative support. "Give me fifty good secretaries, and I can run Washington," I mused during a speech during the Reagan transition in December 1980. I then watched as many high-level Reagan officials spun out of control. This was usually because their receptionists or secretaries were career holdovers who had no interest in their well-being.

In the fourteen years since the dawn of the Reagan era, the information revolution had liberated clerical staff from many mundane duties. The titles of "secretary" and "receptionist" had been banished from most corporate environments. The traditional "gatekeepers" were now "special," "personal," or "executive" assistants.

For the CAO operation, this cadre of traditional "gatekeepers" would become important members of the change team. In fact, in the CAO operation to come, these support professionals would end up being key implementers as they interacted with the line organization and with the CAO's "customer base" in more tactical and timely ways than the executive tier. I began to search my mind for those who had excelled as "doers," problem solvers, tactical decision makers, and crisis managers. It is like the process shown at the beginning of the old *Mission Impossible* television show; you mentally sort through dossiers to find the right mix of skills to make the mission possible.

One in particular was heartwarming: Edith "Edie" Vivian, the former officer manager for Representative Don Young (R-AK). Vivian had been my supervisor when I interned in Young's office. She was now retired and happily immersed in volunteer work. I recalled how efficient she was in running Young's operation and how much she taught me about the ways of the House.

Another upbeat call was from Jane Bennett. She was the office manager for Representative "Buck" McKeon (R-CA). During my days with Representative Ashbrook, she was in charge of computer services, building and managing the massive mailing lists that the congressman had accumulated from his years as a national leader of the conservative movement. I recalled Jane's tireless commitment to meeting Ashbrook's exacting standards and her unflagging sense of humor and common sense.

As I tied up loose ends on FMI with one of my business partners, Armando Chapelli, he offered his own executive assistant to be part of my support team. This was a gracious "house warming" offer. Jennifer Borcherdling had been Armando's eyes, ears, and implementer for several years. She was highly respected within the Washington Consulting Group as a problem solver and had gathered an impressive knowledge of information technology. I readily agreed to add her to the mix. She would prove a key asset in building the cyber-Congress.

As I thought about the world of customer service that we would all enter, my thoughts turned to one of the best "doers" I had ever encountered—Debbie Hansen. We had worked on numerous campaigns with Virginia Young Republicans during the 1970s. More importantly, I had watched her move from grassroots activism to becoming one of the best executive assistants in the Reagan administration. Her ability to sort out details, ferret out documents and facts, and handle difficult people and situations consistently impressed me. She was currently the office manager for the Cato Institute, a major Washington think tank. I called her to see if I could entice her to join the reform team. After thirty minutes on the telephone, she was ready to give notice and join the House revolution.

By the afternoon of Friday, December 16, my small beachhead of Garbett and Simon was focusing on preparations for bringing the main part of the team on board by Monday. Jane Bennett had worked out sharing time between the transition and McKeon's office. She threw herself into preparing briefing materials and arranging the reform team's schedule for next week. She seemed to know everybody, and she procured ID badges, parking spaces, supplies, support, and appointments for briefings in record time. Simon began outlining the procedures that would govern our time prior to January 4.

PERSONNEL MECHANICS

The transition continued to build a rule book for the first transition since December 1954. A key document was the guidance issued by the ethics committee authorizing an "advisory committee" to form and assist the transition.[2] However, it did not address bringing in people who might later fill the various management positions in the House.

Dan Crowley and Jack Howard worked to get additional guidance from the ethics committee. Nussle sent a new request to the ethics committee on December 14. Understanding the need for speed, the committee immediately wrote back, stating that any future employee of the House could become part of the transition, as they "are learning about their future positions before assuming them, but they are not actually doing any Congressional business." The committee concluded, "Accordingly, it is the opinion of the Committee that their 'indoctrination' does not violate House Rule XLV. It is permissible for them to attend briefings, be given briefings, be given materials to read and retain, pose questions, sit in on meetings, interview individuals about their duties, and so forth."[3]

The way was cleared for the reform team to enter the Capitol.

Parallel to bringing people on board was the process of removing incumbents. After our meeting with Medlock's executives, Simon began work on the procedures and documents required to fire the House employees identified on the December 15 list. Working closely with Crowley and other transition staff, and drawing on his years at the Office of Personnel Management, Simon crafted the appropriate documents.[4]

There still remained the details of sorting out the severance packages (paying out accrued leave could total many thousands of dollars for some of the long-term workers). Committee staffs had a wide array of personnel policies and procedures, some not written down. The letters went out on December 17 and cleared the way for the management revolution to proceed.

Thursday, December 15, ended with a round of additional meetings and briefings. While Simon worked on personnel issues, Garbett and I toured the House recording studios. We learned about how a network of robotic cameras, controlled from the basement of the Capitol, broadcast a live feed of the proceedings on the House floor, which was public domain. C-SPAN early on decided to pick up this feed and built a network around it, although anyone could do the same thing. I remembered those early days of C-SPAN in 1979, when the Chesapeake opposition used visuals to create some wonderful "street theater" on the House floor to build public awareness among C-SPAN's small but growing viewership.

We also toured the extensive studios in the basement of the Rayburn House Office Building. There were a number of items of "movie magic" that were created with tax dollars to "better portray" the House, including a series of false backgrounds showing the Capitol during the day and at night that could be dropped into position with the push of a button. The books that lined the fake congressional office shelves were cut in half to save studio space. I left Garbett to get acquainted with the studio staff and had my first meeting with Representative Vernon Ehlers (R-MI), the designated head of the cyber-Congress task force.

FIRST MEETING WITH EHLERS

Representative Vern Ehlers (R-MI) had been elected in a special election in December 1993. In just one year, he had used his formidable science background (the only doctor of physics in the Congress) to become Gingrich's main missionary for bringing the House into the information age. He had taken the lead during the transition in developing a series of recommendations for the 104th Congress. I had already read the "Ehlers Report" for Gingrich's cyber-Congress.

One victory was already within his grasp. With the push for an Open House, he and Gingrich had used the Republican transition to rapidly implement what had been a long-stalled effort to put House documents on the Internet. The Library of Congress, along with its Congressional Research Service and the House Information Systems (HIS) unit within the CHA, was to launch a new website within the first days of the 104th Congress. It would be called the "Thomas" system for Thomas Jefferson.

One of the more sensitive subjects was to be the fate of HIS. While all transition documents pointed to HIS becoming part of the CAO's office, it remained a committee staff. HIS staff provided the House with its telecommunications, its computers, and its data storage, making it an administrative office. Yet the perks, salaries, and privileges of being part of a committee staff were going to be hard to lose. Many HIS employees were busy lobbying the new CHO to ignore the transition recommendations.

Another factor was that CHO members, like Representative Ehlers, were still torn between supporting the transition's and the Speaker's vision of an independent CAO and their longing, after so many years in the minority, to directly control the House's infrastructure. This was particularly true in Ehlers's case, as he had very clear ideas about how to proceed with making the cyber-Congress a reality. He believed his work on creating a similar, although smaller system, for the Michigan Senate was a prelude to his becoming the leader of this historic effort. His hope was to build an "Ehlers system" through his own direct control over HIS and then, when all of his report's recommendations had been implemented, to turn it over to the CAO.[5]

Our first meeting in his Longworth office was cordial. He later admitted that "Faulkner had his head screwed on right,"[6] as we came to a quick agreement that the House had many years of catching up to do if it was ever going to aspire to the cyber-Congress label. He was very much focused on building off the existing mainframe and already had personal and professional ties to Microsoft. During our dialogue, I tried to leave open the possibility of other vendors and a more open framework of servers.[7] Ehlers's system was for highly-prescriptive direction to member offices and the continued use of the homegrown "proprietary systems" built for the House. My bias was more for off-the-shelf solutions, possible outsourcing, and a more general guidance to members. This was consistent with my own "run the House as a business and treat each office as a small business" approach.

It was clear there was potential for us to be either close allies or bitter rivals. He was insistent on interviewing any selections I was going to make for HIS, and began to recommend hiring several of his former staffers and colleagues. Along with Thomas, I now had two Republican members of the CHO who would require agile handling on my part. Several of my former Reagan colleagues, who had worked with Ehlers in Michigan, provided me with detailed information on his background, personality, friends, and foes.[8]

Friday was not over yet. Ed Gillespie caught up with me before I rejoined my team. *"Roll Call* is going to run a major article on you this weekend."

"I thought you all thought *Roll Call* was just a crackpot liberal tabloid?" I countered.

"Well, yes, it is like a comic book, but people are already jumpy about what this new CAO operation might be like. We have to deal with this, at least for now."

Roll Call was laying the groundwork to separate me from the rest of the Speaker's team and to harass my every move. They had cropped me out of the House officers' photo in their December 15 edition and had not spent much time on my background. This was to become an ongoing pattern of this tabloid: not a word against the other two House officers, and never a word in favor of me or the office of the CAO. A clearer picture of their reasons for this would emerge later, but for now it was "static on the radio."

"Please call them and give them some rebuttals," urged Gillespie. "And keep me posted."

I called Mary Jacoby at *Roll Call* and proceeded to hear an onslaught of how I was a fraud and that everything I had done in my life had been wrong and injurious to the Republic. I was sure she was ready to link me to every scandal of the Reagan administration. So much for professionalism and objectivity!

She assaulted my credentials. First, I was too young for the job (the clerk was younger, as were twenty-one members of the freshman class). Then, I did not have House experience (I had worked on House members' staffs for more than five years, double the tenure of current House staffers, and served as head of congressional liaison for the FAA. Neither the incoming clerk nor the incoming sergeant at arms had ever served in the House). She then said that I was too "partisan," even though I had worked with five Democratic governors, receiving commendations from two of them, whereas the clerk had only worked for Republicans, including the Republican National Congressional Campaign Committee.

Jacoby then insisted that I had been just a salesman for Crosby. (Tell that to the five thousand executives I taught in seminars!) She tried to tear apart FMI as a "single shingle" operation. (Tell that to my two partners and twenty associates.) She even tried to split hairs between Crosby and Deming on their approaches to quality and organizational change, as if she were a scholar on their works! For forty minutes I countered her accusations. The next day only two quotes appeared for all my effort. All of her attacks remained in place.[9]

I could not believe that she blatantly ignored the documented truth. Jacoby never called the names and sources I provided. I wrote off *Roll Call* as a third-rate tabloid for the remainder of my tenure. I also wanted, right then and there, to haul Jacoby and her editors into court. "Don't worry—it's only *Roll Call*," advised Tony Blankley. "No one reads it except a few interns. Ignore them. The real media will know what good we are all doing."

THE BEACHHEAD

Monday, December 19 was like igniting a booster rocket. Having my team in place and absorbing their enthusiasm was a major adrenaline rush. Their average age was fifty-three, and all had worked in top jobs and high-pressure environments, but they took on the transition like it was their first campaign. They high-fived and hugged each other like a championship team every time someone discovered some new fact or uncovered some new abuse of the system.

We established a daily schedule of meetings for people to report in, and set up a resource library for documents and reports. Each day, one member of the team would present a short seminar on change management or organizational analysis. This was designed both as a way of introducing the talents each had to the team and to make sure everyone was using similar terms and approaches in their work. I usually started the day with quotes and articles from Crosby and other management gurus as "thought provokers." One of my favorite sources was *High-Velocity Culture Change*, by Price Pritchett and Ron Pound:

"Don't let the existing culture dictate your approach."

"You will have trouble creating a new culture if you insist on doing it in ways that are consistent with the old one.

"Deliberately destabilize your group."

"You must hit with enough shock effect to immobilize the old culture at least temporarily."

"Disarm the Old Culture."

"You must seize control of the energy—turn it to your advantage—so it can't be used to fortify and perpetuate the old culture."[10]

These provocative quotes, fortified by case studies from *Harvard Business Review*, *Quality Progress* magazine, and other journals, became the mental calisthenics to start the day. The A Ring would then fan out into the House buildings to interview staff and collect documents. I would selectively attend these sessions and tours, leaving my schedule free to handle a growing array of legal and personnel issues.

The team set up their operations in HC-8. Worktables were spread with documents and notes, and flip charts accented each corner of the room. New telephone lines were run. Edie and Jane managed the growing infrastructure while Debbie and Jennifer worked on fact-finding.

Kay Ford began building job networks to prepare for all CAO jobs being recompeted. Her intent was to have at least five applicants for every position. Ford brought in a young volunteer from the Heritage Foundation, Scott Granieri, to help build lists and review positions. His enthusiasm for personnel reminded me of my early career.

The morning meetings of the transition team now included most of the CAO team. Our numbers swamped the room. Simon and Dorsey took dominant roles in working with the transition on the many legal issues relating to "cutting over" to Republican rule. Mike brought in Jackie Aamot to assist him with his legal work. She had worked with Mike at HUD and had been the executive secretariat of the department.

The CHO was also staffing up to meet the growing array of policy and procedural issues. Otto Wolff, a longtime Republican activist, was hired to be Stacy Carlson's liaison with the House officers. Otto had been my immediate supervisor on the Reagan campaign. Stacy had used me as a reference in her hiring of Otto. I recommended him. We had remained close over the years since the 1980 campaign. During his eleven years as the deputy assistant secretary for management, he used Philip Crosby Associates to provide seminars on quality management. Otto was very much a hardworking professional, to the point of being overly analytic, but not a crusader or a risk taker. This mixture would severely test our friendship.

I decided that additional input was needed to help the team identify all the reform issues and to help those without political backgrounds understand the political issues surrounding our management revolution. Rick Shapiro, from the Congressional Management Foundation, conducted a brilliant session on what needed to be done to make the House more professional. He also gave several pointers on change management. The best one was how to "paint the buses." This meant finding something high profile, but not necessarily critical, and making an immediate and dramatic change. He cited a mayor who "painted the buses" as a way of showing that the times were different.

Dave Mason and Ed Feulner from the Heritage Foundation also spoke to the A Ring. They provided extensive documents on the House scandals of the early 1990s and lists of contacts within the House that we could draw upon for additional information. The success of these sessions led to a series of speakers over the next two years, including international dignitaries and leading management thinkers.

The firing letters did not sit well with the recipients. Several mounted letter-writing campaigns to remain in office. True to his word, Nussle worked closely with me to deflect this pressure, allowing me to continue building the reform team without political intervention.

In only one case did I have to consider a different course of action. Representative Bill Emerson (R-MO) called me on behalf of Bern Beidel, the director of employee assistance.

"Scot," he began (he had known me for years), "Bern is different from the others. He was hired through a nationwide search that I helped conduct. You will see from his background that he was with the New Jersey State Police for fifteen years prior to being hired by us.

"Scot, as you know I have been overcoming alcoholism for several years. Bern has helped me. While part of my therapy has been to publicly admit my problem, there are thirty-three other members whom Bern is confidentially helping with drug addictions. I speak for all of them. Changing Bern could hurt many of their recoveries."

That clinched it. Kay Ford and I quickly met with Bern. We were impressed with his professionalism and his approach to employee assistance. It took two days of discussions, but with the assistance of Nussle, we overturned "the list" in this instance. We never regretted it. Bern remained an outstanding "holdover" and helped build a positive work culture in the years ahead.

As the A Ring began collecting more data on how the House really ran, the plan for "cutting over" to Republican administration took shape. Our to-do lists grew hourly as January 4, 1995, drew closer. Key to the first days of the 104th was communications and dollars. While the two Toms (Anfinson and Simon) waded ever deeper into the financial swamps, the information team of Rick, Don, and Jennifer was key to solving the communications issue.

How were we going to keep track of everybody when we were spread through six buildings and were all committed to "management by walking around"? The solution was to wrap an advanced communications grid around the A Ring, with possible expansion as the team grew. The foundation would be an e-mail system. Rick was familiar with Novell GroupWise, so we obtained the licenses and began wiring a local area network of computers for the A Ring.

Jennifer found mobile telephones for everyone and recommended SkyTel pagers to handle the immediate needs for connecting people. This would prove the best of all the communication ideas. SkyTel allowed for broadcasting 110 characters to everyone in the grid or to selected people. A page could be sent from a computer. This allowed us to immediately establish a communication protocol: everyone would check e-mails twice a day for routine information, but emergency communications would go out on the SkyTel pagers. If your pager went off (we had everyone set their pagers to vibrate to lessen the noise disruption from beeping), then drop everything, as something important required immediate action.

Such a system allowed us to keep our mobile telephones switched off, saving batteries, and allowed detailed broadcast messages to be sent out on the SkyTel network. This system was a technology and management breakthrough for the House. It would later be supplemented with broadcast voice mail. It allowed us to maximize our time and to be totally virtual and spontaneous in our operations, and eliminated the need for a network of support staff to act as gatekeepers. It proved the winning edge we needed to successfully implement the revolution.

THE GREAT LAND RUSH

"It's like the Oklahoma land rush," remarked Nussle one day. He went on to describe how the downsizing of the Appropriations Committee led to the availability of choice offices in the Capitol. Then there was the elimination of the doorkeeper. His office was available. Then came the fact that Gingrich wanted to use the minority leader's office as his Speaker's office. All of a sudden, instead of the suite off of Statuary Hall and the hideaways on the third floor of the Capitol being the center of power in the House, the second floor was to become the nerve center. Majority-leader-to-be Dick Armey (R-TX) wanted the old third-floor Speaker space and coveted some of the clerk's space off of Statuary Hall. Whip-to-be Tom DeLay (R-TX) now looked at the core clerk's space on the first floor for his office suite. There was also a highly emotional scramble for all those "hideaway" offices that were behind countless unmarked doors throughout the Capitol.

"It's a nightmare," observed Nussle. "Everyone wants space in the Capitol. I am doing all I can to make sure you have at least one office. They say the CAO has nothing to do with floor operations and should be out of the Capitol. I say you are an officer and should be in the Capitol near House leadership."

My heart sank. My team had found a half-dozen spaces in the basement of the Capitol that would allow at least some to remain close to each other. I had assumed I would at least get Medlock's two rooms. I had hoped for the doorkeeper's space as a way of bringing a majority of the A Ring into one suite. Nussle told me that although my team could temporarily use spaces in the Capitol, they would be housed in House Annex 1.

Near the end of the day, Nussle took me aside and asked me to walk with him. "Don't tell anyone else, but I am going to show you two rooms." We walked up the stairs to a set of unmarked doors astride the handicapped ramp next to the "crypt."

Nussle unlocked the unmarked doors and led me into two suites. The interior suite was H-112–H-111; the exterior suite was H-157, with an incredible view of the Mall, a huge chandelier, an elaborately painted ceiling, and a great fireplace. H-112 was dreadful. It was the offices for the House counsel. The windowless rooms were crammed with desks, bookcases, and a large counter. There were ugly fluorescent lights hanging from the ceilings. "In an hour we are going to make the final room assignments. One of these will become my hideaway office; the other will be yours. I am going to let you have first choice," said Nussle.

Although H-157 was clearly the more beautiful and had a view, I saw H-112 as the better choice. It had more space. I could possibly house two or more staff members with me, whereas H-157 had only a tiny alcove attached to the main office. There was space for a waiting area in H-112, whereas none existed in H-157. This would be important, as I predicted that many people would be dropping in on a CAO. H-112 also had an escape door. The inner room, H-111, had a door that exited to a hallway by the crypt area. I anticipated there would be times that I would want to enter and exit without running a gauntlet of people. In H-157, I would be trapped unless I wanted to jump out the window. "I'll take H-112," I announced to Nussle.

THE SECRETS OF THE HOUSE

December 15, 1994

"Oh, that's the free gift wrapping," Jeff Trandahl observed as we walked past a line of twenty people holding small parcels. Two large cardboard candy canes framed an open doorway near the basement elevator lobby of the Longworth Building.

"Free gift wrap?" I stopped and looked back at the gathering.

"Yeah. The folding room has nothing to do during the holidays, so they wrap Christmas presents for members and staff."

"It's free?" I continued to look on with amazement. "You mean the wrapping paper, tape, and ribbon come from tax dollars?"

"I guess so," answered Trandahl. "Everyone looks forward to it."

Welcome to Babylon.

House Rule II states that each House officer "shall take an oath to support the Constitution of the United States and for the true and faithful discharge of the duties of his office to the best of his knowledge and ability, and to keep the secrets of the House."[1]

"To keep the secrets of the House" has for 207 years been used to silence anyone who finds out just how the House abuses public funds and voter trust. The secrets of the House are not nuclear launch codes or names of intelligence agents. The House has no real secrets in the national-security sense. Its secrets are those things it has sanctioned to bend reality in favor of incumbents and to create a surreal world where votes are brokered for creature comforts. Its secrets relate to how the system is polluted and choked with money, and "for the record" has meaning only after much editing. The real secret of the House is a culture of arrogance in which, like Jack Nicholson in *A Few Good Men*, members and staff assume the American public "can't handle the truth," and so the truth is filtered and fabricated.

During the course of the transition, and on into the first month of the 104th Congress, my team and I encountered ever-stranger evidence of the most corrupt, dysfunctional, and surreal operating environment in any of our professional careers. The fact that this abuse and mayhem was being fueled by public funds appalled all of us.

After their orientation session on December 19, the A Ring fanned out into the various operations of the House to find out all they could about what was really going on. Every hour that went by unearthed amazing stories of abuse and chaos. Even Phil Kiko, Bill Norton, and the other veterans of government were awed by the sheer audacity of the corruption. Some private-sector members of the team went so far as to say they were ashamed to be Americans.

FINANCIAL FIASCO

At the core of the House's "secrets" is how it funds its operations and what it actually reports to the public. Until the beginning of the 104th Congress, there were only two documents that the public used to track the finances of the House. Both were works of fiction.

The appropriations for the House were always "reverse engineered." The fiscal year never actually closed the books. Some accounts had activity up to six months into the new year. The key was that many members and committees never spent the entire amount appropriated to them. So, although the full funding of accounts was reported and funded in the appropriation process, a multimillion-dollar wedge of funds was created. This wedge was then reallocated through a series of verbal agreements, without any documentation.

In an attempt to cover this diversion of funds, the Clerk of the House Report became an even greater work of fiction. This report, designed to track the quarterly outlays of funds in the House, was usually not printed until up to a year after the close of the quarter. Only a few thousand copies were ever printed, with distribution tightly controlled by the CHA.

The Clerk of the House Report was formatted to frustrate even the most thorough accountant. All expenditures were listed chronologically within member, committee, and general accounts. The descriptions of expenditures were deliberately vague. A careful review of the totals showed that no member or committee overspent its allotments, yet many actually did. How could this be?

The House Finance Office kept two sets of books. One set was the actual running tally of expenditures. This was kept using a large checkbook-like register compiled in large handwritten ledgers designed for the Second Continental Congress in 1775. With no accrual of ongoing financial obligations (such as the salaries of staff members or the monthly rental payments for an office lease), the ledger passively documented numerous accounts spending beyond their limits. The second set of books then moved these over-expenditures into general House accounts. This is why there was up to a year between the close of a quarter and the release of the fictitious clerk's report. This was made possible because the fifty-four-person House Finance Office had no CPAs and only three people had any accounting training. None of the fifty-four had formal degrees in finance or accounting. "We have one person with a disability on staff," commented Anfinson. "He is numbers dyslexic!"

The other fundamental fiction of House finances was the highly-published allowances for members. Officially, members have their own salaries paid out of a general House account, and then they are provided a lump sum ("clerk hire") to cover all their other office expenses, including the hiring of staff. This figure varies, based on twenty-six round trips to their home districts. For example, the delegate from the District of Columbia would have a smaller allocation ($800,000) than the representative from Alaska ($950,000). Prior to the 104th Congress, this allocation was divided into minuscule accounts with their own spending limits. Because many members spent past these mini-accounts, another series of bookkeeping revisions had to take place so that a member's overall spending conformed to the official guidelines.

Another basic fiction was that the member allocations covered all office operations. Not at all. Many basic support operations for member offices were actually directly funded through other accounts and never allocated to individual members. One example was the House folding room. The folding room was founded in the 1850s to fold letters and stuff them into envelopes. With the machine age, the folding and stuffing stopped being done by hand. With computers and mailing labels, the development of highly-targeted mailing lists became common practice. This $5.5-million-a-year, 120-person operation was funded out of the doorkeeper's account. Some mailing lists were purchased from vendors to target mailings to small businesses or to specific industries. It was all done in the name of "informing constituents," but this entire operation was designed for the reelection campaigns of the House incumbents. Members could even expand their lists beyond their own districts to prepare for statewide races.

Other services for members—videotaping, photography, and radio shows—only had a small portion of their actual expense charged back to member accounts. Therefore, members could stage elaborate "Report from Washington" half-hour television shows, complete with guests, professional special effects, editing, and sound tracks, for only the cost of the videotape. All the staff, staging, and equipment costs were borne by a general account under the clerk. The photos taken of visitors, including those individual color prints of the local high school band posed on the Capitol steps with the member, were also charged back at only a fraction of the true costs. The rest was absorbed by the clerk's accounts.

Members were provided with barbers, beauticians, aestheticians who gave bikini waxes, and a shoeshine stand. Although these providers all charged market rates, their operations lost hundreds of thousands of dollars annually. These losses were all absorbed in general administrative accounts.

Fortunately, the House restaurant system had been outsourced to vendors who paid the House a percentage of gross receipts. However, the architect of the Capitol, under orders from the Senate, was still subsidizing meals provided to the Senate at more than $2 million a year out of general funds.

Prior to the 104th Congress, each member had a government American Express credit card. Members could charge anything they wanted on their cards. They were on an "honor system" to personally reimburse the House for their unofficial expenditures; the House paid the entire balance on the card out of central funds in the clerk's office. The result was tens of thousands of tax dollars spent each year on personal vacations, gifts, cars, clothing, home furnishings, stereo equipment, and entertainment.

All members received personal retirement and other investment counseling from a ring of three $80,000-a-year "payroll clerks." Originally located in the sergeant at arms' office as part of the House banking system, this unit was transferred to the director of nonlegislative and financial services as part of the 1993 reforms.

House leadership received additional operating subsidies. Drivers and limousines were considered "security," and their operation fell under the domain of the sergeant at arms. The architect of the Capitol provided a staff of interior designers to assist in the decorating of leadership offices. When the designers selected silk tapestries for the furniture and designer silk damask draperies for the windows, the central furniture accounts under the director of nonlegislative and financial services absorbed the full cost. This could run up to $50,000 per work order, with multiple orders per room. Custom-built furniture and the purchase of oriental rugs were also handled through these shops without any accounting to the members.

Underlying all of this was the fact that there was virtually no documentation. The normal accounting flow is as follows: a purchase order or contract drives a purchase; a goods- or services-received receipt drives a voucher; and a voucher authorizes a check. Much of this trail was missing when the CAO team began reviewing the House books. When Mike Dorsey began organizing the files for the 1,100 district offices, he found that most leases did not exist. Landlords would just call in to say that the member was renewing for another two years.

"Fine, send us a copy of the signed lease," Dorsey would request. After a pause, the landlords would respond: "Lease? We never use a lease. We have always handled this informally." In some cases, the landlords were relatives or campaign-finance officials of the members. Many offices were colocated with campaign or party offices. In no cases were any market surveys conducted to determine whether rents were reasonable.

Examples of the chronic lack of documents were everywhere. The House had a ticket agency, the Combined Airlines Ticket Office (CATO), with offices in the Longworth Building. No one could find any formal agreement or lease for its existence. No one, not even CATO officials, could remember who authorized them. There was also a Western Union office in the Cannon Building. Once again, no one knew how it got there or could find any documents. We discovered that Western Union was only attracting two or three clients a day. No accountability, no rent paid, no nothing. "They have always been there," was the answer from House staff. This led me to muse that we should have hired some cultural anthropologists, since we had uncovered a previously undocumented oral culture.

The two Toms began a methodical search of the House financial files. They likened their search for vendors and suppliers to astronomers looking for planets or dark matter in the universe. Just like the way astronomers first find unusual gravitational fluctuations as the first sign that there may be something "out there," so too did Anfinson and Simon find unusual fluctuations in account balances as the first sign that a House contractor may be "out there."

It was our conclusion that such a system of loose money and no documents could occur only because of a conscious institutional effort to rob the Treasury. It seemed intentional that there were no CPAs to track and control a $725 million annual budget. What payment processes there were all went through the same people. That meant the person authorizing payment was the same one disbursing the money. The general ledger, still kept by hand, had pages with as many as six different handwritings and three colors of ink. Many entries were crossed out with numerous corrections and mathematical errors.

Anfinson and Simon settled into the Finance Office's suite off the rotunda of the Cannon House Office Building. Their first discovery was the check-writing machine. The Congress is able to write and sign its own checks, the way the executive branch uses the Treasury and the treasurer. The machine held the signature block of the clerk. All one had to do was type in a dollar amount and a payee and push the button for a fully valid check. The machine had no internal log for tracking use.

The check blanks were stored in the room with the machine. A key turned the machine on and off. However, as keys kept getting mislaid, the key was left in the machine. The door was unlocked. The ground floor windows had no bars on them. "I think we have found the ultimate ATM machine," deadpanned Simon. There were no logs of who had access to the machine.

Finance Office staff stated that they could not determine whether any unauthorized checks were produced. "We might know if any were written over $5,000," offered one staffer.

It was unfathomable that such operations existed. The House finance system had no checks and balances. It had no warning systems. Over the course of the next month, the CAO team found twenty-four undocumented petty-cash accounts, some with as much as $25,000 in the box. Money gushed from the House, and the only official response was to hold the books open and manufacture reports that showed that the accounts balanced. But these reports did not necessarily reflect anything real.

The House could conduct itself this way because there was no true outside audit. The GAO was an arm of Congress and would be shown what the House wanted the agency to see and instructed on what the House wanted the agency to find. Our team had decades of certified GAO audits claiming everything was fine, yet we blew the myth apart within hours of having unbridled access.

Over the previous five years, an attempt had been made by a House information-systems team to develop a proprietary financial-accounting and tracking system driven off the House's ADABAS mainframe. After the House spent more than $5 million dollars, the system had yet to be tested. Even if the system could work, it would have only been able to meet sixteen of thirty-four basic accounting requirements. It had no analytical capabilities. A trip to a local computer store to buy a copy of Quicken would have netted better results.

THE SCAVENGER HUNT

Down the hall in the finance suite was the House Personnel Office. Kay Ford had discovered the "soap room." This was a room set aside for watching soap operas on television during business hours, complete with sofas and a refrigerator filled with sodas. She found the human-resources files were nonexistent. There were no position descriptions, no hiring forms, and no performance standards. Personnel files on existing employees were sporadic. There were no résumés on existing personnel and no forms tracking personnel actions.

Though members managed their own personal staff, the Finance Office's payroll operation supported members by processing and tracking their hiring and wage decisions. Ford found this chaotic. There were no standards linking pay to duties. Every office could do whatever it wanted.

The result was a salary range of $50,000 and up for the same position. Members did not have position descriptions, functional statements, performance criteria, or hiring guidelines.

Staff turnover in personal staffs ran over 50 percent a year. For a total employment base of approximately fourteen thousand, which included the more stable committee and administrative staffs, more than twenty thousand W-2s had to be issued for the 1994 tax year. Under House rules, members could not give bonuses to their staff, but nothing prevented them from granting a temporary salary increase and then reducing the salary later. The payroll office was processing five hundred or more such actions a month.

Ford also uncovered the fact that the personnel placement office acted as the support staff to the Democratic Caucus in placing patronage workers for Democratic members. There were even in- and out-boxes and other signage clearly marked "Democratic National Committee" and "House Democratic Caucus." The placement office had an array of obsolete typewriters and still had typing and shorthand testing forms. There were no computers.

The seventh floor of House Annex 1, the O'Neill House Office Building, had been designated the CAO suite. As the CAO advance team walked around the space to determine room assignments and computer cabling needs, a number of surprises were in store. These offices had been used by the Democratic Caucus. Boxes of opposition research and focus-group audio and videotapes from the 1994 elections littered the rooms. Their computer cables still sent messages to wires that dangled from abandoned workstations. "It's déjà vu," I mused during my walk around. I remembered my first weeks in the Old Executive Office Building immediately after Reagan's inaugural. The Carter people had left amazingly sensitive mailing lists, printouts, logs, and drafts in their drawers. It was an intelligence windfall for Republican and conservative groups. Now we were encountering similar material. It was like they were in denial of a Republican takeover up to the very end. One day they just left, forgetting to sanitize anything.

It was during this shifting of debris that we found maps and work files showing that all parking allocations and permits were being administered within the Democratic Caucus and not through the architect of the Capitol. The architect of the Capitol still physically issued the permits and ran the garages, but here was clear evidence that the decision process was hardly apolitical.

It was during this discovery that various sources, such as employees, former employees, outside watchdog groups, and news reporters started approaching members of the A Ring with incredible tales of fraud, waste, and abuse. Were they fact or fiction? Some overlapped with accounts already in transition-team reports and briefing books, but others broke new ground for audacity. The A Ring began to distribute the stories, sometimes with introductions to their sources, to the team members in charge of the relevant areas. Then they returned to their giant scavenger hunt to follow up on these new leads. The work was highly productive.

Debbie Hansen and Paul Sweetland combed the printouts and the garages for parking abuses. Tom Simon and Bill Sturdevant detached themselves from their other duties to assist. The search documented fifty lobbyists, former members, and spouses and children of members who had parking permits. Members were supposed to have eight parking spaces for themselves and their Washington staff—five in the underground garages and three in the open-air lots—but 157 members had more than the eight allocated slots or had all of their allocated spaces shifted to inside garages. Representative Charlie Rose (D-NC), the chairman of the CHA, had twelve. We found that some spaces were being used for long-term storage; both a Bentley and a Jaguar were found under tarps. There were also spaces allotted to the Republican and Democratic Congressional Campaign Committees. No wonder the House had to lease additional parking from the District of Columbia ($225,000 a year) and there was talk of acquiring additional spaces.

Norton discovered that each member received seventy-five free subscriptions to the *Congressional Record* from the Government Printing Office. These were intended for local schools and libraries in their districts. However, a random review of member printouts showed that up to two-thirds of all these taxpayer-funded subscriptions went to lobbyists, lawyers, and interest groups in Washington, D.C. Some members sent 100 percent of their subscriptions to Washington addresses.

Hansen and Sweetland also found problems with the furniture inventory—there wasn't one. Nor were there standards or written procedures for furnishings. There were no policies or guidelines for maintenance, repair, or periodic inspection and replacement of House furnishings, rugs, blinds, or draperies. The result was extensive expedited activity driven by crisis and political pressure. Materials were not always bought in bulk. This meant the thousands of furniture items owned by the House were repaired and maintained on a costly retail basis.

Each year the House furniture shops built and repaired thousands of pieces of furniture. As mentioned earlier, none of this was charged to member accounts. Every two years, with the beginning of a new Congress, members get to choose new offices. It is like a drawing for dormitory rooms at a college. The seniors choose first and get the best. The freshmen choose last and end up in places like the attic of the Cannon or Longworth buildings. The ripple effect can create three office moves for every one freshman elected. For the 104th Congress that meant around 264 offices were in play, in addition to the changes in leadership and committee posts.

The House Building Commission rules state that members may have their personal desks and chairs moved to their new offices. In practice every piece of furniture, even for staff, is moved, resulting in thousands of dollars in overtime and contract charges, since the moves must take place in the weeks before the new Congress. Having all this furniture moved by many different groups of movers results in enough accidents to create more than a two-year backlog of repair. Many pieces are damaged beyond repair. Some of the damaged furniture is disposed of; some is stored for future spare parts.

In all the decades of moving, repairing, and building, no one thought to keep an inventory. There were rumors that retiring members had hauled whole suites of furniture to their homes, that vacation homes on the eastern shore of Maryland were appointed with House furniture, and that when many of the member office alcoves that housed sinks or coat closets were converted to bookshelves, the doors ended up in private homes. Speaker Sam Rayburn even took a one-hundred-year-old crystal chandelier from the Capitol for his Texas library.[2]

There was also an official process of removing furniture from the House. Members leaving House service could take, free of charge, their Washington desks and chairs. The replacement value of this "bon voyage" present was over $4,000. The furniture shops would refurbish the outgoing furniture, prior to shipment, at no charge. Shipping was also paid for from general House accounts.

Outgoing members could also purchase all of their district office furniture and equipment. Once the incoming members who were succeeding them had the opportunity to review the inventory and select what to retain, the furniture and equipment was available for sale to the outgoing members. We discovered how the House defined "sale price" when one departing member was being reimbursed $50 for overpaying on her district furniture. Simon and I went over the bill of sale to find that this one-term member was buying her eighteen-month-old desks for $2 each, file cabinets for $1.50, and chairs for $1.25.

While many official items found creative ways of leaving the House inventory, others items found unusual ways of flowing in. The two Toms not only found undocumented purchase contracts, but they also found something called "perpetual purchase orders," meaning that stuff arrived COD regardless of need, annually. There were storerooms and warehouses full of furniture that had never been used, and no one had a consolidated list of all the storerooms.

Nussle wanted to become part of the hunt when we found a 44,800-square-foot warehouse being leased in southeast Washington, D.C. He took along some reporters and entered what used to be the old *Washington Star* warehouse. The House was renting this 1912 building from its current owner, the *Washington Post*, for $253,000 a year.

Nussle was not disappointed. There were five floors, each roughly a third the size of a city block, filled to the ceiling with every imaginable piece of furniture. There were 1870 Victorian couches mixed in with chrome desk chairs from the 1960s. Obsolete typewriter tables occupied a third of one of the floors. In 1975, the House eliminated the need for steamer trunks that had once been used to ship documents to the members' districts during the time of stagecoaches. Stacks of brand-new trunks were still being stored, some in their original wrappings and with bills of lading dating to 1964. There were two floors of books, including agriculture yearbooks (the practice of members giving away copies had been discontinued in 1985). The inventory was staggering.

Lusby and Sturdevant were finding additional caches of furniture, documents, and debris in other buildings. The attic of the Rayburn House Office Building was littered with discarded systems furniture. There was an underground room full of oriental rugs. There was a small room under a set of stairs that contained House documents petitioning for a navy yard in Charleston, South Carolina, dated March 3, 1838. On and on the hunt went. We joked that we would eventually open a door and find both Jimmy Hoffa and Judge Crater.

Garbett and his team fanned out into the array of service functions that would become "support services" in the new CAO operation. Carole Kordich picked her way through the cluttered Cannon basement hallways that Simon and I visited earlier to determine why so much House equipment was piled up. She found out that, just as in the case of the furnishings, there was no inventory list of the equipment. A few years earlier an attempt was made to control House equipment. Bar-coded stickers were put on all the new equipment, but no one ever bought bar-code readers.

How much equipment the House had, and in what condition, remained a mystery.

There were other problems with House equipment. There were approved vendor lists that not only limited choices to one to three items, but also locked the House into obsolete technology because most of the selections, along with the vendors, had not been updated or recompeted in years. In addition, the House paid full retail! House negotiators never negotiated bulk sales or wholesale pricing. House rules prevented purchases outside of the vendor lists, even when dozens of local stores sold equipment at a fraction of House prices. Office managers for House members told us they felt like Soviet citizens standing in line for overpriced stale bread.

The equipment problems kept being unearthed. No one ever tracked cycle times for purchasing or for servicing. We heard stories of months passing before anything was repaired. The House spent $16 million a year in lump-sum service contracts, funded through central accounts, but no one monitored use or performance. It was possible that hundreds of thousands of dollars were being spent monthly without any services being provided. Most service contracts were missing from the files. Carole worked with Phil Kiko to call or write vendors to ask for copies.

Garbett and Davison worked their way through the recording studios and photography staffs. Work logs showed that both the studio and photography staffs were overstaffed and underutilized. On an average monthly basis, the studio staff provided only 3,694 hours of service for the 10,404 studio staff-hours available. The photographers were worse: only 220 hours of service for the 3,320 hours available, only 6.8 percent of capacity. The staff arrived and worked an established nine-to-five time schedule. Yet because the House usually conducted sessions from noon to midnight, up to 80 percent of the photographers' time was outside normal working hours and paid at overtime rates! No one had ever considered flextime or other staffing patterns.

Several recording-studio staffers complained about their jobs being threatened if they did not do personal favors for members and then fabricate their work logs to cover the time and materials used. Representative Rose used them to produce a video for his campaign for Speaker, which was never used because the Republicans won the House. One staffer provided us with a copy of the script he had hidden away when Rose and his staff swore them to secrecy and collected all production materials, including videotape, after the session. One of the studio supervisors used video crews to film his wedding.

A whole different set of surprises was in store when Davison and Garbett visited the media galleries. There are many stories about the White House press corps, but few know that there is also a congressional press corps. More than 7,500 reporters are credentialed to cover the House of Representatives. They are divided into three "galleries": radio and TV, newspapers, and periodicals. In a long-ago undocumented past, the House decided to use taxpayer funds to support media coverage. A committee of journalists selects thirteen staffers who act as the administrative support to the media. These staffers become House employees with all salaries, benefits, travel, and expenses paid from House operating funds.

The media galleries dominate much of the office space off the third-floor visitor level of the House chamber. This area includes three press conference rooms (complete with bookshelves with books cut in half to save space and fake backdrops); small cubicles reserved for an elite group of individual reporters and their broadcast stations; and support equipment, including faxes, photocopiers, wire-service outlets, televisions, and computers. Another set of media support rooms, including a small interview room, are located in the Rayburn Building.

The media committee controls all policy, hiring, personnel, and spending for the galleries. Requests are channeled through House administrative systems for processing, but House oversight is not an option. In addition, all construction, procurement, maintenance, and supplies are funded by the public. Tax dollars are also allocated for the gallery staff to equip and support party media operations at the Republican and Democratic national conventions.

In the midst of the room-assignment process, Garbett and I toured rooms in the Capitol to explore CAO room options should the doorkeeper's suite not be available. Many people were already gone for Christmas, and rooms were open. We walked into H-105, the clerk's lavish reception area and on into H-104, Don Anderson's (the outgoing clerk's) personal office. We were stunned. The walls were lined with incredible oil paintings. A staffer proudly gave us a tour, explaining that Mr. Anderson had used his contacts with the Smithsonian Institution and the Metropolitan Museum of Art to acquire over $2.5 million in loaned artwork to decorate his office. We later discovered that shipment and insurance for the art, and an upgrade in security for H-104 and H-105, were paid for from central administrative funds, but hidden under miscellaneous expenses.

The information team of Don Mutersbaugh, Rick Endres, and Jennifer Borcherdling were busy exploring the world of House Information Systems (HIS) four blocks away in House Annex 2 (the Ford House Office Building). This former FBI records center housed several floors of information and telecommunications services. Other floors housed the Congressional Budget Office and, at the time, numerous House caucus groups.

"Everyone is writing code!" complained Endres. He and the others found a culture obsessed with mainframe operations. It was a place where software was developed in-house; hardly anyone bought proven off-the-shelf programs.

"They say the House is unique and that everything must be tailored, so they do everything themselves," Mutersbaugh explained, shaking his head. The cost was staggering. In addition, many of these "proprietary systems" were years behind the current state of the art.

Few, if any, House offices were on the Internet. Most computers used by members' staffs were stand-alone word processors. A growing number of offices were experimenting with local area networks that linked computers within the office suite. HIS had an antiquated DOS-based system that linked all offices to the mainframe and the legislative databases of the clerk. They had just begun to support e-mail. However, there were nine e-mail systems in use. The overworked House servers, and their Ethernet protocols that directed the electronic traffic, crashed daily. E-mails that were sent took weeks to arrive, if they arrived at all.

"There is no leadership. There is no plan. They are just short-order cooks," Mutersbaugh observed. He and Endres worked their way through HIS management, asking everyone who reported to whom. The HIS organization was an amazing testimony to bureaucracy. They found twelve layers of supervisors, in some cases leading only a handful of frontline service personnel. There was a small help desk where seven people waited for the telephone to ring. That was worse than a seventy-to-one ratio of offices served to support available. No wonder many in the House thought the cyber-Congress was a futile goal.

Until Lusby joined the team, Norton, Sturdevant, and Kiko took turns delving into the postal and folding-room operations. What immediately stood out was how obsolete the operations were, in terms of service approach, technology, and even management thinking. These were the areas known in the House as the "dumping ground" for patronage. The workforce was demoralized. The operations were also highly overstaffed. The high fixed costs in the folding room drove costs to $480 for stuffing a thousand envelopes, whereas the average price in the private sector was $15, with some volume discounts taking the price below $8! No one had considered outsourcing.

The various search teams returned to HC-8 like conquerors from war. Everyone in the A Ring wanted to know about the latest find and would gather around for the latest report. Outrages and absurdities were greeted with a mixture of "Oh my god!" exclamations, sometimes laughter, and much saddened head shaking and forehead slapping.

Clerk-designate Robin Carle and her deputy, Linda Nave, would walk by shaking their heads or rolling their eyes at the A Ring. It was as though they were saying "grow up" or "get a life." They showed no interest in reform. Jeff Trandahl, who had been assigned to assist the CAO start-up, seemed overwhelmed by the intensity and dedication the A Ring brought to the transition. His interaction with the team lessened as the days passed. Just after Christmas he announced that he would be joining the clerk's staff in the 104th Congress.

On the other hand, Bill Livingood would drop by HC-8 and urge the A Ring to visit him in HC-6. His own review of the sergeant at arms' operations was finding appalling management practices, lapses in training, and serious security issues. Livingood asked some of the A Ring to help him sort through his findings, as he lacked an A Ring of his own. We became close colleagues and then good friends during this period. We saw our mandates in similar ways—change House operations to reflect the best practices in our fields.

THE LAST PLANTATION

The findings from the scavenger hunts were all part of a poisonous culture in which an uncaring elite focused on scooping up money and perquisites. The A Ring heard countless stories of how things were managed or funded, which was of little consequence to those who ruled prior to the 104th Congress. They heard that what really mattered was who got what in return for delivering basic services. Whether it was a bulk mailing that needed folding or a chair that needed repair, each request went from a member to the CHA or to managers with links to leadership. The administrative support system became a network of brokerage firms bartering favors for favors. Evidence and interviews underscored that much of this bartering was being conducted through verbal agreements. Administrative files showing that seven thousand exception letters had been issued by the CHA in 1994 was one indication of the extent of this practice.

Republican members were rarely able to enter the barter system. Instead they found themselves waiting six months or more for reimbursement of their travel expenses, whereas favored Democrats had three- to five-day turnarounds. For a Democratic member, "jumping the queue" to get an earlier slot in the recording studio, or having equipment arrive on time, meant pledging support to an amendment to an appropriation bill, or dropping opposition to leadership-backed legislation.

Lusby and Sturdevant heard stories about the postal scandal, in which House members took undocumented cash and dollars spilled from drawers. The entire A Ring was overwhelmed with explicit details of how the post office, restaurant, banking, and supply-store scandals occurred and how other scandals had been suppressed. For those who had not followed the reform issues during the early 1990s, this was the first time they had heard about the flagrant abuses of congressional power. "It's almost too much to bear," observed Lusby. "What kinds of people are running this place? This is madness!"

All members of the A Ring were approached by House support staff who complained about an abusive work environment in which people were told to break House rules and ethics guidelines and were then threatened with firing if they ever spoke about it. We would ask, why not "blow the whistle" or get a job elsewhere? Many workers told of daily harangues by supervisors about how worthless they were and how they were lucky to have a job because they would never find one anywhere else. They told of the reprisals that occurred when people did try to go to the CHA or to House leadership.

They went on to tell us of arbitrary and capricious promotions, bonuses, firings, and hirings. They told us about the many cliques within the support services. Some were dedicated professionals and craftsmen who somehow made it into the operation. These people had to work side by side with hacks, relatives, and mistresses. There were extended family networks in which one staffer would be hired through a political connection and then proceed to bring in his or her entire family over the course of several years. Unlike in the executive branch, in the House there were no policies regarding nepotism, except that direct blood relations to members had to be documented.

The A Ring walked through poorly lit and poorly ventilated windowless workspaces where the folding room and postal operations were housed. They found obsolete, poorly maintained, and dangerous equipment. No wonder the House had exempted itself from workplace and employment laws! The Occupational Safety and Health Administration and an array of federal regulatory agencies would have shut most of the support operations down within minutes had they seen what the A Ring saw. The A Ring was also told of a lack of training, a lack of supplies, and a lack of supervision. Many of the support operations seemed like a "Devil's Island" where people were thrown into dark obscure corners to be forgotten and abused.

The worst stories related to how sexual favors were demanded by both supervisors and members. They told of how stress and hopelessness led to fist fights and, in one case, a knife fight. They told us of how their supervisors and the Capitol police looked the other way. Everyone seemed scared of what powerful members and their handpicked managers would do to them. The seasoned professionals of the A Ring assumed some of these stories were designed to provoke us into keeping certain people and firing others. We had seen similar fratricide within "career" ranks during the Reagan transition. But we also assumed that some portion of what we were hearing was indeed true. The thought of even a fraction of the stories being true sickened us. Was this really happening in 1995 in America?

8

★ THE WILD HORSE ★

January 4, 1995

"Turn around, Bill," said a bemused Speaker Gingrich. In the "well" of the House, Bill Livingood had faced the audience for the swearing-in ceremony. Everyone had a good chuckle, and Bill looked a little dazed as he pivoted to face the Speaker.

Everything else was going like clockwork. The hours of dress rehearsals were paying off. The first hours of Republican House rule projected professionalism and clarity of purpose.

The officers of the House—the clerk, the sergeant of arms, the CAO, and the inspector general—were voted on as a slate. The resolution for my new position, along with those of the other House officers, passed on a voice vote.[1] Reverend James D. Ford, the chaplain of the House, was voted on separately and was unopposed. The House then went through the formalities of having a majority and minority candidate for the other House officers even though the outcome was preordained.

While the parliamentary machine was efficiently shifting gears from one party to another, my team was making sure the management end went through a similarly smooth transition.

THE CUTOVER

The members of the A Ring returned from their respective Christmas breaks by Tuesday morning, December 27. With eight days to go before the start of a new Congress, our morning transition sessions increasingly took on the substance and tone of an operating unit. We now took time from the A Ring's scavenger hunts to develop and review ever-lengthening transition checklists. The team's collective years of managerial experience were paying off as we went over every detail involving the "cutover" to Republican rule. We brainstormed "Murphy's Law" scenarios regarding every possible thing that could go wrong, including malicious actions by outgoing officials or by holdovers.

Part of this "cutover" process was bringing the A Ring up to speed on existing operating procedures and equipment. The team threw themselves into nearly around-the-clock training regarding computers, office procedures, communication, security, and file systems. At the same time, Edith Vivian and Jennifer Borcherdling made arrangements for new computer access accounts, stationery, forms (fax, telephone, etc.), signature fonts, and e-mail addresses that reflected both the A Ring's existence and the fact that it would now be the 104th Congress.

In addition to the steep learning curves and general start-up tasks, members of the A Ring also had special assignments. Garbett was meeting with Tony Blankley to develop ways to improve floor coverage, including camera placement and better audio capture to relay a more accurate picture of the proceedings on the House floor to viewers. He and Davison also supported Tony's initiative to credential talk radio as part of the ongoing coverage of the new Congress. There was great resistance from the media galleries to expanding credentialing to this relatively new and conservative-leaning dimension. Therefore, the talk-radio reporters and commentators were housed in the old transition offices. New cable lines were run to this part of the Capitol.

Paul Sweetland and Debbie Hansen were in charge of refurbishing the seventh floor of the O'Neill House Office Building, House Annex 1, and turning it into the operations center for the CAO's office. It did not take many trips in the O'Neill Building's elevator before they nicknamed O'Neill the "tower of terror" for how the elevator bounced, suddenly stopped, and made strange noises.

The legal team began building a legal reference library. They were also supporting Nussle's major revision to the *Congressional Handbook* and helping draft the "Dear Colleague" letter that would be issued by Nussle and Thomas on the first day of the new Congress.

The legal team's main concern remained scavenging for legal documents and finding and diffusing any "ticking bombs." They discovered that the House restaurants still owed $711,000 from fiscal year 1992 to the Washington, D.C., government for unemployment insurance. They also began building a "suspense calendar" of contracts, such as for the "Republican" and "Democratic" printers, which were set for renewal and renegotiation in 1995. They would make sure there would be no automatic rollovers or renewals without a full review. This contract-renewal schedule would play a key role in the timing of the reforms.

I was also going through the paces of learning and preparing for my role as head of this new enterprise. On Friday, December 30, I had my first meeting with George M. White, the architect of the Capitol, to learn about his operation and open discussions on how our two offices should collaborate. This was an important relationship, since our operations were intertwined in a myriad of ways. For example, if a House member wanted his or her office renovated, the architect's team painted the walls, but the CAO's team laid the carpet. The architect's electricians ran the electricity, but the CAO's electricians ran the telephone and computer cables. The architect's craftsmen repaired the windows, but the CAO's staff repaired the venetian blinds. The architect's designers designed the room renovations, but the CAO's designers coordinated the interior decor, including furnishings, curtains, and upholstery. If this ballet of skilled individuals and inventory management misfired, members and their staffs could be disrupted for weeks if not months.

The scope of this collaboration was driven home during my countless journeys through the House tunnel system. Furniture was stacked up in every nook and cranny of the tunnels. Major staging areas arose at intersections of hallways and by elevators. The smell of fresh plaster and paint permeated the office buildings. The flotsam from the previous Congress—copies of the *Congressional Record*, bill reports, newspapers, legislative files—commingled with carpet remnants and discarded wire in countless large wheeled waste buckets stationed outside offices.

The architect of the Capitol's domain stretches across the west front of the Capitol building in the basement. His executive suite is entered through SB-15. This is just around the corner from the most hallowed part of the Capitol—the crypt. It was originally designed as the final resting place for George Washington. It remained empty for decades, after the Washington family declined the honor in favor of a tomb at Mount Vernon. After the funeral of Abraham Lincoln, the crypt became the storage area for the catafalque on which his coffin lay in state. At many times during my tenure, I would walk down this quiet corridor under the west stairs and pay homage to this symbol of the nation's grief and reverence. It was a place for contemplation and for putting a day's events in perspective.

White had arrayed his senior team throughout the room. Simon and Sweetland joined me in this first of many sessions between the two teams. There was much to discuss, including the architect's curiosity about how the House reforms might ripple into the architect's office in particular, the ice-bucket people, the elevator operators, and the parking-garage attendants. I assured the architect's team that the reforms were still evolving and that decisions remained months away. We would consult on anything that effected his operations.

I was drawn to the wonderful array of artifacts that filled George's office. As the meeting adjourned, we discussed some of the items. Sensing my interest in history, he graciously offered his curatorial staff, and several other team members, to personally assist me as I planned for the restoration of the CAO suite. As we parted, he also let me know that one of the "perks" of my new office would be unlimited access to the Capitol dome. I expressed amazement that there was any such thing. He briefly described the "outer" and "inner" domes and the walkways that snaked between the two, leading to the viewing platform underneath the *Goddess of Freedom*. The dome would hold a number of very special moments in the years to come.

I made mental notes about the sense of calm and graciousness that the architect and his staff exhibited. It was the kind of image I hoped to project while implementing a revolution.

The placid and historical environment of the architect's office quickly gave way to the final push toward the "cutover" as we returned to the transition office. Simon and I repeatedly went over checklists and talked to the A Ring about control of in-boxes and out-boxes and capturing all calls starting the morning of January 4, 1995. Jane Bennett introduced me to a representative from SkyTel to discuss an experimental communication grid for the A Ring. This system would allow any member of the A Ring to send 120-character e-mails to pagers. The pagers worked throughout the House campus, including the tunnels. No cell phones were able to do that. I authorized the SkyTel pagers on the spot and laid the groundwork for a communication grid that would serve us well in the coming years.

Bill Sturdevant and Gloria Wright-Simmonds reported on their project-management preparations for the reforms. They were working with Rick Endres on finding the necessary graphics support, including both the software, plotters, and other tools for developing flowcharts, organizational charts, and project-tracking systems. They also maintained an "idea board" in the transition office so that the A Ring could post issues and reform ideas, real time. We would then sort them out once the "cutover" was completed.

Gloria was also working with Jane and Debbie on locating space for the A Ring, setting up offices, and scavenging furniture, especially for the seventh floor of the O'Neill Building. Some of this literally involved "rattling door knobs" to find empty and unclaimed offices. There were no central room inventory or even accurate floor plans. Records of the innumerable renovations during the past forty years lay somewhere between the archives of the architect and the ether.

Kay Ford and I devoted hours to sorting out final salaries for the A Ring, and fitting the new team into existing personnel slots. Since my office would not "officially" exist until the House Rules were passed and would not be fully authorized until the House Oversight Committee met, we had to live in a parallel universe, temporarily using the old system. Key to this was the "Speaker's pay order," which authorized salaries for staff and offices reporting directly to the Speaker, including all the House officers. This was a major change, as many of the offices under the CAO had reported through the soon-to-be-abolished CHA. Kay and I also looked at providing a model personnel policy to members and their staffs, since none existed. We conferred with former congressman Don Ritter and the Congressional Management Foundation on how to develop and roll it out.

Every day, Jim Nussle would convene a transition meeting to see how everyone was doing and determine what, if any, additional assistance was required. Sue Wadel, counsel to the Speaker, took on an increasingly proactive role as the "exec-sec" for tracking transition issues and the primary point of contact for Gingrich. We were all running on adrenaline. Our enthusiasm was driven more by the thrill of seeing how it was all falling into place than by the prospect of the curtain rising on January 4. It was clear that Bill Livingood's team was similarly involved in cutover activities, which included "bug" sweeps of all leadership offices. The only people who seemed bored by it all were Robin Carle and her team. Her mantra was "keeping busy—hanging in there," and she offered no details unless specifically asked by Nussle or Wadel.

Some of Carle's disengagement may have been due to the shrinking role of her office. The Speaker's inner circle wanted to make major changes to the House Rules to achieve both efficiency and transparency. One of these changes would be to have filings go directly to the Federal Election Commission (FEC) instead of having them go first to the clerk. In part this change was designed to end the practice of the clerk's office "tidying up" member filings, giving incumbents an advantage over their challengers. Another was moving all "ministerial" approvals and filings from the clerk to the CAO. This would include all financial documents and all legal documents relating to members and staff (court orders, wage garnishments, divorce decrees). Until the CAO's office was fully authorized, the CAO's office would prepare all documents and the clerk would sign them. Once the CAO's office was official, the CAO would sign all documents, leaving the clerk out of all these loops.

Another contemplated shift from the clerk to the CAO was for the quarterly report on member and House spending to be both prepared and issued by the CAO. The "Clerk of the House Report" would become the "Financial Report of the House." Simon and Anfinson were already looking at ways to improve the accuracy and clarity of this report and to turn it into a true management tool for tracking the budget, accrual accounting, tracking against plan, and analyzing budgetary patterns and trends.

During the transition meeting on Wednesday, December 28, Simon floated an idea: what about a "finance public record office" where citizens could review the financial documents of the House the same way they could view FEC filings? This drew immediate fire from Bill Thomas and Stacy Carlson. "We never anticipated these records would be *that* public," snarled Thomas. We asserted that the clerk's report already had this detail and that document access was just another way of assuring the public of the accuracy of the public record. Thomas would hear none of it. "That is more information that we should give out." Simon, Anfinson, and I beat a retreat, but privately decided to revisit this matter at a later time.

January 4, 1995, finally dawned. Jane, along with Vicki, made sure everyone knew where and when things were occurring. The first day of a new session is like a massive party. Members' families and staffs fill the hallways along with well-wishers from their districts. It is also like opening day of fishing season for thousands of lobbyists who use the swearing-in parties and open houses to meet the new players and renew contact with old colleagues.

In my case, there was to be a series of very special moments—to be sworn in, officially, and later in a photo op with the Speaker. My parents drove in for the occasion, getting a chance to enjoy a moment that made their years of grassroots politics all worth it. As important, this was a day for the entire A Ring to glory in their work to date and finally receive the "starting gun" for the revolution that lay ahead.

Jane, Edith, and Gloria did a masterful job of creating party food and making the CAO suite look festive. I left my own swearing in on the House floor and strode to the CAO suite. There, in front of the A Ring, I first signed all the termination papers for the executives of the old regime, and then signed all the A Ring's personnel papers. Jim Davison arranged for Keith Jewel, one of the official House photographers, to swing by and take photos of the A Ring.

Before the group photos, I swore in my team saying, "You are going to do things that you will tell your grandchildren about. You are going to make history." I looked at the members of the A Ring arrayed in a semicircle around my desk. Everyone was choked with emotion. This was a great "sense of moment" for the team. They had accomplished much in the previous sixteen days. They were about to accomplish so much more.

The CAO suite filled with friends and families. Many colleagues from the Reagan years dropped by to say hello. Many had become part of the "Reagan diaspora" that had fanned out to think tanks, law firms, associations, and lobbying firms in the late 1980s. We had all worked for this moment, a Republican Congress, and it was definitely time to rejoice.

The House then went back into session and changed the "world" as Washington knew it. In one of the longest sessions in its history, the House passed House Resolution 1, a massive reinvention of the Rules of the House. It was a compendium of every "wish list" item the insurgents believed would, in one decisive stroke, erase years of administrative and ethical abuse. Much of the bill related to parliamentary and committee issues. They also passed HR1, the "Congressional Accountability Act." This was the Shays Act which would end Congress' exemption from eleven federal labor and employment laws and establish an independent compliance act. My office cross-walked the operational reforms embedded in this legislation into action plans that we set in motion on January 4.

NO GOING BACK

House Resolution 1 eliminated many offices—most prominently, the Office of Technology Assessment and the thirty-seven "legislative service organizations" (LSOs). That meant that their budgets, assets, and offices were to be reclaimed and absorbed into the general operations of the House. Their eighty-nine employees would have to be paid for out of private funds. Carole Kordich and Bill Sturdevant went door-to-door inventorying the offices and making sure they were shut down. They completed the shutdown in less than ten days. All equipment and furnishings went back into the House inventory. Another $1.2 million in revolving funds was reclaimed into House accounts. Much of the equipment and furnishings were castoffs from member offices. Carole and I decided to ship the castoffs to the General Services Administration's (GSA's) resource disposal program.

While supervising the loading of GSA trucks at the Longworth loading dock, a former LSO staffer struck up a conversation with Carole. "Where is all that stuff going?" he asked. "To the GSA for disposal," Carole answered. "But what if you change your mind?" queried the staffer. "That is not going to happen—there is no going back," said Carole. The word was getting out that the revolution was real and rapidly becoming a reality. Unlike other times in Washington, this was not to be a "press release" effort. With the A Ring as the phalanx, the reforms would happen quickly, decisively, and irreversibly.

Each day was filled with decisive action. The A Ring hit the ground running and then picked up speed. Linked by the SkyTel pagers and fully empowered, the A Ring fanned out to create the new reality.

One of our immediate goals was to clean up the hallways. We all felt that the more physical changes we made, the more everyone would realize change was real and here to stay. It also helped professionalize the work environment and set a higher standard for all. Skids of 1993 consumer catalogs and other obsolete government publications were sent off for recycling as fast as they were discovered.

Just as before January 4, the A Ring had their own priorities and then worked in cross-functional teams on special projects. Don Mutersbaugh and Ben Lusby tightened their control of mail operations, and in particular, ended the mailroom's practice of absorbing postage due for members. Mike Dorsey and Bill Norton compiled lists of recurring reports and their deadlines so that we could proactively comply with all requirements. Endres and Borcherdling sorted out HIS consultant contracts and discovered different payroll systems. Ford and Anfinson both raised flags about possible phantom workers or people being double paid. Phil Kiko, along with Norton, developed major procurement reforms, including dollar thresholds, procedures, and standards for assessing vendors.

A major and immediate change was launched by Anfinson and Simon and announced via a "Dear Colleague" letter from Bill Thomas. One of the major scandals had been members not paying their American Express card accounts. Many members made personal purchases on these accounts. Annually, the House had to pay off and absorb tens of thousands of dollars in American Express claims or face termination of card privileges. The masterfully simple solution was to do what most of the "real world" does—have each member be responsible for his or her own card accounts and be billed directly. The members would then have to add qualifying American Express charges to their travel reimbursement forms.

In the rudimentary surroundings of the CAO suite, Jane, Gloria, and I established operational procedures for the new entity. Our stationery would have no names—allowing it to be used for years. All executive-tier CAO officials would purchase their own business cards. We checked out whether the exclusive House contract with Bethesda Engravers had ever been competed. Ford helped us complete all the personnel paperwork for the "cutover." We also sorted out terminations for the LSOs and committee staff, including computing leave accrual.

Garbett and I took a brief break from the intensive implementation drills to attend the unveiling of the Library of Congress's new "Thomas system" (named for Thomas Jefferson). On Friday, January 6, we strolled over to the Madison Building of the Library of Congress. Bill Thomas and Newt Gingrich, along with library officials, were launching the first system for online access to congressional records and data.

After the ceremony Gingrich waved me over. "Scot, your team is doing a fantastic job! Everyone is very pleased with how you and your team are performing. I am only hearing positive things about your operation. Keep up the good work!"

To keep up that positive momentum, I knew my team had to constantly evolve to meet changing circumstances. First, I ended the daily A Ring meetings and shifted them to once a week to allow the team to focus on operations. The SkyTel pager system tethered everyone to each other anyway. This would be the first of several refinements in striking the right balance between having face-to-face meetings and fully leveraging information technology.

It was also clear that the shift into operational mode required redeploying the inner core of the A Ring. Jane Bennett was an amazing resource who knew more about the Hill than all the rest of my team. We spoke, and agreed that she should become my office's overall service coordinator and ombudsman. This freed her from my schedule and allowed her to directly establish and monitor service standards for the CAO. More importantly, it freed her to interact with her vast personal network of members and staff to find out what was on their minds and garner intelligence about issues and concerns that might effect my office. Anticipating the next steps in the "revolution," I freed Gloria from "front-desk duties" so that she could divide her time between creating the internal procedures for the CAO's office and, along with Bill Sturdevant, prepare to head project management for the major reforms still to come.

This redeployment meant that I needed a new person to be "my brain" when I was in countless meetings on any given day. This person would be my "keeper," advancing meetings, taking notes, reminding me of follow-up actions and commitments made, and keeping me on schedule. Vicki had an idea—Terri Hasdorff.

Vicki and I had first met Terri when she was working at the White House in the Office of Public Liaison. We had gotten together at several White House functions relating to my role as treasurer of Friends of Dan Quayle. Terri had always struck us as energetic and very detail-oriented. Since leaving the White House, Terri had worked for several Native American groups and was currently director of legislative affairs for a technology firm. I gave her a call.

"Well, I'd like that! Thank you for thinking of me," Terri said in her Alabamian cadence.

Terri started on Monday, January 9, and her value was immediately realized as she visited with her many friends on Tom DeLay's team. DeLay's office wrapped around the CAO suite and we shared an "escape door." Being neighbors, combined with Terri's friendships, would form the basis of a close alliance in the coming years.

MORE EQUAL THAN OTHERS

The start of the new Congress shook loose a number of items overlooked by the transition teams. Lobbyists were flooding Bill Livingood's office with calls about their "special passes."

In one of the Speaker's meeting rooms (H-128) on January 9, Representatives Thomas and Nussle, Wadel, and the officers gathered to address the rising chorus of lobbyists demanding their "special passes."

"It seems that previous Congresses handed out special passes to lobbyists so they could enter the Capitol building after hours," stated Livingood. He went on to explain that the Capitol was open to the public from 9:00 a.m. to 4:30 p.m. seven days a week. The rotunda remained open until 8:00 p.m. during the summer. However, prior to the 104th Congress, over seven thousand lobbyists were regularly issued special passes to roam through the Capitol building twenty-four hours a day to visit House leadership and attend hearings.

"Then we just have to issue passes for the 104th Congress and honor 103rd passes until then," commented Thomas.

"Not so fast, why should we give them more access than the public?" asked Nussle.

"The Speaker wants this settled. He is getting lots of calls," Wadel interjected.

"If public hearings are public, then the public should be allowed in, not just 'special people,'" I asserted, leaning forward and looking at Wadel.

"I disagree. Attending hearings is part of their job. We can't prevent them from doing their jobs," remarked Thomas. "Exactly," Carle said, nodding.

"No. This is about whether we are going to be different from the Democrats," Nussle began. "I agree with Scot. If a hearing is public, then we need to make arrangements for the public to enter after hours. Otherwise we are granting special rights to a class of people."

"The media can come and go, and we give them special credentials," retorted Thomas.

"The difference is that they are a bridge to the public. Lobbyists are only a bridge to who is paying them," I countered.

The discussion went on for another twenty minutes. In the end, Wadel sided with Nussle and me, and she would take her recommendation to Gingrich. Thomas shook his head in disgust.

The reformers had prevailed—the "special passes" ended. However, the issue raised some disturbing insights about the Washington culture. There definitely was an "us" and a "them," and the "them" was anyone who was a mere mortal, a mere citizen. It also displayed two different

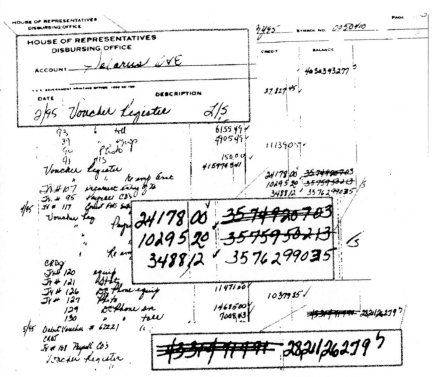

Typical page from handwritten ledgers used prior to the 104th Congress. This page, for fiscal year 1995, shows a mathematical error of over $15 million in just one account.

Ceremonial swearing in held on January 4, 1995.
From left to right: Clarence "Ki" Faulkner, Irene Faulkner, Scot Faulkner, Vicki Hunter, and Newt Gingrich.
Photograph by Keith Jewel, House photographer.

Photograph of swearing in of A Ring, January 4, 1995, in Faulkner's office.
From left to right: Bill Sturdevant, Jane Bennett, Jennifer Borcherdling, Tom Simon, John Garbett, (
ole Kordich, Paul Sweetland, Scot Faulkner. Seated: Don Mutersbaugh, Ben Lusby, Gloria Wright-S
monds, Tom Anfinson, Rick Endres, Edith Vivian, Mike Dorsey, Jackie Aamot, Bill Norton, and Det
Hansen. Not pictured: Jim Davison and Wendy Younk.
Photograph by Keith Jewel, House photographer.

Rick Endres (standing) presents draft Gantt chart for Office 2000, the forerunner of the cyber-Congr
Mike Dorsey is seated on right. Taken during the implementation workshop held in the O'Neill Buil
on February 24–26, 1995.
Photograph by Keith Jewel, House photographer.

...e of the planning sessions during a two-day quality-management workshop. This shows participants ...ating an "affinity diagram" using "yellow stickies."

...tograph by Dwight Comedy, House photographer.

...ober 2, 1995, "gala opening" of the privatized shoeshine and shoe repair service in the Cannon ...ement rotunda. Tom Anfinson (right) tries on his engineer's cap while Scot Faulkner looks on.

...tograph by Dwight Comedy, House photographer.

Members of the public wait in line to register for the House's "yard sale" held in the old Washington Star warehouse on September 23, 1995. Over 7,000 participated.
Photograph by Dwight Comedy, House photographer.

The team that made the "yard sale" a success.
Left to right: Cosmo Quattrone, Tom Van Dyke, Carole Kordich, and Jim Davison.
Photograph by Dwight Comedy, House photographer.

Scot Faulkner presents an awareness session to one of the teams in support services.
Photograph by Dwight Comedy, House photographer.

ss graduation of all CAO employees held in the Cannon Caucus Room on January 18, 1996.
otograph by Dwight Comedy, House photographer.

e of the presentations to the American Society for Quality Control (ASQC) on September 13, 1995.
t to right at witness table: Rep. Dick Chrysler, Rep. Peter Hoekstra, Scot Faulkner, and former rep-
entative Don Ritter.
otograph by Dwight Comedy, House photographer.

ot Faulkner and representatives from Pitney Bowes sign the postal-services contract on December
, 1995, in Faulkner's office.
otograph by Dwight Comedy, House photographer.

Speaker Newt Gingrich and Vice President Al Gore thank Israeli prime minister Shimon Peres after address to a special meeting of Congress on December 12, 1995. Scot Faulkner stands behind Pe to the right.
Photograph by Dwight Comedy, House photographer.

Bill Crain presents achievement awards at a ceremony in the Rayburn Gold Room on June 28, 199
Photograph by Dwight Comedy, House photographer.

Senator Robert Byrd (left) greets Brad and Ginny Nash (center) for their wedding photos in the Cap Scot Faulkner is in the background.
Photograph by Dwight Comedy, House photographer.

1. Bob Ney (seated, left) meets with Joab Eilon, Director of the Israel Democracy Institute (seated, ~ter), with Scot Faulkner (seated, right) on September 17, 1996, in Faulkner's office.
ptograph by Dwight Comedy, House photographer.

~n Atkinson (left) and Trent Coleman (center) take a break with William Summerfield, portraying ~rge Washington, during filming of the orientation video in the Sam Rayburn Room of the Capitol on ~ober 29, 1996.
ptograph by Dwight Comedy, House photographer.

~motional poster for the orientation site on the CAO intranet.

Reps. Ron Packard, John Boehner, and Jim Nussle announce the passage of the fiscal year 1996 legislative branch appropriations bill on June 22, 1995.
Photograph by Laura Patterson, *Roll Call*.

Rep. Bill Thomas and Inspector General John Lainhart confer at a CHO hearing.
Photograph by Maureen Keating, *Roll Call*.

Vicki Hunter confers with Scot Faulkner at a CHO hearing.
Photograph by Laura Patterson, *Roll Call*.

frames of reference within the transition. Nussle and what was left of the "Gang of Seven," along with Gingrich, DeLay, and Armey, wanted a real change in the way things worked. Thomas wanted to just put a Republican label on the old ways and leverage those ways to consolidate control. *Roll Call* and other newspapers screamed in pain and defended special lobbyist access.[2] This would prove ironic given their later crusade against lobbyists.

This dichotomy, erupting within the transition's inner circle just six days after the start of the new Congress, bothered me. I recalled similar battles in the early Reagan years. Back then the inner circle remained united.

STATE OF THE UNION

Congress is punctuated with a variety of special events. The two most elaborate are the joint meeting and the joint session. During a joint meeting, both houses of Congress convene to hear a foreign leader or to commemorate a major event. The president pro tem of the Senate and the Speaker of the House preside. Officials from the judicial branch, the executive branch, and the embassies also attend.

The biggest event of the year is the joint session of Congress for the President's State of the Union address. Everyone in the Washington power structure attends, save for one cabinet member who gets to hang out with the Secret Service in an "undisclosed location" just in case something unfortunate happens.

Both types of events require extensive planning and security preparations. During the House officers' meeting on January 18, Robin Carle decided to launch her first of many efforts to reclaim turf lost to the CAO's office. She interrupted our State of the Union planning discussion to argue that the recording studios should be under her office because they filmed and broadcast floor sessions. These were part of her responsibilities of keeping the "integrity of the public record." She also wanted the publications office returned to her domain. It had become clear that Robin was to be the most status quo-oriented of the House officers. Wadel rolled her eyes; less than one week from the State of the Union was not the best time to fight over control of the floor cameras.

Sue shut down Robin's rebellion by saying that these were issues settled by the transition prior to any of us being appointed, and the matter was not open for discussion. Robin pouted.

Later that day, the CAO team commenced work on their first State of the Union. In EF-100, the Secret Service presided over the coordination meeting. The room was packed with military, White House advance, and congressional staff. This would be the first State of the Union "run" by the Republicans since President Dwight Eisenhower's address in January 1954. The agenda covered a vast array of details, including security, tickets, and holding rooms.

While this event planning focused on who would do what, when, and where, Garbett and Davison were cloistered with Tony Blankley and representatives of the media pool covering the State of the Union. The media representatives stated that their coverage had been frustrated by previous Congresses. New technology allowed for smaller remote-controlled cameras to be placed around the chamber, affording new and varied views of the event. Tony and the CAO team jumped at the chance to try these new approaches and readily approved the media's ideas. New camera placements included a "lipstick" camera behind the podium facing the audience.

Tuesday, January 24 arrived. The layers of security started tightening and expanding the controlled area around the House chamber hours before the State of the Union was scheduled to begin. As a House officer, I was assigned a seat on the podium and could hand out tickets for both the floor and the gallery. Not all of the A Ring wanted to be sealed in the Capitol until after midnight, so my tickets covered everyone. Vicki drove in, and we had a quiet dinner at the members' dining room before the festivities.

Television, even with new camera positions, can never capture the full range of what happens during a State of the Union address. First and foremost, it is a festivity. Members, families, officials, media, and lobbyists mingle in the hallways and cloakrooms before the event. Even after the session is convened, there is much mingling on the floor as everyone waits for the various delegations to arrive and be seated and for the official escorts to leave the chamber, only to return fifteen minutes later with the president. There is also extensive mingling in the holding rooms by various officials and dignitaries waiting to be ushered onto the floor.

Bill Livingood, as the sergeant at arms, had the honor of preceding the president and the escorting members into the House chamber. Standing by the center door of the House chamber, he then uttered the words that symbolize the beginning of the State of the Union: "Mr. Speaker, the president of the United States." The chamber erupted into applause as the president and his escorts strode down the center aisle. Livingood would later relate the story about how a number of his Secret Service colleagues freaked out when he announced the president. They did not realize he was now the sergeant at arms, and thought he was still part of the president's security detail. For a brief moment they worried that Livingood had gone crazy. Fortunately, no one was wrestled to the ground.

I was seated on the podium "stage left," so I was on the "Republican side." The crowd for this State of the Union was rowdier than normal, as most Republicans wanted to remind President Clinton that it was a whole new world. Many Republican freshmen vigorously waved copies of the "Contract with America" at key points during Clinton's remarks.

My seat did not allow for a comfortable view of the president. The viewing angle was too severe for me to crane my neck upward for extended periods. Since I was "off camera" for all but the wide shoots, I used the opportunity to survey the chamber and get a flavor for how others watched the president. There was quite a spectrum of expressions.

The House Republicans watched DeLay and Armey as much as they watched Clinton. The Republican leaders were following along with their written copies of the speech. Whenever they stood, the rest of the Republicans stood. Whenever they sat, the rest of the Republican members sat. They all knew that their actions would help or hurt the president's effort to reclaim some dignity, and momentum, after the horrendous November loses.

Senator Phil Gramm (R-TX) leaned forward and was fully engaged in the speech. He sometimes taunted the president, acting as if he were at a major sporting event, clapping and gesturing emphatically at points he liked or disliked. On the opposite end was Senator Al D'Amato (R-NY).

He clearly wanted to be someplace else. About twenty minutes into the speech, he closed his eyes. I watched in great expectation as D'Amato's head rocked from side to side and finally pitched back. With his mouth wide open, he snored through Clinton's address.

The Supreme Court justices sat with "poker faces," clapping politely only during the most universally patriotic references. The exception was Chief Justice William Rehnquist. He glowered and grimaced at Clinton throughout the State of the Union address.

Surprisingly, the only other person who maintained a contemptuous facial expression was First Lady Hillary Clinton. The body language between the president and the First Lady was disturbingly frosty. It was as though she was projecting "look how you have messed up your administration, you jerk." When Clinton introduced Hillary and he knew the cameras would focus on her standing and waving, he shot her a similar frosty expression as if to say, "I'll show you."

Clinton's speech was a long one. About fifty minutes into his remarks, Republicans began filtering out of the chamber. Representative Henry Hyde (R-IL) even made a dismissive "who cares, enough already" arm motion on his way out the door. By the end of the speech, over a third of the House Republicans had left.

Everyone in the chamber stood for the last ovation as Clinton completed his remarks and worked his way out. The remaining Republican House members used this opportunity to leave the chamber for the evening. This created a slightly embarrassing moment for the House leadership. A joint session is still a session of the House and, therefore, must formally adjourn like a normal session. Representative Solomon, chairman of the House Rules Committee, had been designated to make the motion to adjourn. He had already left the chamber and had to be found and brought back. The chamber was now nearly empty. I left my seat and made my way over to where Simon and the A Ring had watched from the floor. When the "ayes" were called on adjournment, we all shouted "aye" just to give the handful of Republican members a little more volume to carry the motion. It was very amusing, and we figured it was the only time we could get away with the A Ring forming a voting bloc.

THE FIRST HEARING

Most of the contemplated House management reforms would require some sort of consideration by the newly created Committee on House Oversight (CHO). It was therefore important that the first meeting of the CHO go smoothly and that each of the new House officers make a good first impression on the panel.

Thomas called me to outline the hearing and urged me, along with the other officers, to keep my remarks brief and not to raise any "future tense" issues. "We will deal with the reforms later. This is a 'get-acquainted' session. It is not the time or the place to discuss reform. If asked a direct question, keep things very general." During this call, we briefly discussed Vern Ehlers's attempts to insert himself into the selection process for technology consultants. "Vern wants to turn the computer shop into his sandbox," mused Thomas. "Leave him to me." I thanked Bill for his support on this sensitive matter.

I had touched base with the Republican members of the CHO either in person or by telephone in the days prior to the hearing. I also took time to visit with Representative Christopher Shays (R-CT), as he was a leading voice on ethics and reform. Our meeting was very upbeat. Shays shared a number of fact sheets and "think pieces" he had developed on what needed to be done. He was especially interested in having input on parking, citing a number of abuses, some of which my team had already uncovered.

Remembering how successful I was in forging a bipartisan coalition for aviation safety measures during my time at the Federal Aviation Administration, I decided to reach out to the CHO's Democrats at the earliest opportunity. I knew that for the reforms to succeed and be viewed as truly business-based, there needed to be bipartisan support. I met with Tom Jurkovich and Perry Pockros of the CHO minority staff. Unfortunately, Representatives Steny Hoyer's (D-MD) and Vic Fazio's (D-CA) schedules did not permit meetings until after the first hearing. Tom and Perry seemed genuinely surprised that I would meet with them and be so solicitous, but the sincerity displayed by everyone would lay groundwork for collaboration in the years ahead.

The officers met with the CHO majority staff before the hearing. The CHO had grown to twenty-one people. Except for the core team of Stacy Carlson, Otto Wolff, and Dan Crowley, the new staffers came off as immature, unprofessional, and officious. Their demeanor signaled that they had already forgotten that they were just "oversight" and no longer "administration." One of the worst violators was Chris Wright, who would oversee parking and facility issues. Mary Sue England, the liaison for appropriations, took one look at me at realized that we had butted heads back in 1991–1992 over bringing total quality management to the Congress. I made a mental note that this new crew could be the weakest link for the reforms.

Most of the A Ring attended the CHO hearing on Wednesday, January 13. I sat in the front row with the other officers. Vicki sat behind me and Terri sat next to her. There were a few photographers from print news darting about the room, shooting photos of the CHO members as they filtered in. Vicki leaned forward to give me pointers on sitting at the witness table. "Remember to sit on your coat," Vicki instructed, "so that your coat doesn't ride up." Vicki had worked with Roger Ailes on a number of early Fox News productions, so she had a good eye for framing a photo and proper posture during interviews. A *Roll Call* photographer snapped a photo of us conferring. Then it was time for the hearing. They would later publish this photo with the caption "Chief Administrative Lovebirds."[3]

Thomas and several other CHO members made brief opening remarks. Hoyer opened with a cordial nod to my meeting with the minority staff and trying to get together with members of the panel. Thomas shot me a look as if to scold me for not clearing these interactions with him.

The officers sat as a panel, but each made brief opening remarks. I spoke extemporaneously: "Today, we are in the midst of a major revolution. A consumer revolution." Terri let out a soft sigh of relief. She had feared I was going to say "conservative." I then briefly laid out the tenets of quality management as it related to meeting the needs of the customer. "The CAO office's role is to make sure every member is fully successful in serving their constituents. We will measure our success by how effectively and efficiently this is achieved."

Once the pleasantries were over, Hoyer launched into an attack on the firing of executives from the previous Congress. "This attack is more for the record than grounded in close ties to the 'recently departed,'" I mused to myself as he misstated Nancy Glorius's name as "Nancy Doria."

I learned from my years in Washington that witnesses should try to limit their speaking time, including answering questions, to less than 30 percent of their total time at the witness table. Members like to dominate the proceedings. Witnesses exceed this 30 percent at their own risk. Therefore, I hesitated for an imperceptible moment to allow Thomas and the other Republicans to engage Hoyer. I was not disappointed. Thomas opened up on the Democrats with "both barrels," citing specific abuses of power during the previous Congress. The fracas wore down Hoyer and Fazio, so when they turned their attention back to me, it was much smoother sailing. Hoyer opted to ask me about whether, as a Republican, I had any ulterior motives.

"Congressman, good management is just good management," I began conversationally. "There is no 'Republican' or 'Democratic' way to pay bills, purchase supplies, or meet customer needs. There is only what works and makes sense."

The A Ring heaped praise on me after the hearing. The next day the inner circle of Thomas, Nussle, and Wadel conducted a debriefing on the hearing with the officers. "I recommend that we only hold hearings after the fact on the reforms," offered Thomas. There was general agreement that work on the reforms should remain "under the radar screen" and be implemented through administrative action as much as possible.

At the next A Ring meeting I spoke effusively about the "air cover" provided by the CHO's Republican members. I declared, "Thomas is our friend!"

THIS OLD HOUSE

"He's a frickin' Bob Vila!" Jane Bennett exclaimed. She was musing about Representative Dave Bonior (D-MI), who had taken the helm as the new Democratic whip. January may have been the start of a new Congress and a new era, but renovation, not revolution, was all the rage.

Bonior's first order of business was not girding for battle but launching massive alterations of H305–308.

Every member of the leadership, both Republicans and Democrats, ended up with new offices in the 104th Congress. This was not only because of the change in party control, but also because Gingrich opted to make H-227–H-233 the Speaker's suite. This change rippled through the Capitol. With new rooms came a natural desire to "nest" and imprint each new office with the member's own personality.

It started with Gingrich. He wheeled in the glass-enclosed head of a *Tyrannosaurus rex* to be the focal point in H-230, his formal meeting room. It would serve as his constant reminder that we must all "evolve or die."

Armey proceeded to create a Texas-themed suite in the old Speaker's suite in H-327A–H-332. DeLay took over the old clerk's suite in H-104–H-115 adjoining the CAO's suite in H-111–H-112.

Having DeLay as a neighbor was wonderful. Vicki had known DeLay during his days in the Texas legislature. Terri Hasdorff knew many of De-Lay's staff: Ed Buckham, Jim Lafferty, Grace Crewes, Louis (Lou) Ambrose, and Bill Jerrell. We quickly established a close-knit "neighborhood," which had immediate benefits as we negotiated for Terri to have her desk in the "escape corridor" (H-105A) just outside my back door. This allowed Gloria and Jane to maintain their desks in the crowded front section of the CAO suite.

The need to personalize offices had to be balanced with the fact that these were all government-owned spaces with significant history. My most pressing task was to remind everyone that the "perks" had to be kept within the limits of responsible stewardship of public resources.

I met with two longtime colleagues, Kerry Knott, Dick Armey's chief of staff and an alumnus of the same Georgetown program I attended in 1975, and Ginny Thomas, the wife of Supreme Court justice Clarence Thomas and a longtime member of the Conservative Network. We discussed overall cooperation on the reforms to come. I also obtained their pledges to run any major furniture purchases past me for a "smell test."

However, we had a "near death" experience with Tom and Christine DeLay. During this "nesting" period, Terri poked her head inside my office. "Scot, you got a minute?" She said Christine had some questions for me. I dropped what I was doing and followed Terri into DeLay's main reception area. I greeted Christine and she, in turn, introduced me to her interior designer. Her question was how to place the designer on DeLay's staff so that they could pay her for her services. Alarm bells went off in my head. "Tell me about what you had in mind."

The designer proceeded to walk me through DeLay's suite, effusing over her plans for new drapes, carpets, and furnishings. I began to inquire about costs. "Well, I found the most wonderful couch in New York for around $20,000," she answered, enthusiastic about her find.

I turned to Christine. "Do you realize how many pieces of antique furniture I could buy in Baltimore for $20,000?"

She looked a bit sheepish.

"Christine, I understand your desire to redecorate Tom's offices, but that kind of money would be a lightning rod for the media. Have you worked with our in-house designers?"

Christine didn't know my office had designers. I went on to tell her about the historic furniture sitting in various House storage areas and warehouses. Finally, I diplomatically expressed concern about placing an interior designer on the payroll. "This effort would bust Tom's budget and break several House rules."

I apologized to the designer, telling her it was not personal. I recommended that Christine use personal funds if she wanted to retain the designer, but not to try to place her on payroll. I then pledged to give Christine the full attention of my staff to help her with every aspect of redecorating DeLay's suite.

DeLay was not the only one needing to be reminded of the rules and the mission. One of the first major acts of the new Congress was a major across-the-board reduction in committee staff. The staff reductions occurred, but no space was released. Nussle and I met with Wadel to determine how much "persuasion" we could count on from Gingrich to shame the committee chairs into freeing up their newly emptied space. She pledged to us that this would be "issue number one" at the next leadership meeting.

During this time, we decided to resolve two "urban legends" once and for all. The first "legend" was that the Capitol was a toxic site.

Employees of both the CAO and the architect of the Capitol had approached the A Ring with concerns that they were being exposed to asbestos and chemical cleansers. Our search of various tunnels and workrooms did uncover some shoddy handling practices for industrial-strength solvents. However, asbestos would require testing.

Paul Sweetland and I had a vigorous exchange over what to do. Paul felt that we should inform the architect and have his office do the test. I insisted that the architect had some credibility issues and only our test would be viewed as objective. In the end, I prevailed and arranged with Wadel to have an independent lab come in and conduct an unannounced test for asbestos and other contaminants. The tests came back negative. I sent the report to the architect and the CHO. It once and for all put an urban legend to rest. It also signaled that I would move swiftly to resolve rumors and act independently of the old system.

The other urban legend was that Foley and his wife had built a condo for themselves inside the Capitol. Both the A Ring and the transition team had found a number of undocumented renovations completed in the prior forty years. We now wanted to see if H-324 was the Foley condo. The agenda for the transition meeting of January 17 was to visit the suite and see what was inside. Bill Livingood brought the key. Thomas, Nussle, Wadel, and I eagerly stood by the door. At that moment Representative Pat Schroeder (D-CO) rounded the corner. Thomas looked sheepish, but quickly greeted Pat and chatted with her until she passed the scene.

The first surprise was the floor within a floor. A mezzanine level now existed where before there had been a high ceiling. We raced up the stairs to see what secrets the mezzanine held. There was a kitchen unit and sleeper sofas, but no bathroom. The kitchen cabinets were brimming with liquor bottles. But the middle of the mezzanine held the biggest surprise.

Two long lines of tables dominated the middle of the mezzanine. Telephones littered the tables, and coils of telephone wire indicated that there had been many more phones, recently removed. What were they for?

Nussle and I solved the mystery when we went up yet another flight of stairs into a small storage room. It was filled with union membership lists. There were several anti-NAFTA scripts lying on the floor. It was clear that this had been the command center for the effort to stop the North American Free Trade Agreement that was part of the special session in December. Nussle mused at what the White House's reaction would be if they knew about this.

We adjourned back to our regular meeting room to discuss our expedition. It was decided that the most private and mysterious of places would ironically become the most accessible. I was given the mandate to develop a "members' families room" as a place for spouses and children to "hang out" while visiting the Capitol. This major innovation would eventually become one of the great contributions to making the House more "family friendly." It would also become a crowning achievement for Debbie Hansen and Representative Frank Wolf (R-VA).

With the "nesting" efforts well underway, but being closely monitored, I turned my attention to my own nest. H-111 and H-112 had been poorly used and abused. Fluorescent lights blocked the views of soaring vaulted ceilings. The aging rugs were stained and torn. All the electrical wiring was exposed, with metal conduits running up the walls and across the ceilings.

Vicki and I tapped all our years of renovating historic houses for the task of remaking the CAO suite. I also received extensive cooperation from the architect's office. He was true to his word of making his staff available. The first order of business was research. In a few days the architect's curator informed me that my suite was the only section of the Capitol not damaged by the British burning of August 24–25, 1814. This meant that the walls were original to Benjamin Latrobe's design and construction. My actual office, H-111, had been a committee room, but it was the front room that solved the mystery of why this part of the Capitol had not burned—it had been the privy.

The moisture from the internal privy had saved the day for the CAO suite. I shared this research with the A Ring. Our ongoing inside joke was that the CAO suite had been returned to its original purpose—we were once again handling all the crap in the Capitol!

With history in hand, Vicki and I worked with the architect's team to restore the suite to its former glory. All the electrical wiring would be hidden. Damage would be repaired and historical colors would be applied. The greatest windfall came when the architect offered a pair of large magnificent brass chandeliers that had been salvaged from a Maryland home but were sitting in standing water in a basement storage room.

I combed the warehouse spaces for historical furnishings and rugs. Vicki worked with the CAO design team on drapes. This first phase would lead to other phases over the course of a year. In the end, at minimal cost, the CAO suite would do honor to Latrobe, including displaying his architectural renderings of the Capitol, Thomas Jefferson's damage report on the burning, and one of the only two portraits of Latrobe.

The initial work required that the suite be vacated for a week. So Gloria, Jane, and I migrated to the "tower of terror," leaving Terri behind as our on-site presence.

The seventh-floor CAO offices were the antithesis of the "island of calm" I aspired to in the CAO suite. Every few minutes, someone from the A Ring dropped by to show me things and to discuss some proposed action. Though this immersed me into the full magnitude of our undertaking, it left me with no time to myself. The entire point of the A Ring was to bring together professionals who were far brighter than I was in their particular specialties, giving them full reign over their enterprise and allowing me to become the "facilitator in chief" able to tie everything together and run the political traps with leadership. I counted the days before I could return to the Capitol.

As the work on the CAO suite progressed, I noted that both Livingood and Carle were in the midst of their own "nesting" efforts. Tourists had to thread their way past stacks of furniture and pails of paint arrayed along the ground-floor hallway that linked our offices.

On Monday, February 6, something was different about the hallway. All of the CAO office furniture was missing! Jane Bennett knew exactly what to do. She contacted her friends with the Capitol Police and reviewed the security cameras. Low and behold, there was Barry Jackson, executive director of the House Republican Conference, directing interns hauling the furnishings down to his suite in H-132–H-133. Jane, with the police in tow, stormed down to Barry demanding the return of the furniture—case closed!

My telephone rang. It was Wadel. John Boehner was furious about Jane's detective work. Jane had to apologize to Barry, and I should consider firing her. "What?" I was aghast. "Are you telling me that Barry steals our furniture and we must apologize to him?"

"Exactly," Wadel confirmed. "Scot, we have to maintain good relations with everyone. Jane overstepped herself. You both should have come to me."

"But we didn't know what became of the furniture. Jane did the right thing in checking the security tapes."

"But you should have come to me. I would have worked things out with Barry and John."

"Sue, inventory control is a key part of establishing financial integrity. Having a senior staffer to leadership pillaging the halls is not setting a very good example."

"This has gone beyond my control. Jane apologizes or leaves."

I was nonplussed. Barry should have been the one penalized, not Jane. I had a heart-to-heart with Jane about the injustice of it all and recommended that she outdo herself in making amends. Ever the master at customer service, Jane personally took Barry, John, and their staff over to the warehouse and helped them select historical furnishings, and then expedited reupholstering, rugs, and draperies. It was another example of the parallel universe I had entered.

AT YOUR SERVICE

The A Ring was proving itself in the efficiency with which it handled the "cutover" and in taking charge of operations. We now needed to take it to the next level.

The 104th Congress welcomed eighty-eight new freshmen. I decided the most vivid display of the new era would be for the A Ring to personally visit each freshman office to check on their settling-in and to offer assistance in resolving any remaining housekeeping matters.

We divided the three office buildings into sections so that each A Ring person, myself included, only had to visit eleven offices. I brought Jane along on my rounds so that we could discuss aspects of her customer-service initiative.

My section was part of Longworth. Jane and I would drop by each office, introduce ourselves, and ask a series of questions about whether everything had been installed, set up, activated, and made operational. Representative Mike Ward (D-KY) ushered us into his office. He needed help getting his long-distance calling cards activated. Without hesitation, I picked up the telephone and called over to Mutersbaugh, resolving the matter on the spot.

Ward looked at me with amazement. "You actually helped me."

"Of course. That is why we are here."

"But you are a Republican and I am a Democrat."

"You are a member," I explained. "Your constituents elected you to serve them. My role is to make sure you have everything you need to fulfill that responsibility."

"Then the stories are true," he mused. "You really are here to make things run like a business. You are not a partisan."

SCARING PEOPLE

The "retiring rooms" are a large lounge area directly behind the Speaker's podium, just off the House floor. On January 3, this was a waiting area for the officers waiting to be sworn in. During this downtime, Paul Rodriguez, an investigative reporter for the *Washington Times*, walked over to me and introduced himself. I had never met him, but respected his work on many hard-hitting stories about the House.

Paul wanted to share his findings as a way of providing a road map for reform. I invited him to meet with the A Ring, saying that they would all benefit from his years of research.

On January 11, during one of the A Ring's regular meetings, Paul dropped by and spent about an hour regaling them with horror stories about the House. Most of what he said verified our work to date. However, Paul went further by linking a number of actions to a conscious and strategic intent by the Democrats to subvert democratic processes. His conspiratorial take on what to us was a dysfunctional culture in which a corrupt few took advantage shook some people. I ended the session by stating that we benefit from hearing many perspectives and that it is useful to draw on the tireless work of those who expose wrongdoing.

The reaction to Rodriguez was not long in coming. The very next day, Thursday, January 12, Jane and I had just completed our last office in Longworth on our "freshman" tour and were looping through the Rayburn subway en route to the Capitol when Jim Nussle rounded the corner and greeted us. He clearly wanted to talk. Jane continued while we moved over to the side.

"Scot, you are scaring people." Jim looked serious. "That Rodriguez meeting was a mistake. Some members are concerned that you will engage in a witch hunt instead of reform."

"Jim, I have no intention of doing anything other than making the changes we are discussing and making them stick." I felt a pit in my stomach.

"Rodriguez doesn't fit that mold."

"You're right. It was a onetime opportunity to let my team know that there are bears and wolves in the forest."

"I am on your side on this." Jim lightened. "We both know a lot of illegal stuff has gone on. But we need to stay focused on the reform. If we can change this place, we will drive out the bad guys and make sure they never come back. Just ease back a bit on the 'digging up the skeletons' issue. You have developed enough momentum for reforms. Don't hurt yourself with being too zealous for 'righting all the wrongs' at once, okay?"

"Okay." I said. He smiled and we parted.

That evening Otto called to tell me that members were really angry about the fact that Rodriguez met with the A Ring. "You may not be in trouble on this, but I would watch whom I invite to meetings in the future."

The next day, Jim and I were in a meeting on space reduction. Wadel had just told us that Gingrich was leaving us on our own regarding the "space wars," since he was reluctant to take on the committee chairmen during the first hundred days. After the meeting, Jim wanted to talk, so we walked together back toward his office.

"Scot, I want to apologize for coming off a bit strong yesterday," Jim began.

"That's okay. I value your feedback. I can pace myself to make sure we get all these reforms through," I responded warmly.

Jim lowered his voice. "We both know that not everyone up here wants us to succeed. In fact, many of our friends are worried about how this place will change if we do everything we are planning."

"I understand. We are breaking a wild horse."

"Exactly!" Jim beamed. "When you tame the wild horse, you don't put the saddle on him right away. Try the bridle for a while, then a blanket, *then* a saddle. We have to ease the members into accountability or they will throw us off their backs—and if we bridle them too fast, they may throw us *all* off."

As I returned to the CAO suite, I pondered Jim's comments. I also pondered the fact that someone in the A Ring chose to take their concerns to Otto instead of to me. Loyalties were to prove a complex, and transitory, factor in the years ahead.

BLUEPRINT
FOR REVOLUTION

February 23, 1995

We are serving our country by serving our Congress.

—Management credo, chief administrative officer

How does a leader turn a vision into an operational reality? The challenge facing the revolutionaries in the House required more than better accounting and some internal controls to resolve. It would require creating an entirely new culture and way of doing business. This would be the largest reinvention since 1789.

I pondered this during my first fifty days in office. The A Ring had collected voluminous evidence of corruption and dysfunction throughout the House. They had also gained an understanding of how things could work and identified those among existing CAO employees who were potential allies in making things better. This was a similar process to what happened during the cleanup of the General Services Administration (GSA) in 1981–1982.

It was up to me to make all the parts work and to drive the process forward. Thinking back to the GSA, I remembered how President Reagan appointed Gerald Carmen, a businessman from New Hampshire, to head the agency. Gerry had been an early supporter of Reagan, but his strong suit was being a no-nonsense owner of a network of tire and auto-parts stores in New England. Reagan gave Gerry a clear mandate: develop a plan to clean up the most inefficient and corrupt agency in the federal government in six months or shut it down.

Gerry brought together a small dedicated team of skilled managers. I was lucky enough to be brought in to drive the personnel reforms and ultimately to organize and lead the team that tracked the progress of the reforms. We had the additional advantage of several whistle-blowers who had voluminous files on what had gone wrong in the agency. With a clear change agenda, and support all the way up to the president, we proceeded like emergency-room doctors. We triaged the ailments of the agency, addressing "life-threatening" illnesses first, then taking on lesser matters until the GSA was on the road to recovery.

Two fundamental sets of principles guided the GSA effort. We lived the mantra of internal control: prevention, early detection, and limiting the damage. Implementing these three bulwarks methodically eradicated the corruption and stopped the hemorrhaging of millions of public dollars.

The second principle was changing the culture. The "Carmen Dozen" could not outwork thirty-four thousand employees. Allies had to be found, and the entire agency needed to be retrofitted. Step one was for me to create the "war room." This was a room where we could put the entire agency's personnel on the walls. I cut up the payroll records and pasted them onto poster-sized card-stock modules. Each module was covered in translucent acetate, and holes were drilled along the top edge. Each module could then be placed on large hooks protruding from the walls, going from floor to ceiling. One pattern of modules would create a GSA division from headquarters into each region. Another pattern would create a region across divisions. Gerry and I would spend hours going over each pattern. "What's that?" Gerry would ask, pointing to some inexplicable office with no apparent reason to exist. "Who's that?" Gerry would jab his finger at a high-level official who had no one reporting to him.

Throughout these sessions, we would use colored grease pencils to annotate the modules. We even had a tall, wheeled ladder that allowed us to roll around the room and reach the top modules. The Carmen Dozen, along with whistle-blowers, would join us to give their input. Ultimately, plans evolved to outsource and downsize the agency to twenty thousand employees. The leaner, more streamlined, GSA would then arise within a new culture of professionalism, ethics, and customer service.

The GSA experience inspired and guided me, starting with my appointment in December. That was one of the reasons I wanted Simon on my team, as he was part of the second wave of reformers who joined us at GSA. I then sought to replicate the spirit and expertise of the GSA team with my A Ring. Finally, our fanning out to discover and document the disastrous management practices in the House was designed to give us what the whistle-blowers gave us at GSA back in 1981. Throughout this period, I also thought about Reagan's and Carmen's sense of urgency—six months. In my case, we had fewer people and dollars to address, so my goal was to have a plan ready by the end of January.

In addition to mounting a strategic reform of operations and internal control, I considered the broader implications of what my team and I were about to do. We had a once-in-a-lifetime opportunity to reinvent Congress and the nature of American government. My first step was to give these different levels and concepts of reform a driving vision.

A REVOLUTIONARY VIEW OF THE
U.S. HOUSE OF REPRESENTATIVES

I viewed the House as a small town. Peopled by eleven thousand individuals, it is like any small town in America. It has good and bad people. It has lots of friendship circles, cliques, and factions. It has many secrets known to many who live there but not told to outsiders. The townspeople know the bullies, the drunks, the fools, the corrupt; they also know the good, the saintly, and the wise. Because this town is historic and important, three million tourists a year, from around the globe, visit to watch, photograph, and fill its hallways. The Capitol of the United States is the only complex of working parliament buildings in the world that anyone can enter and wander through unescorted. Once you clear the metal detectors, it is up to you what tunnel or hallway you wish to walk through. Just like a small town, you cannot enter every room—some require permission, but you can linger outside and occasionally peer in.

I also saw the House as a large conference center. Meetings are what the place is all about. The House floor can seat five hundred comfortably; with folding chairs and people willing to stand, it can fit the Senate, the Supreme Court, the cabinet, the Joint Chiefs of Staff, and more than a hundred diplomats for the State of the Union address and other special sessions or meetings. There are dozens of committee rooms for meetings; there are also forty special rooms, from the cavernous and opulent Cannon Caucus Room to small, modern but mundane rooms tucked under the western terrace of the Capitol. In addition to these general-use spaces, members have their own office suites, where a constant flow of constituents and lobbyists come and go to meet with members and their staffs.

As with a conference center in a city or a large hotel, each of these meetings requires a range of basic things: tables, chairs, microphones, coffee, bagels, linens, flowers, water glasses, nameplates, and name tags. Some meetings may be noteworthy to the news media, so media credentials (seven thousand issued during each Congress), cameras, outlets for telephones, and lots of cables become important. All of this occurs in the House of Representatives and requires the same management of resources, planning, implementation, and customer service that it does in the private sector. The rules and challenges of logistics are not suspended because one is supporting a major national parliament.

The House is also like a large office park. Every member is like a small business, controlling an annual operating "allowance" of $840,000 to $950,000 (the figure varies based on the distance from Washington, D.C., and the size and nature of the district itself). Each member can hire up to twenty-two full-time staff members (most stay at eighteen or below). Given members' independence to hire staff, organize their offices, and procure equipment and supplies, including leasing office space in their home districts, they truly operate like "Second District of Florida, Inc." or "Twentieth District of California, Inc." Each has the member as chief executive officer, who has a two-year contract from the voters to operate in their interest. This means voting, speaking, conducting casework, and listening.

Add to this array of member operations committee staffs, leadership staff, and various support offices, and you have five hundred very independent businesses sprawled throughout a well-landscaped office park of six buildings and a separate day-care facility. Within this complex, these separate enterprises and their employees need mail service, food, information and communication systems, supplies, and a variety of personal services, such as day care, haircuts, shoeshines, banking, and travel ticketing. The models for meeting these needs can be found in every multitenant office building in the world. Once again, the rules and challenges of logistics are not suspended because these business operations are supporting a major national parliament.

Lying astride meaningful reform was the basic flawed premise that the House was a political body, not a business. Every action, even how event rooms were reserved and how travel was reimbursed, ultimately led back to how each member voted on various issues.

Prior to the 104th Congress, the majority constantly punished the minority by abusing mundane administrative activities. For most of its two-century history, this abuse of power was the domain of whichever party held the majority. Since 1955, the legacy of preserving, expanding, and perfecting these abuses fell to the Democratic Party. For forty years, by withholding basic information on how the House operated, by politicizing the parking allocation, the furniture and equipment allocation, the personal services, the travel, the mail, the telephones, the payroll, the food, the Democratic majority crippled and harassed the Republican minority. The Republicans talked about reform, but many aspired to simply turn the tables on the Democrats. For them "payback," not change, should be the fruit of victory.

Prior to the 104th Congress, the management that oversaw these support activities operated like the worst-possible third-world government. Bribes, in the form of favors, votes, and money, made dysfunctional and nonexistent systems run smoothly, for a price. All was protected from outside scrutiny because nothing was written down. Those in charge of the record keeping were political loyalists who themselves had no background or training in the operations for which they were responsible.

There was also a climate of fear that stemmed from owing your very existence to the political elite you served. My goal was to end this culture once and for all.

A REVOLUTIONARY VIEW OF WASHINGTON

I placed the House in the broader context of Washington, D.C. The House can also be viewed as a neighborhood inside of a larger small town. Much of what has previously been said about the House can be said about the nation's capital. It too has its secrets that remain undisclosed to outsiders.

Those who enter this bizarre world quickly realize that the normal laws of reality are not allowed to work here. Those who try to change the way Washington works are either closed out or driven out. It is like taking the old story of *The Emperor's New Clothes* and giving it a very different ending. In the Washington version, the climax of the story has a child in the crowd crying out that the emperor, instead of wearing a magnificent set of new clothes so wonderful that they are invisible to the untrained eye, is, in fact, naked. Security forces wrestle the child to the ground and silence him. With the crowd cheering, the child and his family are arrested and deported. The emperor continues with his parade, and the crowd is thankful that no further outbursts of truth will be tolerated. Awkward realities are thus suppressed.

For Washington to operate outside of reality requires those wanting change to always be a diffused group of outsiders. As long as those inside Washington remain focused and alert to threats, there will never be a serious challenge to the status quo. A major preventative tactic is to constantly warn outsiders, "If you knew what we know, you would understand why it must be this way." These naked emperors are ever watchful to make sure their posturings of power are never unmasked like the Wizard of Oz. No one is allowed to get close to the curtain. My intent was to tear down the curtain, let everyone see how the government really worked, and level the playing field for real democracy to exist.

The first step was to clearly summarize these themes in my own management "manifesto." I thought about the Ritz Carlton's management credo, "three steps of service," and their "basics." The CAO's culture should echo similar themes of excellence and service. I also wanted to address the deplorable morale of employees from the start. Building pride in what people do is a major building block of an ethical and quality culture. I wanted to make sure the CAO team understood their vital role in making Congress happen. "Ennobling the effort" would be key to establishing the new work culture and environment.

My credo and manifesto were completed on Saturday, January 21:

> The House of Representatives deserves the best service in the world, and that is provided by those of us who work for the Office of the Chief Administrative Officer.
>
> As service professionals, we are proud to have the Congress as our customer. Its members are independent elected officials, ultimately responsible and accountable to the people who elected them. Our role is to serve each and every member equally and impartially.
>
> To ensure an enduring tradition of world class service for our customers, we will devote every action and thought to the following:
>
>> As Service Professionals, we will constantly and consistently listen to our customers, meet their needs, and seek ways to continuously improve our services to them.
>>
>> As Stewards of Public Funds, we will constantly and consistently account for every action and expenditure based on the highest standards of ethics, honesty, and integrity. We will make our every action documentable, and measurable.[1]

I shared the manifesto with the A Ring on Monday. They were wildly enthusiastic, seeing it as both accurately capturing the essence of our revolution and giving everyone common focus and terminology to proceed. The next step was consolidating our findings into a manageable set of actions.

The best approach was for the A Ring to take all their notes along with the voluminous ideas from the transition "idea board" and spend the afternoon of January 25 doing affinity diagramming. Every idea and finding was written on individual "yellow stickies" and placed on a large blank wall. This process, refined from various strategic workshops and the National Governors Association Education Outcome Team process, was highly interactive and energizing. Anyone can add yellow stickies at any time. Anyone can move and consolidate yellow stickies in any way. After several hours of this nonlinear free-for-all, seventy-five reforms took shape on the wall. Under each one was anywhere from ten to fifty yellow stickies adding detail to what needed to be done and why. I congratulated everyone on an incredible work product. Dorsey's team volunteered to transcribe the work product into a document for further review and comment by the A Ring.

The A Ring reviewed the draft set of reforms over the weekend. We then discussed and made revisions during our Monday staff meeting. Next we clustered the seventy-five reforms into themes: internal control, openness, privatization, customer service, and the cyber-Congress. We were now ready to share formal briefing books with the CHO and the transition team.

Throughout this period, the A Ring was managing a herculean effort. They all had to balance their days between running House operations and collecting additional data on reform.

The A Ring also began the process of identifying "career" employees who could be allies in our revolution. First, they personally distributed paychecks and stubs to all their employees on January 31. This served to determine whether there were any "ghost" employees or duplicates on the payroll (there were a few), and to finally meet everyone. After this first introduction, the A Ring began experimenting with working sessions with small fledgling teams. Carole and Kay facilitated problem-solving sessions and process-analysis sessions to flesh out selected reforms and to further test their teams' ability to think in management terms. The process flowcharts were extremely helpful. The "careerists" had never been asked how things happened or didn't happen. We gained many insights simply by methodically asking, "What happens next?" and, "Then where does the request go?" Large flowcharts on brown paper began emerging from these meetings. We confirmed that there was no documentation for anything. Most processes had too many steps, wasting time and adding opportunities for error.

Dorsey and I were also working with the CHO staff and Sue Wadel on sorting out our own flow charts. So much was happening that everyone was getting blindsided by everyone else on something. We ultimately designated points of contact: Dorsey, Wadel, and Wolff would act as the executive secretariats for each organization to make sure paper flowed and everyone was in the loop. Hasdorff, Bennett, and Hansen became my brain trust regarding processing and tracking individual member requests.

REALITY CHECK

The management revolution of the House formally began on February 2, 1995. On that day, all the major players in the revolution gathered around the witness table in the CHO committee hearing room to decide how to proceed. Nussle, Wadel, and Thomas cochaired the meeting. Many of the CHO staff attended, along with Lainhart. This was also the first time Representative Ron Packard (R-CA), the chair of the Legislative Branch Subcommittee of the Appropriations Committee, was included. The transition team intended to have the CHO approve the specific reform initiatives and then to have the financial aspects of these reforms reviewed and approved in the appropriations process. Thomas arrived twenty minutes late from another meeting. I then began my presentation with the manifesto.

"I am not your customer! I own the store!" exploded Bill Thomas.

We all looked at Thomas as he vigorously shook his head.

"Well, owners, as bosses, are the customers of those who work for them," I continued, trying to keep the focus on the reforms. Nussle leaned over and calmed Thomas down. Stacy and Otto fidgeted in their chairs, not looking very happy. Packard's eyes got large, and he looked over at me sympathetically. I continued to lay out the themes and walk through the seventy-five reforms. Thomas interrupted, demanding to know where my team and I came up with these ideas. Nussle took control of the discussion and cheered the proposals as clearly arising from the transition reports and significant due diligence by the A Ring. He asked about next steps.

"I thought it best for everyone to review the reforms and give my team feedback on them. Especially if we have missed anything. Once we have all agreed that this is what should be done, I propose an implementation workshop—"

"What's that?" asked Thomas.

"The implementation of each of these reforms will need to be carefully planned. We also need to figure out our respective roles. Some of these reforms can be done administratively; some may require Oversight Committee approval; many will impact appropriations. By mapping out each reform, we can figure out which ones can happen simultaneously, and which ones need to occur sequentially."

It was agreed that everyone would take a week to provide feedback and that my team would organize and run the implementation workshop on the weekend of February 24–26.

After the meeting, Ron came up to me. "We need to talk." He mentioned that the first Appropriations hearing was scheduled for February 15. He then took me aside. "Bill may be our fly in the ointment. You and I need to make these reforms happen."

To make sure we were all on the same page, I had most of the A Ring attend the session. I gave each of them a "listening points" worksheet to provide feedback on the meeting. Their answers and observations would shape the fight for reform in the House:[2]

1. Relationship of CAO to Oversight Committee?

   - Thomas is boss.
   - Too much control—can't let go.
   - Plantation attitude
   - We are unique compared with clerk and sergeant at arms.
   - Can there be an effective team, with internal customers, between CAO and Oversight Committee?
   - Style issue—Thomas wants more formal approach.

2. "Center of gravity" for fundamental reform?

   - Policy versus operations—Committee does policy.
   - 25 percent if Oversight is in charge; 75 percent if leadership is in charge; Thomas off-track; it is surprising they are not more in tune with each other.
   - Definitely the Appropriations Committee. Thomas's staffer wanted to dissent but didn't. Gingrich et al. need to be seen as

center of gravity, but taxpayers/voters are the ones who voted for reform!

3. What do we still need to know in order to do our jobs?

- Who gives the orders?
- What are the decisions?
- Which changes are "no goes" for now?
- Can we hire staff in February?
- Lack of timely decisions prevents effective budget and project schedules.
- We need to stay in front of curve.
- Make allies with Appropriations Committee w/o alienating the CHO or Thomas.

4. What worked?

- Goal, vision statement
- Group pulled together as more of a cohesive force.
- Having Mr. Packard there helped overall understanding and communication.
- Presentation to members of CAO credo was good. Members wanted to talk and Scot engaged them with his intro. This led to immediate discussion and strategic conversation.
- Scot's communication process with his own people—we fed enough information to Scot to allow him to speak with force and explanation.

The next week was filled with multiple meetings and calls between the CAO and CHO offices to flesh out and clarify the reforms. During this time, Thomas and I met specifically on human-resources policies and procedures. He was pleased and impressed with the first draft of a new revolutionary members' handbook hammered out by Dorsey, Simon, and Anfinson, which included Thomas's priority project—the merging of member accounts.

He was interested in how I was going to create and manage a parallel organization. This "ideal" would rise up as the "status quo" structure withered and disappeared. In the process, 1,200 people would go away on paper, and a new organization of 630 would take its place. The challenges were to downsize without legal entanglements, maintain the quality of services, and make sure "worthy" careerists transitioned to the new organization. Thomas was skeptical that it could be done as fast as I was proposing. I explained that those issues would be discussed during the implementation workshop.

Nussle and Wadel were fully engaged in the reform vetting process. They were instrumental in making sure the CHO signed off "in principle" on all seventy-five reforms.

ENTER PACKARD

Packard and I met in his office on Monday, February 13. David Coggins, Ron's liaison to the Appropriations Committee, joined us.

Ron came to Congress in 1982 as the fourth person in history to win as a write-in candidate. His unique understanding of grassroots politics and government reform came from his years serving on the city council and as mayor of Carlsbad, California.[3] Ron had heard much about my background from his friend, Tom Anfinson, and his fellow Mormon, John Garbett.

Our discussions were highly collegial from their onset. Ron outlined how he saw the reforms as vital to fulfilling the voters' mandate of 1994 and to solidifying the reputation of the Republican Party as the party of reform. He provided several insights into the agenda and psyche of Representatives Bill Thomas (R-CA) and Vic Fazio (D-CA), as they had all served as members of the California congressional delegation for the past twelve years. "We are going to have to stay one step ahead of them if we are going to succeed," Ron counseled.

He then outlined the first hearing that was scheduled for Wednesday of that week and also recommended that I meet briefly with Ed Lombard, the professional staff member in charge of the Legislative Branch Subcommittee. "The hearing will be just a general get-acquainted session. You should not talk about the future, just state that you look forward to working closely with the subcommittee on improving the operations of the House. I will divert Vic should he try to press you on details."

I agreed, and we ended our meeting with plans to communicate regularly to make the reforms happen. "David also knows Tom Anfinson. They can work out the numbers when we get closer to markup. Remember, you can always count on me."

True to his word, the February 15 Appropriations hearing was a non-event. The most interesting element was its setting. The elaborate mural of Lucius Quinctius Cincinnatus in hearing room H-114 was the first work by painter Constantino Brumidi, the "Michelangelo of the Capitol."[4] Brumidi completed the mural on March 17, 1855. Cincinnatus was a farmer who left his field to defend Rome, became a military hero, and then returned to his farm. The Society of the Cincinnati was formed as an alumni organization for George Washington's officers. Their descendants maintain the tradition of "unwavering public service, and a willingness to lay down personal power for the good of the Republic to this day."[5] The other unique feature of the room was a large conference table where meetings were conducted. This promoted a far more collegial atmosphere than having members look down from a dais.

IMPLEMENTATION WORKSHOP

On the morning of Friday, February 24, the A Ring gathered in the newly opened CAO meeting room on the seventh floor of the O'Neill Building. Each member of the A Ring had taken lead responsibility for individual reforms since the January 25 planning session. Rick had taught each of the A Ring members how to use the project software. Gloria had given everyone templates for what to include on the Gantt charts. This all culminated in poster-sized Gantt charts for each of the seventy-five reforms.

The workshop used another stack of yellow stickies. We placed ten charts at a time on the walls around the room. We asked everyone to review the charts and add comments and questions from their various perspectives to better define each implementation plan, as well as the who, when, and how of each plan, along with requirements and processes for documentation and measurement.

With this process, legal, finance, human-resources, information-technology, internal-control, training, and logistics issues were all addressed at once. We also had lively discussions about project tracking, data collection, and scoping. We clarified communication flows to the "reform caucus," CHO, Appropriations Committee, and leadership teams, and how we would inform our customers, garner customer feedback, and promote ongoing evaluation and continuous improvement.

The A Ring spent an hour on each set of ten charts. We then spent another hour going over each set and discussing the yellow stickies. Through it all, Gloria and Jennifer compiled extensive notes, questions, and to-do lists that would refine the implementation of each reform.

My role was that of lead facilitator. I had also invited the staff from the CHO, the Appropriations Committee, the inspector general, and leadership to give their input. Lainhart brought two new players in the reform effort. These were the leaders of the Price Waterhouse (it did not merge with Coopers & Lybrand until 1998) audit team, Bill Pauli and Tom Craren. They were fascinated with the process we were using and asked many questions during the day.

Sue Wadel was also fascinated by the process. She commented on how it truly made her realize that the reforms were real and going to happen. Stacy and Otto kept looking for where the CHO fit in each reform. I spent much of my time explaining to them that that is why they were there, to let us know the appropriate place for CHO input or formal approval.

As the second day dawned, we completed the final set of reforms. Our attention then shifted to pacing the reforms. Everything was initially premised on happening all at once. Now that we had refined each reform to cover all bases and disciplines, we had to step back and figure out which ones might need to be rescheduled so that we could devote adequate resources to properly implementing them. It became clear that the House post office would be the largest of our endeavors, requiring major renovations to be coordinated with the architect of the Capitol and a historic outsourcing process. There were many other reforms that could happen fairly quickly and administratively.

There was a clear set of reforms that would require CHO action. These included the House post office; the folding room; printers; the barbershop and beauty salon; the photographers; the studios; information systems; and parking. I turned to Sue and commented that these addressed the core of the scandals that brought the Republicans to power. "Everyone will be watching these. They will make or break the revolution." Sue nodded in agreement.

"You also see that, except for the post office, we can cut over to the new operations over the summer, when people are out of town. That will allow us to work out any kinks during the lowest need for these services," I remarked. "That means we need Oversight approval by April so we can run the RFPs and select the vendors."

"Let me take care of that," Sue concluded.

The thoroughness and speed of the CAO operation was garnering supporters and momentum. This juxtaposed with the clerk, who had just fallen out of favor with the Speaker.

The dark days for the clerk had begun at the CHO hearing on February 8. It was to be Representative Jim Nussle's (R-IA) formal handoff of the transition team. I did not need to attend. In his testimony, Nussle emphasized the broad policy guidance role of the CHO: "The mission of the House Oversight Committee would be to provide greater emphasis on developing broad policy recommendations and alternatives to the House rules that govern administrative procedures. It would concentrate its oversight responsibilities on major management issues and limit its involvement in day-to-day administrative operations."[6]

The hearing made it clear that Nussle was going to phase out his primary role in the reforms, since his duties as a member of the House Budget Committee were taking center stage. Robin Carle saw her chance to reopen the turf fights with the CAO office. She drafted a scathing critique of the House reforms with a plea for reversing most of the House's reorganization as her testimony before Packard's Appropriations subcommittee on February 15.

Thankfully, Wadel had set up a clearance process on all testimony by House officers. Carle's testimony was a bombshell that went off on Tuesday before the hearing. It did not take long for Nussle and Wadel to schedule a "come to Jesus" meeting with the Speaker and Carle. Gingrich made it clear: stand by the transition team report or resign. Carle ended her rebellion and allowed Wadel to rewrite her testimony.

There was tension all around the officers meeting on Wednesday, February 15. Carle came in and glared at everyone, remaining silent throughout the meeting. Stacy and Otto were also sullen, as Wadel and Nussle had had their own "come to Jesus" session with them on Monday over the role of the Oversight Committee. Wadel made it very clear that Stacy and Otto were only staff and therefore needed to be more deferential and respectful to House officers. I viewed these actions not only as a vote of confidence in the revolution we were launching, but also as a sign that the old ways would not die quietly and that the CHO would be a battleground in the months and years ahead.

At the next A Ring meeting I gave a "mini-sermon" on political "air cover" and political sensitivity. I cautioned everyone that the reforms were not a "done deal" and that we would need to be watchful for signs of a counterrevolution. I urged discretion and cited news reports about the future of the House elevator operators. A handicapped elevator operator had become a "poster child" for portraying the reforms as harmful and hateful.[7]

A WALK IN THE WAREHOUSE

With the various rebellions temporarily vanquished, the A Ring turned its attention to an array of "quick victories." We were all working nearly around the clock and it became clear that I needed to move my base of operations closer to the Capitol. Vicki found a condo in the Pennsylvania Building, near the National Archives, that we could rent. Harpers Ferry would now become our secondary home until mid-1997.

During this period, I took the first small steps toward modeling the new service culture by sending out thank-you notes and letters to "careerists" who contributed to the CAO start-up. One in particular was Susan Zeleniak, from HIS, who capably oversaw the changeover to the new telephone system and coverage of all incoming calls within the CAO offices. Jane Bennett and I worked out a customer-request tracking system, which included a weekly list of actions, evaluation of service and cycle time, and a status report to associate administrators

(AAs). We also established processes for looking for patterns and trends among the requests that might point to root causes and improvement opportunities.

Every night, Simon and I went through boxes of unpaid bills and vouchers. Payee names, service or product descriptions, and document and accounting numbers were missing, wrong, or did not track from one part of a package to another. Minor but necessary items also took my time. I had to establish a comprehensive snow-emergency procedure using color codes, taped telephone messages, and links to leadership for guidance, and create an emergency personnel list for when the House is in session and not in session.

Kay Ford became a Republican hero for stopping 324 Democratic staffers from using the Ramspeck Act to "career into" the Clinton administration.[8] Bill Norton gained control of all the gasoline cards and the seventy-seven vehicles in the House motor pool. He also tightened control of free copies of the *Congressional Record*. In both cases, the numbers were greatly reduced and tracking systems were put in place. Anfinson shut down all the petty-cash accounts. Sturdevant cleared out squatters from various empty offices and made sure the Speaker's office had complete and exclusive control of all excess space.

Sweetland freed up 1,400 parking spaces and completed his space-management survey of all the House buildings. Lusby stopped the holiday gift wrapping. Simon uncovered that legislative service organizations (LSOs) were end-running their prohibition. The LSOs were charging inflated "subscription fees" to skirt the law preventing the use of House funds for their operating expenses. Thomas took great joy in issuing a letter closing this loophole in the House Rules.

Dorsey and I crafted a new newspaper-distribution policy. Various companies were dropping off thousands of copies of their publications, which were then distributed by House employees to congressional offices. We determined that "free newspapers" violated Rule 45 on gifts. These free newspapers artificially inflated the circulation figures for *Roll Call* and the *Hill*. In essence, it was taxpayer price support of the advertising rates for these newspapers. "You are now their favorite dartboard," mused Jane Bennett.

Carole Kordich held inventory party weekends throughout February. She worked out an agreement with the GSA to take away surplus and obsolete equipment. Bar-code readers were acquired, and the first real inventory of the House's personal property was underway.

Don, Rick, and Phil proceeded with the HIS audit. They reviewed funding, operations, and needs analysis; defined tasks; and developed a strategic plan for what HIS should be doing, all in coordination with Ehlers. Kiko began unbundling maintenance contracts and establishing the first procurement guidelines.

The CHO and leadership were busy implementing their revolution in House Rules. We worked together to set up a "compliance timetable" to bring the House into full compliance with all federal laws, including employment, health, safety, and environmental regulations. The "official printers" were eliminated, forcing members to use their own office accounts to obtain printing services. Mass mailings were banned prior to members appearing on ballots. The first of the incumbent-protection "cookie jars" were smashed.

We did not win on all issues. There was the matter of the American flags "flown over the Capitol." Every day thousands of flags are hoisted for a few seconds on the roof of the Capitol. Three short flagpoles are used and are hidden from public view. The flag raising itself was not the only part hidden from the public. How these flags assist incumbency and their true costs were also a "secret of the House." Members promote themselves by sending these flags to their constituents, but their allowance is charged only for the cost of shipping. The balance of the costs—the flag, the flying, the certificate, and the packaging—were all tucked away in either the House stationery store's overhead or the architect of the Capitol's facility operations. Sweetland suggested creating a central 800 number for citizens to directly order the flags, without having to go through a member, or even "outsourcing" the entire process to a patriotic nonprofit group.

"That is a fight you will lose," offered Nussle. "Members will never give up their flags."

As a compromise, we let members handle all flag orders, but charged their allowances full price. The result would be adding accountability to members' accounts and creating additional pressure to economize within their members' representational allowances. Members could request that citizens reimburse them for at least the cost of the flag. "It will also put pressure on the architect to either reform or outsource the operation," I observed.

The old *Washington Star* warehouse continued to fascinate me. John Kostelnick, one of the senior "careerist" holdovers, resigned after realizing that his management of the warehouse was moving onto my priority list. On March 9, I took my second tour of the warehouse and furniture shops. This was the first time I met two "careerists" who would eventually solve the warehouse problem—Tom Van Dyke and Cosmo Quattrone, who was also the nephew of Joe "Q," the longtime Rayburn barber. The tour overwhelmed me with the disarray and dysfunction of the operation. I shared my experience with Thomas at our next meeting. "I'd like to see it for myself," he declared.

On Friday, March 31, Thomas, Terri, Stacy, and I drove over for a tour. Thomas immediately understood why this facility had to be dealt with sooner rather than later. We then moved to a floor where Van Dyke and Quattrone had moved the more historic and "upscale" furnishings. Much of the furniture was tagged for eventual use in leadership offices. Bill walked past some items tagged for Boehner and the Republican Conference. Thomas tore the taped tag off a blue silk wing chair and attached it to a hideous orange recliner lounge chair. "We'll see what the asshole thinks of that," smirked Thomas. "Imagine him wanting to choose before me."

★ COUNTERREVOLUTION ★

March 3, 1995

"What do you think?" Sweetland smiled as he presented the flag-pole with a flourish. The formal display pole had a standard military finial, complete with hooks for "battle ribbons."

"Perfect!" I enthused, examining the array of hooks.

Every House member and officer may have two official flags in his or her office. One is the American flag; the other is a flag of the member's choosing. Most ask for and receive an official state flag. I decided to have the flag of the House of Representatives, as I served all members. I was the first person to request a House flag since Speaker Tip O'Neill. I had asked Sweetland to acquire the "battle ribbon" attachment as part of a long-term awareness project. Everyone in the A Ring knew that our revolution would be a struggle. Each reform would only become reality after a major battle with Thomas or some other force in the House. Therefore, each reform would earn a "battle ribbon" and would be displayed on the flag as each battle was "won."

It did not take long for the first casualties in our "war" to occur.

Later that day, reporters at *Roll Call* announced they had Price Waterhouse's critique of the draft reforms.[1] This was less than a week after the February 24–25 implementation workshop, and *Roll Call* was planning to run a story about the "revolution." Tom Craren was mortified. There had never been such a leak from Price Waterhouse. He took immediate steps to replace several members of his team and crafted a detailed set of audit and confidentiality procedures.[2]

On March 8, I presented my first staffing plan before the CHO. My staffing plan was the codification of the A Ring plus several junior staffers, including Doug Fehrer and Joan McEnery. It was my first CHO-approved action, netting $365,611 in yearly savings because of the elimination and consolidation of executive positions.[3] This first small reform went like clockwork thanks to the hard work on human-resources and legal issues by Ford and Dorsey, and my road show.

Over the previous weeks, Bennett, Hasdorff, Dorsey, and I met with most CHO members and members of both the "reform caucus," including Representative Chris Shays (R-CT), and the "privatization caucus," including old friend Representative Scott Klug (R-WI), one-on-one, to discuss the "revolution" and its various stages. It became clear that Representatives Pat Roberts (R-KS), John Boehner (R-OH), and Jennifer Dunn (R-WA) would be active allies. Representative Lincoln Diaz-Balart (R-FL) candidly stated that he supported the reforms but that his first priority was to district issues. "I will be there if you need my vote, but otherwise, I must focus on my constituents."

The final Republican member of the CHO was freshman Representative Bob Ney (R-OH). Ney and I bonded immediately. His district included parts of Ashbrook's old district, and he had known Ashbrook during his early years in Ohio politics. Bob had served in both the Ohio House and Senate and was very savvy about parliamentary procedure. He was also one year younger than I, with his birthday on July 5 and mine on July 3. He was earnest in wanting reform and pledged to help in any way he could.

This "road show" with CHO members included the Democrats. I had met early on with Representative Vic Fazio (D-CA). He was the ranking minority member on both the CHO and the Legislative Branch Subcommittee. He and his staff were to be key links to the Democratic members. However, Fazio was personally close to Thomas and tended to view things through a partisan lens. Representative Sam Gejdenson (D-CT) was fiercely partisan and very liberal. I felt like a lion tamer during my meeting with him. Vic and Sam were both willing to give the reforms a "fair hearing" and gave me credit for taking the initiative to meet with them. Fortunately, Sam also sat on the International Relations (renamed Foreign Affairs in 2007) and Appropriations Committees. It was clear that his mind was focused elsewhere.

My one hope for a bipartisan reform effort lay with Representative Steny Hoyer (D-MD). He had the reputation of being reform-minded and fair. Prior to his House service, he had served for twelve years in the Maryland Senate and was its youngest president in Maryland history. Late in the afternoon of February 16, we finally met.

"I do not envy your task," Steny began. "The Maryland Senate was just as antiquated back in 1975. It took every ounce of will to overcome those wedded to the old ways. In the end, I succeeded, but few were willing to admit that things were better."

We proceeded to discuss transformational leadership and change management. It was clear that Steny understood that House reform was long overdue. He talked candidly about how Democratic members had opposed corruption but were outvoted in their caucus and powerless to press for change. I chose not to press him on why they remained silent during the scandals.

Our wide-ranging discussion continued as we reviewed the priority reforms and their basis. Steny leaned forward and looked me in the eye. "Scot, if you base your reforms solely on management and there is no hint of seeking partisan advantage, I will support every one of them. In fact, I can say that if we continue this level of dialogue, I will make sure my colleagues will not stand in the way of what you are doing."

I smiled broadly. "Congressman, I can assure you that is exactly what this is all about."

Hoyer smiled back. "I want you to bring the House into the twentieth century. Clean it up and bring in your business ideas. It is going to be hard work. I want it ready for when my party retakes Congress in 1996."

"That is my goal, but you may have to wait a few more elections."

ENTER BOB LIVINGSTON

I had known Representative Bob Livingston (R-LA) since he and Representative Arlan Stangeland (R-MN) served together as freshmen on the House Public Works Committee (subsequently renamed the House Committee on Transportation and Infrastructure). I was handling Stangeland's committee assignments. During a Water Resources caucus, the ranking Republican yelled at Livingston for supporting a reform without first consulting him. "You need to understand your place—and that place is behind me," snarled Representative Gene Taylor (R-MO). I observed Livingston as he cooled toward being a revolutionary and over the years became part of the establishment. We had had better days together. In January 1980, we were both part of a congressional team sent to Guatemala to assess Sandinista support of rebels in the region. We had stood on the aging runway used in the Bay of Pigs invasion and discussed our commitment to thwarting communism.

Bob was in a jovial mood as he welcomed me into his Capitol office. We reminisced about Guatemala and our times together. Then Bob got serious.

"Scot, I really want to help you and Newt on these reforms," Bob began. "But I must say, we have to pace ourselves. We are all new to this." He spread his arms and looked up at the palatial surroundings of H-216. "We need to be sure we are not throwing out babies with the bath water."

I nodded and looked serious. Nussle had cautioned me on how Livingston had retained most of the Democratic staff members on Appropriations. "We are bracing for some real confrontations with Bob," Jim warned. "Newt thinks he's an ally, but I think he's trouble."

I was also careful not to mention my contacts with Packard. I agreed to keep Bob posted on the reforms and to coordinate with his key Appropriations people.

My attention returned to moving the reforms through the CHO. A detailed reform package, complete with flowcharts and projected savings, and incorporating the comments from the workshop, had been submitted to the CHO. The remainder of the finalized reform action plans were presented to CHO staff on March 10. This was a very strange meeting. Otto and Stacy rejected all the reforms as too vague. They demanded a CAO "business plan" and a detailed study of existing operations to substantiate the need for each of the seventy-five reform proposals they had already approved and in fact, had already designated "priority" proposals.

It became clear that the CHO staff was not going to allow any of the seventy-five reforms to be considered by the members of the committee until the staff itself was "fully comfortable" with every detail of what was going to happen and why each step was necessary. They also wanted assessments of various options, including no reform and partial reform, in addition to the full-scale reforms we had proposed. "This is what we want," asserted Stacy, crossing her arms smugly.

This was totally opposite of my recent discussions with CHO members. Every one of them pledged support to "full speed ahead" on reforming the House. In fact, Pat Roberts, John Boehner, and Jennifer Dunn were hoping for CHO votes on key reforms by the end of March. I tracked down Nussle on the House floor.

Jim and I huddled in the Republican cloakroom. "Bill is totally out of control," he said with exasperation. "Newt is swamped with the 'Contract [with America]' votes and has abandoned the effort." I looked at Jim with amazement. He continued, "I have not been able to get Newt to return my calls. He hasn't met with me since January."

"What should I do?"

"Let me talk to John and Jennifer. You should update Sue."

Sue Wadel's office was at the top of the spiral staircase hidden within the leadership section of the Capitol. Starting on the ground floor, the spiral staircase still had the bullet holes made by the British as they entered to burn the Capitol in 1814. On the second floor, I would then jog into the Speaker's hall and to a second spiral staircase leading to Sue's office. Her office was my destination several times a week to discuss reforms and leadership issues.

She was not surprised to hear about the CHO rebellion. "You have to understand, many members are getting cold feet about making any changes up here."

"But Sue, we all knew we had to move fast before Republicans got used to the perks. Pat, John, and Jennifer are all ready to vote on the reforms. What can we do to break them loose?"

Sue agreed to talk to Stacy and Otto. The next day Sue dropped by my office to report on what had transpired. According to Stacy and Otto, they were under tremendous pressure from other CHO staff and the staff of CHO members not to do any reforms.

"I thought members could think for themselves. What does staff have to do with any of this?" I countered.

"Work with them, at least for a while," counseled Sue. "Meet and hear them out."

WHACKING THE HORNET'S NEST

Stacy and Otto gathered the Republican staff from the CHO and from CHO members. I brought along Dorsey and Hasdorff to take notes and be witnesses to the "festivities." Their notes outline the disconnect between the election, the transition, and ninety days into the Republican era:

- Such fundamental restructuring of legislative operations had never been tried anywhere. We should go very slowly.
- Why change at all? We are now in charge.
- Why can't you just use better accounting and leave everything else in place?
- Why don't you automate everything? Won't that solve the problem?
- Why move so fast? Why change so much at once?
- Shouldn't you study things longer? You are jumping to conclusions!
- Shouldn't we try making the existing system work? We can then change things later.
- How about some small pilot projects? If those work, we can try something bigger.
- Why should we deprive ourselves of what the Democrats had for so long?
- We have earned the right to these perks. Don't take them away!
- Won't the changes limit our political influence?
- Won't the changes limit our advantages as incumbents?
- Why should we trust what you say is wrong with Congress?
- What makes you think these changes will solve the problem?
- We are a political body, not a business. Your assumptions are flawed.

- We are unique. There are no "best practices" that are applicable.
- Why should we learn new ways? We already know how things operate.[4]

"Now you see what we are up against," declared Stacy after the meeting. Otto then handed over a stack of letters from various members requesting that various functions or people be left alone.

"The Speaker wants reform," I began. "He should have it."

"The Speaker is just one member," countered Otto.

"Then what about your committee members? The Republicans are all on board."

"But not their staffs!" countered Stacy. "Scot, we are not going to put anything on the agenda until we are certain it will pass. It is up to you to convince us, and the staffers, that the reforms should happen."

Upon hearing my report, Sue suggested that we let things cool down through the Easter recess and then regroup. She also referenced the need to get through the "hundred days agenda" before leadership could focus on the reforms.

I took some solace in the fact that many of the administrative reforms were proceeding without CHO approval. Fortunately, only the "big-ticket items" required CHO sign-off, and the A Ring was proceeding as if those approvals were imminent. Kiko and Norton were working with the A Ring on drafting the requests for proposals (RFPs) for each outsourcing, and Kay Ford's staff was creating a state-of-the-art outplacement process. The other reforms were speeding along under the radar screen.

Don, Rick, and Jennifer were completing their desk audits and needs analysis of HIS. Debbie Hansen, working closely with Representative Frank Wolf (R-VA) and numerous congressional spouses, had implemented the family suite and family services program in record time. This earned large reserves of goodwill for the CAO operation.

Anfinson and Simon had brought in Ernst & Young to work with Price Waterhouse on building a new accounting system. They were also conducting forensic accounting to reconstruct cost centers and identify vendors. We were also negotiating to move the House payroll to the Department of the Interior to take advantage of the government-wide "cross-servicing" initiative begun by Simon and me through our work with the Cabinet Council on Management and Administration.[5] We had also made a key policy change, forcing all members to personally pay for their House-issued American Express card charges and then submit forms for reimbursement of official expenses. This resolved a huge area of abuse where members' allowances covered the card's entire balance and only rarely did members reimburse the House for personal charges.

During this period, the entire A Ring moved to the next level of analysis and reform. They drew on the methodologies of both quality management and President Reagan's Private Sector Survey (also known as the Grace Commission).[6] They began to measure outcomes, cycle times, and accuracy for the numerous CAO operations. This gave us vital baseline data to meet the needs of the CHO and to help us anticipate and ultimately track the results of our reforms. I conducted a training session on "cost of quality" for the A Ring and some of our "careerist" allies on March 17. This is a method of determining what it costs to do things wrong or do things over. One can then extrapolate how many times these costs may occur or reoccur as part of current operations. From these costs, managers can then objectively understand the full scope of what is happening in their organization and prioritize actions to address each problem.

The month of April saw further progress on the financial reforms. Carole Kordich and her team were methodically developing "House-Smart," a complete directory and explanation of all House services and operations. She and I developed the questionnaire and report format. Every House office participated except the clerk, who labeled it a "Mickey Mouse" exercise. This "user's guide" for the House was designed to strip away all vestiges of the "caste system" of Capitol Hill and allow everyone to have the same unfettered access to information and services. After compiling and refining the directory, via customer feedback and use, we planned to make it the centerpiece of the future House intranet.

Also in April, Gingrich met his deadline for floor votes on all parts of his "Contract with America" within the "hundred days." Congress then went on recess. Unfortunately, the contract votes and the recess allowed the CHO to nearly come to a standstill on the reforms.

It got worse. Otto and Stacy were refusing to sign off on numerous CAO personnel actions. As with any large organization, people retire, leave for other jobs, and leave for personal reasons such as marriage, maternity, and a spouse locating to another city. This "churn" allowed us to consider eliminating positions or reformatting the positions ahead of the overall reorganization, which was languishing with the CHO. Stacy and Otto refused to allow these tactical changes, stating even these slots should be considered only when the strategic reorganization was approved. This resulted in a "stacking up" of basic personnel decisions, including normal in-grade pay increases and other mundane actions. It was ironic that this was identical to the situation criticized by Representative Thomas in the 103rd Congress relating to the CHA's micromanaging of General Wishart.

I appealed to Sue Wadel, contending that I should be allowed to handle the "churn" as part of normal day-to-day management. I also suggested that Otto and Stacy, who were in the midst of expanding the CHO staff, did not want to be "outnumbered" by an expanded A Ring. Sue agreed, but she was also rebuffed by Otto and Stacy. Sue had to admit that Gingrich and the leadership were now swamped with dealing with Livingston over appropriations. Confronting the CHO on the reforms would have to wait.

This did not sit well with the A Ring. Morale improved on April 27 when Phil Crosby graciously spent an entire day with the A Ring to personally review transforming an organization's culture and implementing quality management. Phil was pleased to see Gloria and hear her plans for employee training and recognition. Phil and I hosted lunch in the members' dining room with Nussle, Boehner, Dunn, Packard, and several other allies to discuss applying quality principles to legislative decision making. This group included Representative Peter Hoekstra (R-MI), who was tasked by Gingrich to develop new decision mechanisms for the House. Prior to entering the House in 1992, Peter had been an executive with Herman Miller, a leading furniture manufacturer known for its innovative approaches to management.

As May began, the reforms, and the burgeoning personnel backlog, languished before the CHO. During the May 3 meeting on the fiscal year 1995 appropriations, Otto and Stacy rebuffed the Appropriations staff, and the CAO team, regarding spending reductions.

"Don't assume there will be any savings in the new fiscal year," announced Otto. "The committee is not considering major reforms. It is way too early for us to move on them. We are waiting for more information."

This came in the wake of another a major blow—John Garbett, my de facto deputy and sounding board, had left. I had always known he would not last long. His availability was due, in part, to his turning down several film opportunities. It was only a matter of time before one would be too good to pass up. He had been contacted by Universal Studios to work on *The Frighteners* with Michael J. Fox. He was to work in New Zealand for at least six months. Fox personally asked for John. More importantly, this would be the American film industry's first opportunity to test the special effects and production capabilities of a new generation of young New Zealand filmmakers. It led to the *Lord of the Rings* series and a revolution in digital film effects. His departure left a gaping hole in my operation and changed the A Ring's dynamics.

MEMO WARS

The May 10 CHO meeting approved Phil Kiko's package of procurement reforms for the House. This was a major milestone for preventing future contract abuses. The CHO also approved an antiquated internal "squawk box" audio system supported by Thomas to head off strategic reform on opening hearings to the public. *Roll Call* mused, "The House may finally be ready to take a technology leap the California State Senate made back in the 1950s."[7]

These were the only reforms the CHO considered. Everything requiring CHO approval, including now hundreds of personnel actions, gathered dust on Otto's desk. Otto was sending a steady stream of "Ottograms" to the A Ring and me, demanding increasingly pedantic details about the CAO operation and the reforms.

I had had enough. The A Ring had created a voluminous set of reform proposals. Each reform, individually and collectively, met the strategic decision standards of any Fortune 500 company. Each day, more members signed letters or called the A Ring, or me, to lobby for exempting some person or practice from the reforms. Bill Livingood and the Capitol Police had briefed me on the crime and drugs problems festering in the postal and folding operations. It had been ninety-five days since the reform "summit" and sixty-one days since the "implementation workshop." Something had to happen.

Earlier, I met with Simon, Anfinson, and Hasdorff to sort out the counterrevolution.

"Reforms stick in his craw," began Anfinson. "Our battle with Thomas is over who ultimately provides customer service to members and staff. Thomas wants it all done through the CHO, with CAO carrying out directives. That is totally at odds with Open House reforms. Thomas's approach continues the old culture, but with Republicans and him in control."

"Can't we just lay out what is at stake?" offered Simon. "Just tell the members and leadership, this is what we can do. This is what it is costing not to do anything."

"We need to remind these guys what they were elected to do," stated Hasdorff.

I agreed and put together a fact sheet and sent it out. The war had begun.

Thomas fired the first shots. He made sure *Roll Call* had my memo. On Thursday, May 11, *Roll Call* published my briefing memo. A barrage of "Ottograms" attacked me for making baseless charges about the crime problems and the inefficiencies of House operations.

On May 12, Bob Livingston and Thomas requested a meeting with the Speaker to discuss delaying reforms until such a time when they had more confidence in the CAO and his team. Thomas then sent a blistering memo to me stating he was canceling any consideration of reforms at the CHO meeting scheduled for May 17. He promptly leaked it to *Roll Call*.

Roll Call published a front-page article quoting Thomas's memo to me. His primary focus was asserting that I was operating on my own and outside the direction of the CHO. The article quoted unnamed sources, including one stating, "He [Scot] is the Speaker's creation. I don't know how much input he's getting from the Speaker [personally], but I think he is operating on the presumption that he has the Speaker's support [and that] he's got the ball. If Faulkner makes a mistake," the observer said, "then we'll all see how much [Gingrich] support he has."[8]

Otto then wrote to Ed Lombard on the Legislative Branch Subcommittee of the Appropriations Committee, stating that he and Stacy were uncertain of the accuracy of the reforms' savings and that they may be overestimated. He counseled Lombard that the reforms needed more time and more analysis.

I had been in constant contact with Wadel, Blankley, and Nussle since the war began. Wadel assisted me in crafting a written response to Thomas defending my actions.

Blankley took Stacy aside. "When any real media calls, say that the *Roll Call* article is misleading—say that everything is 'hunky-dory.'"

"You're kidding!" exploded Stacy.

"No, I am serious. You are going to say, 'Everything is hunky-dory.'" Stacy stormed off. "I enjoyed that," he mused to me.

I had already scheduled a second round of member meetings before the war began. Jennifer Dunn summed up the situation best. "Bill is the most despicable man I have ever known." Boehner, Ney, and the others all expressed solidarity with my efforts. Earlier, on May 3, Hoyer expressed concern that the reforms were languishing. "I just don't understand what Bill is up to." On May 15, I met with Armey's staff in H-226. I had known Ginny Thomas, Kerry Knott, and Michelle Davis for years. They expressed sympathy, but were absorbed with moving the legislative agenda. "You are in good hands with Tom [DeLay] and Jim [Nussle]," said Ginny.

During my second meeting with Chris Shays, on May 16, he waved off the Thomas war as "typical Bill" and focused on outlining his ideas about parking reform.

The next day, Representative Albert Wynn (D-MD) distributed a letter implying that I was racist for alleging criminal activity among the minority workers in the postal and folding operations. With the assistance of Wadel, I wrote an apology letter to folding-room employees. It was one of those typical Washington apologies that gave Wynn a sense of victory but did not back off from the core facts that leadership knew were true.

At Hoyer's urging, I met with Tom Jurkovich and Perry Pockros of the CHO minority staff to "make peace." They were angry about my not giving them the same level of information as the Republicans. Hoyer also recommended that I be very candid about the gauntlet I had been through over the previous months. They were surprised to hear about the divisiveness among the Republicans. "Just keep us informed, and we can find common ground," advised Jurkovich. Several Democratic colleagues had informed me their leaders were secretly cheering my reforms, as they saw me as the only person preventing Thomas from unleashing a reign of terror on them.

Nussle and Wadel urged me to consolidate my individual CHO submission into a complete set of the "big-ticket item" reforms. This massive document, with twenty-two tabbed sections filled with support data, went to Thomas on May 17.

Later that day, Jim dropped by my office to review the war. "Scot, just lay low right now. You don't need to fight anymore. Help is on the way."

At the end of the day, I was in Sue's office reviewing the battlefield. Sue was in an upbeat mood. "Bill has emptied his guns, and you are still standing. Now we are going to let him have a train wreck of his own making. Once that has occurred, the field is ours."

THE TRAIN WRECK

"Scot, you got a minute?" Terri popped her head through my escape door. This was her way of letting me know Tom DeLay wanted to see me. As always, Tom smiled broadly and waved me into his office. We had become good neighbors. I kept him informed of the reform effort and socialized with his team over the giant buffets of food brought in for lobbyists and Members during the late night Floor fights.

"Scot, how are you holding up?" asked Tom with genuine concern.

"It has been a tough few days."

"Well, we are all behind you."

"Thanks, that means a lot."

"You just hang in there. Thomas is going to get his."

The plan was for me to temporarily cede the field to Thomas. The May 23 CHO meeting would be the venue. Parking reform would be the issue.

Parking had been a major issue of power in prior Congresses. The A Ring had uncovered numerous abuses. Most importantly, it was costing money as the House leased expensive vacant lots for the overflow. It was also a major symbol of the new openness because in his April 7, 1995, speech, Gingrich had promised the American public a paid lot near the Capitol by summer.

The CHO staff had laid claim to parking as one of their major interests. They were intimately involved in every detail and every step of the A Ring's development of a new parking allotment and set of operational policies, sometimes driving Sweetland and Hansen to distraction.

They demanded that every piece of parking data be immediately shared with CHO staff. They also demanded that all of Sweetland's analysis and options be immediately shared with CHO staff.

A younger member of the CHO staff, Chris Wright, had the committee's lead on parking. As May progressed, Sweetland handed off Chris to Simon and me. "He's all yours. I can't talk any sense into him." Paul related how Chris could not even do the math regarding parking allocations and had never toured the facilities to better understand the situation. The bombing of the Alfred P. Murrah Federal Building in Oklahoma City on April 19, 1995, had raised serious concerns about the security of Capitol Hill. Parking was now an issue involving Bill Livingood, a person Chris had not met.

Tom and I went up to the CHO staff offices and proceeded to review all our parking options, including banning overnight parking on weekends. "What if one of my friends gets drunk and leaves his car over the weekend?" Chris interrupted. We rolled our eyes.

We reviewed the priority for creating a public lot. Chris again interrupted, "House staff will grow again. There is no way we can have a private lot. It reduces our options if we ever need more space."

Chris declared his intention to give every office an additional space. "We should promote use of the Metro," offered Simon. We grew tired of this parallel universe and ended the meeting.

A little while later, Stacy dropped by my office. She scolded me on not being more cooperative with Chris. "Chris Wright is brilliant! He is the driving force behind parking reform!"

I countered, "He doesn't know diddly about parking. We have had to redo his parking counts every time!"

"He doesn't know diddly?" Stacy gasped with incredulity.

"That's right, he doesn't know diddly."

Stacy frowned and stormed out.

The final version of the CHO proposal was shared with my office only days before the hearing. In fact, the final version of the resolution on parking was not available until ten minutes into the May 25 hearing. Sweetland and Simon were not allowed to comment on the CHO parking plan and were barred from attending the CHO member caucus and the CHO staff briefings. However, at these meetings CHO staff provided their own critiques and criticisms of the A Ring's original parking plan, even though no CAO personnel were present.

On Monday, May 22, Sue dropped in to hear my prediction on the next day's parking meeting. "They are not prepared. They are contradicting everything Newt wants."

Sue smiled. "Let them sail over the cliff. That is what we are waiting for."

Later, I walked across the hall to visit with Nussle in his hideaway office. "The trap is set," Jim announced. I ended the day sitting in Blankley's office. He was still chuckling about my "diddly" comment. "Tomorrow, all this insanity ends," Tony declared.

The May 23 hearing was a fiasco. Boehner and Dunn embarrassed the staff with basic questions they could not answer. Thomas fumed. The end result was the adoption of the CHO staff version of the parking allocation and policy. It reassigned parking operations to the sergeant at arms, with allocation decisions residing in the CHO. No public lot was offered or authorized.

On Wednesday, May 24, at 2:00 p.m., Boehner, Nussle, Packard, and Dan Meyer met with Thomas and Livingston in H-126. They first explained, in no uncertain terms, that CAO reforms would happen or the CHO would be abolished. Meyer then told Livingston that he would defer to Packard's budget cuts for the legislative branch. The CAO reforms would be integral to the first appropriations bill passed by the House and a major symbol in the coming battle with President Clinton over federal spending.

The next night I was working late. Sue Wadel walked into my office and reported on the "come to Jesus meeting" with Thomas. "Things will be different now. They got the message."

★ END RUN ★

September 11, 1297 (Stirling, Scotland)

"**H**old! Hold!" William Wallace shouted to his men. The heavy cavalry of Edward I bore down on the Scottish line.

"Brrrrzzzz" went my vibrating beeper.

"I'll be back," I whispered to Vicki and made my way out of the darkened movie theater. I trotted up the escalator and into the main foyer of Union Station to gain the best reception for my mobile telephone. This was the third time Tom Anfinson and David Coggins had beeped.

It was actually the night of May 25, 1995. The Appropriations staff, frustrated by CHO inaction, had begun writing most of the seventy-five reforms into the fiscal year 1996 legislative branch appropriations. Anfinson and Coggins were building a new budget that slashed committee staffing allowances by $38.4 million, franking by $19.4 million, and all other administrative costs by $11.7 million. Prior to the formation of the CAO, administrative services were growing at 21 percent a year. The reform-based appropriation cut this spending by nearly 44 percent. This included forcing the reduction of CAO personnel from 1,120 to 630.

Going the Appropriations route meant reforms could begin in October 1995. Our hope was to force the CHO to act out of embarrassment or self-preservation and therefore obtain approval to move forward over the summer. This was still four months later than we had hoped, but at least the reforms were back on track.

Planning for the end run began on February 6, over a private lunch with Ron Packard at the Capitol Hill Club.

"I have never trusted Thomas," Ron stated matter-of-factly. "He has undermined conservatives all his life, and now he is sabotaging our revolution."

"Why is he so powerful?" I queried.

"God only knows. It is like he has some hold over Gingrich."

We proceeded to discuss the details of an audacious act. If the CHO did not move expeditiously on reforming the House, Ron would write all the reforms into the fiscal year 1996 legislative branch appropriations. Even better, he would reduce funding and staffing levels to reflect full implementation of the reforms, thus forcing them into existence.[1]

Ron smiled. "This will happen, even if it is over Bill's dead body."

Nussle was very amused with the end run Ron and I had orchestrated. This, coming on the heels of the "come to Jesus" meeting with Thomas, turned the tide back in favor of the reforms. Jim made sure the full impact of the changing fortunes for House reform were made clear to the media.[2]

Hints of the end run had been apparent during the Appropriations working session on April 12, and again at the Legislative Branch Subcommittee hearings on April 19. Packard and several majority members clearly expressed their own support for rapid progress on implementing the reforms. Thomas assumed that Otto's and Stacy's May 3 outbursts had quashed the appropriators, or that his alliance with Livingston would bottle things up. He certainly had not anticipated losing the "memo wars."

The May 31 CHO meeting was to be a general briefing on human resources. This meant reviewing plans for complying with federal laws and previewing the CAO reorganization proposals, which were to be part of the June 14 reform ratification session. This mundane curtain-raiser to the main event took a brief, but amusing, detour.

One of Hoyer's staffers had displayed dismay at his convivial interactions with me, especially during our last meeting, where we reviewed the A Ring's financial disclosures and how many of them took major pay cuts to serve. She displayed partisan zeal and seemed horrified that common ground and purpose could be so easily established. During the rather bland round of questions, Hoyer held up an annotated version of my organizational chart. Various symbols indicated who was a Republican or who had worked for the Republican National Committee. "Mr. Chairman, this supposedly nonpartisan office is, in fact, staffed with partisans," Hoyer declared.

"Congressman, I have never worked for the RNC," I pounced, seeing the annotation by my name. Hoyer frowned and shot a look at his young staffer. She had clearly not done her homework. She even had Sturdevant and Sweetland listed as Republicans. Just as I was about to further pick apart the chart, Pat Roberts interjected.

"I'm shocked, shocked to find that partisanship is going on in here!" he said in his best impersonation of Captain Renault from *Casablanca*, complete with some inspired gestures. The room exploded in laughter. Hoyer gamely smiled at me, said something about keeping a close watch, and then put away the document.

RATIFICATION

In the run-up to the ratification meeting, Stacy and Otto did everything they could to derail the end run.[3] Livingston summoned me to his office on June 13 to basically state that he opposed everything that was occurring and that Ron and I would ultimately be proved wrong. He was still smarting from a separate "come to Jesus meeting" that he had with Armey, which further reinforced leadership's commitment to keeping the reforms in the legislative branch appropriations bill. The bill passed on June 22. It cut $154.9 million, becoming the first reduction in House spending in the twentieth century.

I put the A Ring into overdrive to develop graphics that vividly made the case for each reform. Jim Davison oversaw the creation of large measurement charts showing waste, and Doug Fehrer laid out a huge before-and-after organizational chart showing how twelve layers of management were to be reduced to two, as the CAO was to shrink from 1,120 to 630.

This, along with the "come to Jesus" meeting, forced the CHO to act. A "ratification of the reforms" meeting was scheduled two days before subcommittee markup on the legislative branch appropriations, which was to mandate that the seventy-five initiatives be completed prior to, or during, fiscal year 1996.[4]

Calls and brief meetings with CHO members from both parties ensured passage of each of the "big-ticket" reforms. Hoyer informed me that some votes would remain party line because of the Democratic Caucus's concerns about privatization in general. He also pledged that no amendments or stalling tactics would be used. "Good luck," he said as he rang off.

In meetings with Wadel and Nussle, I obtained a free hand to work directly with the Price Waterhouse team to clean up the House's financial system. This allowed Anfinson to cut Otto and Stacy out of the process and move expeditiously. I also obtained immediate approval of all personnel actions that had been bottled up since late January. The second wave of the A Ring would start arriving on Monday, June 19.

The June 14 CHO hearing was indeed the ratification session we had been working toward. Thomas put the best spin on the proceedings by singing praises of each reform and taking credit for each proposal, positioning the A Ring and me as implementing the will of the CHO.

I presented each reform, explaining why each was needed, what options we evaluated, why the recommended action was the best, and what benefits would accrue by their implementation. Doug Fehrer and Jim Davison efficiently displayed large placards illustrating findings and actions on three easels arrayed around me. The most interesting one was the massive chart showing the old organization (see table). The twelve layers of management and duplicative staffing patterns generated much comment and head shaking from the panel. It was clear that the old ways had to go.

The five-hour hearing was over, and the reforms were now a reality. I was energized by it all. It was a great day for the "good guys." The A Ring was jubilant.

THE PRICE OF REFORM

The hard work lay ahead. Gloria updated the project-management charts to reflect the June 14 starting date. Kay and her team had all the

House Oversight Committee: Reform Votes, June 14, 1995

Reform	For	Against
Reform human resources	8	1
Abolish House post office	11	0
Privatize postal operations	6	5
Abolish folding room	6	5
Abolish printers	8	3
Reform studios	11	0
Reform photographers	8	3
Adopt Office 2000	11	0
Reorganize HIR	11	0
Reorganize CAO	6	5

personnel paperwork on my desk the afternoon of the CHO hearing. I spent hours signing hiring and reassignment documents to implement the reorganization. Anfinson and Simon moved forward with moving the payroll to the Interior Department and began a series of direct meetings with the Price Waterhouse team along with the Ernst & Young team. Mutersbaugh and Endres gladly "pulled the plug" on the in-house software development and commenced the "sex change" of transforming "HIS" (House Information Systems) into "HIR" (House Information Resources).

Sue Wadel dropped by my office on June 16. "It has been quite a week," she remarked.

"Absolutely!" I responded, settling into one of the wing chairs by the fireplace.

"Scot, we need to talk." She began looking serious. "The Speaker and Thomas met, and some changes must be made."

"What kind of changes?"

"Thomas viewed the approval of your reforms as something requiring a quid pro quo."

"He got his quid pro quo. He stays chairman, and the Oversight Committee still exists."

"Bill doesn't see it that way. He told the Speaker your organization is top-heavy, and will be especially so once the personnel reductions and outsourcing are complete. You are going to have to reduce your executive team."

"Huh?"

"The Speaker says you will have to reduce the number of executives that report to you."

"By how many?"

"Two."

"I have already lost Garbett and have not yet replaced him. Can that count?"

"No." Sue took a deep breath. "Scot, you need to fire Endres, Mutersbaugh, and Sweetland."

"What a minute. That's three."

"Vern Ehlers wants his own team implementing Office 2000. In the case of Paul, you can't justify his position now that parking is under the sergeant at arms."

"Oh no!" I shook my head. "I was told there would be no must-hires or must-fires."

"Scot, you have to work with me on this. The Speaker was adamant that Thomas be given something to offset his embarrassment."

"It was of his own making. If we had not sat on him, the reforms would never have happened. They are already four months behind schedule."

"That is not how the Speaker sees it."

"What's going on? Why is Thomas still in the equation? After the stunts he's pulled, he's lucky to sit on a committee, let alone chair one."

"Scot, you can't talk that way. This is not negotiable."

We continued our discussion. Luckily, some things were negotiable. I had to remove one person immediately. I could keep one person to run HIR until a new leader was selected. But all three had to go by the end of the year. It was a terrible decision. How could I punish three of the A Ring for doing exactly what I hired them to do? Should I appeal directly to Newt and force him to choose between reforms with me or status quo with Thomas?

"Scot, you have been put in a horrible position," sympathized Nussle. "I wish I could help you, but Newt hasn't spoken to me in months. It was all we could do to get Dan [Meyer] to weigh in against Thomas."

The next week I agonized over how to proceed with Don, Rick, and Paul. On Tuesday, June 20, Vicki and I attended the annual White House congressional picnic. Livingston turned away from me in the food line, refusing to even acknowledge my presence. I did see Newt and went over to him. "I can't get involved in this," said Newt taking a step back.

"Mr. Speaker, I just wanted to introduce my fiancée, Vicki Hunter." I ushered Vicki forward, sidestepping a confrontation. Vicki poured on her Texas charm, reminding Newt of the many meetings she and Lee Atwater had with him during the Reagan years. He brightened and reminisced, relieved that the discussion had gone in a more positive direction.

ENTICEMENTS

Social gatherings take up the largest portion of time for anyone in political Washington. These events are not about socializing as much as they are about networking, influence brokering, intelligence gathering, and fund-raising. The House's legislative schedule even takes a backseat to these events. It is common practice to delay legislation, and even to adjourn for the day, to allow members to attend fund-raisers. Congressional staff, in particular the administrative assistants who run member offices, usually coordinate these fund-raising activities and serve as the main point of contact for lobbyists, PAC coordinators, and contributors in the office and at the receptions. This is against House rules, but no one has ever complained.

My high profile as the first CAO made me a curiosity. Many interest groups invited me to their events, across the political spectrum. There were also events that I was invited to just because I was an officer of the House. Tom DeLay wanted me at every Republican fund-raiser, to showcase the reform agenda. Some nights I would be invited to five or more events.

Some of the more noteworthy events included Representative Gary Ackerman's (D-NY) annual fund-raiser. It always featured a full deli buffet provided by a hundred-year-old family-owned restaurant from his district. It had the best food of any reception I ever attended. Another was the annual White House correspondents' dinner, which I was invited to because I now oversaw all the media galleries. I knew many reporters and columnists, so it was a great night to "table hop."

I viewed many of these events as "relationship banking"—building relationships and being seen as a value-added member of the leadership team. These "deposits" build an inventory of credits that can be tapped in tougher times. I put Jane Bennett in charge of working with DeLay's office and with various GOP fund-raising consultants to prioritize which receptions would maximize this banking effort.

Early on, another whole world opened. During the transition, Don Mutersbaugh took me aside. "Do you realize you have your own foreign policy?"

The House works with the Library of Congress to provide technical assistance to emerging democracies. I met with Dan Mulhollan, the director of the Congressional Research Service (CRS) and his staff. They explained that there was a cooperative agreement between the House and the library to provide technical assistance to new parliaments in helping them establish their procedures and operations. HIR staff had been sent to several Eastern European countries to help them with data systems for voting, documentation, and public information.

I reported this to Sue Wadel. She smiled. "Then that makes it easier to ask you for a favor." She proceeded to lay out the duties of the Speaker as they relate to foreign dignitaries. The House hosts a steady stream of foreign guests. Most attend events sponsored by the House International Relations Committee (renamed the Foreign Affairs Committee in the 110th Congress). Heads of state are invited to speak to a joint meeting of the Congress; this is different from a joint session, as the president is not present and the executive and judicial branches send only one representative instead of all their top officials. The president pro tem of the Senate sits next to the Speaker instead of the vice president. There may be six or more of these each year. Coordination of these events, along with visits from parliamentary delegations, is usually handled out of the Speaker's office, with coordination with relevant House offices. "The Speaker wants to limit his involvement, except for major heads of state. He would like you and your office to take the lead."

I embraced this new responsibility. Thanks to the fact that Gloria was the former First Lady of St. Kitts, I had protocol covered. It was also a great opportunity to test-drive the reforms on a global scale and to identify and adapt best practices from other parliaments.

My office suite was an excellent stage for these diplomatic meetings. I worked with Barbara Wolanin, the House curator in the architect's office, to turn my office suite into a mini-museum in the Capitol. One of the only two original paintings of Benjamin Latrobe, the architect who designed the Capitol, came on loan from the Library of Congress. Copies of Latrobe's blueprints and Thomas Jefferson's "damage report" on the British burning of the Capitol were framed and put on display. In the main alcove of my reception area, Barbara added a huge portrait of Tomáš Garrigue Masaryk, the first president of Czechoslovakia. It was given to the Congress by Czech president Václav Havel in 1991 and had been languishing in storage every since. The Congress receives many "protocol gifts" each year and is always challenged to find appropriate venues for their display. Most remain in storage. In this case, it would be a wonderful symbol to greet visitors from emerging democracies.

Over the next two years, I hosted forty-four separate delegations, including heads of state and parliamentary leaders, in my office. Gloria established the protocol procedures and guidelines for my office and set up the liaison with Pamela Ahearn, Newt's chief of protocol,[5] for all major events and visitors. We acquired an inventory of beautifully-bound books on the Capitol and the history of Congress to serve as gifts for the visitors. I sent Terri Hasdorff to a Dale Carnegie course to polish her protocol skills. Then, I added one more major resource.

I knew Gloria would be spread thin in handling visitors, managing the implementation of the reforms, and leading the cultural transformation. I needed to find a person to become part of my front office, full-time. Tom Anfinson's wife provided the solution.

Susan Marone had served as assistant to former president Richard Nixon during the last years of his life. She oversaw the steady stream of world leaders who wished to meet with and remain in contact with the former president. Tom's wife was the daughter of Donald Nixon, one of the president's brothers. She told Tom that Susan had been looking for a new challenge since closing the New York office after Nixon's death on April 22, 1994.

The end run had broken the dam on personnel. The second wave of the A Ring flooded into the CAO, including Susan. Another key person was Joan DeCain, who had run the White House correspondence shop and handled special events under President Reagan. She was to organize and oversee all meeting and event rooms in the House. This wave also mollified the careerist allies we had been identifying and brought them into key leadership roles. The blending of old and new moved forward at "flank" speed.

In the dark days of spring, some friends and colleagues noted my despair and counseled me to ease back and enjoy the perks of my office. Sue Wadel had linked me up with Representative Ben Gilman (R-NY), chairman of the International Relations Committee. Ben and I became close colleagues, and he invited me to attend his committee's luncheons and meetings with foreign visitors. As the CAO, I also served as liaison to various organizations, like the U.S. Capitol Historical Society. I had known former representative Bud Brown (R-OH) from my days with Ashbrook. Bud elevated me from being his House contact to being on his board of trustees.

By May, I had already met with leaders of the Russian Duma, and we had planned the improvement of parliamentary systems in the Russian Federation. Joseph Connor, the under-secretary-general of the United Nations, and John O'Sullivan, general manager of the Parliamentary Service of New Zealand, had already visited my office. Nearly every night I was attending events and standing by DeLay, Nussle, Boehner, or other key Republicans, meeting lobbyists and discussing the reforms. Even the Grand Old Party Action Committee (GOPAC) had me hold briefings for their top donors. I was also meeting regularly with my original base of support, having lunch with Rick Shapiro of the Congressional Management Foundation and Don Ritter.

It would have been very easy to back away from confrontation. This is how the Washington establishment wins. The steady diet of meeting VIPs and eating free food is very enticing. One could even justify this lifestyle as being important to maintaining communication and building relationships that promote your agenda to key decision makers and promote American democracy to the world. At some point, though, you realize that someone else did this before you and that someone will do this after you; therefore, nothing changes.

ENTER ABRAMOFF AND THE LOBBYISTS

I first met Jack Abramoff back in 1982. Kathy Royce had brought me over to the Republican National Committee during a break from forming the International Young Democratic Union with our colleagues from various European conservative parties. At the time, Abramoff was chairman of the College Republicans. He and Grover Norquist, his executive director, were laughing about a meeting they had just finished with GOP operatives Rich Bond and Ron Kaufman.

"You wouldn't believe those jerks," Jack started off. "They were trying to get us to demand Reagan not run for reelection, so that Bush could be president in 1984!" He and Grover started laughing again. "They wanted me to say Reagan was too old. I asked them what I should say about Bush being too liberal!"

Jack would visit my office during my tenure as CAO. Jack was like the thousands of other lobbyists who swarmed Capitol Hill. Every lobbyist wanted the most up-to-date Rolodex, so networking was their main activity. Knowing who is who and, even better, who was to be who, was the coin of the realm.

My years of building personnel networks made me a magnet for these lobbyists. They knew I had nothing to do with legislation but was privy to every personnel action in the House and was in personnel loops relating the Senate and the association community. I was, therefore, viewed as a "one-stop shop" for them.

One of my first acts in January was to declare a zero tolerance for gifts to the CAO office. This went further than the House Rules. It harkened back to the GSA reforms, when Carmen stated that reformers had to be cleaner than anyone else because we were under more scrutiny. The opponents of reform were always looking for hypocrisy, while fellow reformers were always looking for consistency.

Dozens of lobbyists wanted to take me to lunch or dinner. I countered by offering to get together in the members' dining room either as a "Dutch treat" or with my paying for both of us. This way I could be gracious to old friends and colleagues while remaining open and consistent regarding my own ethics policy. Many opted for a brief visit in my office. The others worked within my guidelines. They respected my long history of being a "straight shooter." It cost me hundreds of dollars directly, and maybe thousands in unrealized free meals, but it set a consistent example for the professional culture we were creating for House operations.

I had mixed feelings about lobbyists. Many were longtime friends. When I was a young legislative aide, they schooled me in parliamentary procedure and provided invaluable research for the amendments and floor speeches I drafted. One even recommended me to John Ashbrook, which launched me on a trajectory that took me to the White House. On the other hand, lobbyists, by their nature, filter information to and from the general public. Just like the other enticements of Washington, it is easy to depend on lobbyists and avoid the harder work of fathoming the minds of normal citizens. This is another way that the establishment wins.

I could not be a recluse. Out of duty and the need to "relationship bank," I had to spend countless hours doing the protocol and making the social rounds. To beat the system and the odds, I simply worked more hours. I would arrive around 8:30 a.m. and sometimes not leave until midnight. I would come in on weekends. Vicki and I would return to my office after a reception. She would watch television or visit with DeLay's staff, or with a member of the A Ring, depending on who was still around. The guards got to know both of us as the night owls of the Capitol. Vicki's outgoing personality and charm won her the nickname "Miss Vicki," and she became a fixture in the Capitol, as I made sure the reforms remained my priority.

Not everyone shared my zeal. Bob Livingston had quietly unleashed members of his personal staff and friendly reporters to dig into every aspect of my life. They fanned out, researching everything I had done since my first campaign in 1970. At a Capitol Hill Club reception in mid-June, Bob was in good spirits. "Faulkner will be gone by Labor Day," Livingston smirked.

SMASHING THE ★ COOKIE JARS ★

September 23, 1995

The line stretched for three blocks. Nearly seven thousand people waited patiently to make their way into the old *Washington Star* warehouse. They came from as far away as New York and Chicago to attend. They filed past twelve camera crews and dozens of reporters. Jim Lafferty, the top media aide to Tom DeLay, and Jim Davison had worked around the clock to generate this amazing media coverage and public interest.

Once inside, these thousands of average citizens were given bidder cards and allowed to roam through the five-story structure. On each floor, television monitors displayed the item up for auction while an auctioneer, linked to a central data bank, processed their bids.

Nothing like this had ever happened. The House was holding its "yard sale." When the amazing day was over, $203,800 in sales were processed. The House's auction led all national television news shows that night and was featured in all major daily papers and wire services the next day. Within a week, the warehouse was empty and ready to be returned to its owner. The House would be out of its $253,000-a-year lease.[1]

This was how it should always have been. A major public event, symbolizing the new era of government openness and fiscal responsibility, going off like clockwork. In the end, the symbolism was backed up with real tangible—and sustained—savings to the taxpayer.

Carole Kordich and her team, headed by Tom Van Dyke and Cosmo Quattrone, had made sure the yard sale was the embodiment of perfection. All pre-1940 furnishings had been inventoried by the curator, repaired, and moved into various displays around the House's campus. Other unique items were absorbed into the greatly reduced personal-property inventory. Everything else was on the auction block.

The masterstroke was adding a "certificate of authenticity" to each item certifying that it was from the House's inventory. At the last minute, Gingrich opted out of using his name on the certificates, so Carole's and mine were substituted. To this day, antique stores within a hundred miles of Washington, D.C., still feature these certificates with items from the sale.

The promotional run-up also worked like clockwork. Members were provided opportunities to be interviewed in the warehouse, and the House recording studio provided equipment for remote videotaping. Most did not comprehend what was happening. It was only a surplus furniture auction. Representative Ney and other reformers traveled to the warehouse and recorded short programs for their constituents showing that Congress was reforming.

Tony Perkins, the popular weatherman from the local Fox channel, broadcast his weather reports from the warehouse. Tom and Cosmo did the stand-ups for CNN, C-SPAN, and other news outlets, explaining the sale and featuring unique items. They had asked if I wanted to do these. I deferred to them, since they were managing the sale. I also wanted to clearly show that everyone within the CAO's operation would gain recognition, even on a national scale, when they achieved excellence. It was a gesture that signaled a new era and a new culture for the House.

The weeks that preceded the yard sale were a victory roll for the reforms. The wisdom of having the A Ring move forward as if every reform would happen paid off. The requests for proposals (RFPs), the personnel processes, and the financial arrangements were all in place to rapidly implement the reforms over the summer. One by one, the reforms became reality. Every member of the A Ring and every "careerist," in what was now just becoming known as the "CAO team," accomplished each task as part of a well-oiled machine. Every reform and every detail happened on schedule without a single misstep. The months of planning, the countless hours of reviewing and resolving "Murphy's Law" scenarios, the training, and the bonding of the larger team had all paid off. To this day, I have never again witnessed such a sustained level of excellence, spanning so many disciplines, on so many projects, in such a short amount of time.

THE ENGINEERS

On Monday, October 2, we held a gala opening for the new shoeshine stand and repair shop in the basement rotunda of the Cannon Building. We hung old bunting from the presidential inaugural, since we were replacing the worn material in time for the January 20, 1997, swearing-in ceremony.

I decided to give out railroad engineer's caps to Anfinson, Aamot, Kiko, Kordich, and the new head of HIR, Ken Miller, as "all trains left the station on time":

- The folding room had closed on August 15.
- The barbershop and beauty salon were privatized and set to reopen October 17.
- The printers were to be eliminated by December 31, 1995.
- The RFP for privatizing the House postal operations had been issued.
- An agreement for the U.S. Postal Service (USPS) to operate new 24-7 postal stores had been signed. The first store, located in the old "gift wrapping" room, would open October 19.
- The House's payroll had moved to the Department of the Interior.
- House finances had cut over to a new automated system set up by Ernst & Young.
- "HouseSmart" had been published and the "ONECall" service center was open.
- The recording and photography studios announced new rates and services.
- Satellite communications were set up for direct broadcasts to districts.
- The first CAO website portal was online, and the House intranet was operational.

- The House gift and stationery store was completely reorganized and reformed.
- The first network of CAO "process improvement teams" (PIT teams) had met.
- Ice delivery to individual offices had ended.

The festivities marked a major turning point in the CAO operation. In the audience were many of the "careerists" who had become part of the CAO team. The blending was apparent as everyone intermingled and equally shared in the moment. Through their collective skills and diligence, they had achieved the political equivalent of Hercules cleaning out the Augean stables.

Throughout the summer, we had methodically implemented each reform. A steady stream of communications fanned out from the CAO's office to leadership and the CHO. Detailed updates were given at the weekly officers' meeting. "Dear Colleague" letters were sent out to all members announcing one major change after another.

One by one, we were "smashing the cookies jars." Every action eliminated a perk. Every action shined daylight into the recesses of the House's secrets. Every step brought the institution closer to integrity, efficiency, and business practices. We had eliminated all general accounts and forced each member to pay market rates for services, all out of their consolidated office accounts. Every transaction would now be processed like a normal business transaction, and every penny was tracked, documented, and reported.

Ironically, most people did not stop to consider the revolution that was happening around them. The new services led the announcements. We leveraged Crosby's "WIIFM" ("what's in it for me") concept—if people experienced improvement, then they would not fight the change.

These successes were due, in large part, to Ben Lusby and his team. Ben was one of the more "low-key" members of the A Ring. However, he had several of the most daunting tasks of the reforms, including the outsourcing of postal operations, which would become the largest contract in House history. His attention to detail and his longtime friendship with Bill Sturdevant well served him and the reforms.

The underlying issue in both the closing of the folding room and the outsourcing of postal operations was space. Bill and Ben worked closely with the architect's team to redevelop rooms in the Longworth and Ford buildings. They also worked closely with Bill Livingood's team to develop enhanced security screening for incoming mail and parcels. It was decided that a remote screening location would be created to examine delivery vehicles. They would also construct a bombproof screening area, complete with X-ray and other sensing units, in the Ford House Office Building. This would be the entrance to a completely new postal sorting facility. In future years, moving these screening functions out of Longworth prevented the disruption that occurred on the Senate side during the anthrax scare.

While mail delivery would be outsourced, there remained a need for normal window services. Marvin Runyon, the postmaster general, was planning a revolution in postal operations. This included self-service equipment with 24-7 availability. Runyon was also planning to create a new USPS experience, complete with gifts and one-stop service for packages. A pilot store in Arlington, Virginia, had been testing the equipment and services. Bill Sturdevant arranged for a field trip for Ben and me. He then set up negotiations with the USPS to take over window operations in the House and to pay for all renovations. In exchange, we would lease them space for one dollar a year. We got state-of-the-art service, $275,000 in renovations, and equipment at no cost. The USPS got a venue to promote their new services.

The ribbon-cutting ceremony for the Longworth USPS service center and store occurred on October 19. It was a major media event, with Runyon and his executive team all in attendance. It proved a major success. When the windows closed, a bank of vending machines remained available 24-7 to even weigh and ship parcels.

The closing of the folding room also occurred without any glitches. At a time when the Senate could not even move one cashier without garnering national media attention and lawsuits, we were able to close a 150-year-old operation, lay off 120 people, and do it without a ripple of discord. A key element was Kay Ford's outplacement process. We made sure every person received the type of retraining, counseling, and support usually reserved for corporate executives. We made it clear that all layoffs were based on strategic management decisions, not personal issues. For many, it was the first time they had been treated like professionals.

The architect of the Capitol's team was thrilled with the speed and scope of our reforms. For the first time in sixty-two years, they could re-think the layout of the Longworth basement and redevelop an entire city block of space.

Not everyone was so thrilled. Stacy and Otto seethed from their perches at the CHO. They sniped at every action, derailing some of the peripheral reforms. This included sinking my idea of leasing space to a Kinko's-type store to offer printing services as an alternative to the folding-room. They also tried to trip up the USPS opening ceremonies by demanding to handle them, only to cancel at the last minute. Fortunately, Joan DeCain and her team made everything happen, better and on time.

Stacy and Otto fought for members' attention by issuing competing "Dear Colleague" letters and organizing competing briefings regarding the major changes in House service operations and policies. Although we would invite them to our briefings, they would bar us from theirs.

One example was the series of briefings relating to the termination of folding services. No CAO employee was allowed to participate in the CHO-sponsored sessions. The result was that numerous questions went unanswered or the answers were later found to be wrong. The leaders of the Systems Administrators Association met with me shortly after one of these sessions to complain that these CHO briefings were causing con-fusion. Similar criticisms were raised regarding CHO sessions on finan-cial reform and regulatory compliance.

Discussions with the CHO after the auction were contentious. Stacy was furious that I had made little effort to involve the CHO in the de-tails of the auction. She exploded, "We authorized an auction and the next thing we know it's done!"

"That is what oversight is all about," I countered. "You authorize it. We do it. We report back to you when it is completed. We are paid to sweat the details, not you."

The "Ottograms" kept coming, but they did not have the same weight as earlier ones. We were briefing CHO members individually. Leadership was constantly in the loop. Bennett, Dorsey, and Hasdorff joined my road show to explain the reforms to more and more House members. Most importantly, services were improving, service offerings were expanding, and information was flowing. Wadel was happy. Nussle, Boehner, DeLay, and Packard were all happy. That is what counted. "The CHO staff has become as relevant as ants at a picnic," I triumphantly declared at a Monday morning staff meeting.

These confrontations spilled over into the release of Price Waterhouse's financial audit. This report would be the first truly independent audit of House finances and a key "deliverable" from the "Contract with America." It was also to be an independent validation of why the reforms were necessary. Thomas, for some reason, wanted to downplay the report and its findings. Nussle and the leadership wanted a high-profile release.

On July 7 and again on July 12, Otto and Stacy assured leadership that they would lead all efforts to publicize the historic Price Waterhouse audit of House operations. Repeated offers of assistance from Anfinson, Simon, and Davison, as well as from Tony Blankley, were rejected, as the CHO "had all the resources we need."

Stacy flew into a rage at a meeting with Davison and me on July 14. "It is our report!" she thundered. "We can do with it what we want! You and the leadership just want to run things so you can take all the credit!"[2] The report's release received minimal media coverage. Stacy shrugged it off. "The story was not that big after all."

Blankley decided to call the CHO's bluff. He authorized me to conduct an experiment. "Call one of your best media friends and see what can be generated." Within two days, the *Wall Street Journal* ran one news story, two op-ed pieces, and a featured editorial about the report.[3] This proved that the CHO had stonewalled.

Leadership was furious at Thomas for subverting the report. Stacy and Scott Montrey, the CHO's media liaison, were called into the Speaker's office to explain themselves to Dan Meyer, Blankley, Lafferty, and Wadel. Montrey was fired shortly afterward as the scapegoat.

The second part of the Price Waterhouse report was released on August 2, 1995. Price Waterhouse outlined 226 recommendations to improve the support operations of the House and stated that the shift to business-based systems would aid in implementing these recommendations. It validated everything we had been saying since December 1994. The report acted as a booster rocket to propel a broader and swifter implementation of the reforms.

MUCKRAKING

The rollout of the reforms was played out against a personal ordeal. True to his word, Livingston's minions in the media had conducted a full background check of everything I had done over the previous twenty-five years. By mid-June, I was receiving warnings from various former employers and colleagues about this opposition research. They all said that they had been asked many accusatory and leading questions. When they gave factual answers, they were berated by *Roll Call* reporters for not giving them any "dirt" on me. "They really hate you," commented one former boss. "You must be doing the right thing!"

Just before lunch on Friday, June 30, Nussle and Wadel came to my office to discuss the *Roll Call* probe. They were most bothered about my bankruptcy. "You should have told us," declared Jim in a grave tone.

"I did."

"When?"

"Remember our first lunch meeting back in December? You asked me if there was anything that was potentially embarrassing. I told you about the bankruptcy and how it was tied to legal issues arising from my divorce."

Jim stared in stunned silence. "You're right. I forgot."

"You remember that you told me you didn't want to hear the details because it was obviously a private matter." Sue looked over at Jim for validation. He grimly nodded his head.

The tone of the meeting, and I believe the outcome, dramatically changed. Jim was concerned about how *Roll Call* unsealed the divorce records. Sue was concerned about the review being demanded by Thomas and Livingston. It was decided that the Speaker's office would allow Ehlers, as the CHO's representative, and Linder, as the leadership's representative, plus Boehner, with ties to both, to review the allegations. "We want to believe you, but we must have proof," Sue declared.

Sue sent me a list of questions on Monday. Basically, they were a rehash of the *Roll Call* article from December. It challenged all my professional credentials and experience. I easily provided explanations and rebuttal documents. On July 7, Sue asked for more information to counter the flood of rumors emanating from *Roll Call* and Livingston.

To add fuel to the fire, Livingston wrote a series of letters to me questioning every aspect of the reforms. He accused me of moving "too far too fast" and of not understanding the service needs of members.[4] In another letter, he opposed making any staff changes.

On July 26, Tim Burger, a reporter for *Roll Call*, wanted to review my financial records as part of a story he planned to run. Jim Davison recorded the call. It was clear from his detailed questions that Burger had somehow unsealed my bankruptcy records and had spoken to either my former wife or her attorney. His line of questioning proved he clearly wanted "blood." It also proved he had no idea how divorces were handled in the judicial system. My comprehensive and straightforward answers contradicted his hoped-for headline.

He stuttered and stammered many times during the call. Sensing that I had the upper hand, I concluded, "I think this whole thing is a personal matter, and I think that it's not something that is worthy of a newspaper like yours."

"Um, unfortunately, it's so late in the process. I'm going to do what I can to . . . um . . . to um . . . note what you have said, but at this time, you know, that's all I can say, especially with the late time. . . . I appreciate you taking the time. I'm sure this is difficult subject matter. I . . . you . . . you know, am sensitive, so anyway. . . um . . . if there's anything else, feel free to call."[5]

Roll Call published a story about my financial "problems" the next day. I assumed it was an attempt to overshadow the Price Waterhouse report.

The assault did not go away. My former wife wrote a letter to the editor of *Roll Call* stating that I had fabricated everything relating to the divorce. A few days later, Representative Kweisi Mfume (D-MD) came up to me at the African American Staff Association reception. "I can't imagine what you must be going through," he began. "For them to dredge up your ex-wife to attack you really crosses the line." I thanked him for his kind words.

"Steny has told me you are trying to do the right thing. I respect that. You don't deserve these attacks." He patted me on the shoulder. "Let me know if I can ever be of assistance."

Roll Call's "muckraking" continued through the summer and into the autumn. I was bewildered by the onslaught. "They are probably mad because your downsizing is eliminating all their news sources," suggested Bennett.

After Labor Day, Sue received word that they were preparing an extended story assailing my professional credentials. Jim Lafferty, Vicki, and I drove to Harpers Ferry to pore over my archives. Since my time at the Minnesota Historical Society, I had saved and filed copies of all my work. There were nearly a hundred boxes dating back to my first campaign. We methodically collected the relevant material and returned to Washington at 3:00 a.m.

Roll Call's last major assault spread over three pages. It attacked everything about me. It altered many events and ignored many facts. Their opening analogy on my cleaning up the program in Malawi while I was a Peace Corps country director was written over the protest of *Washington Times* reporter George Archibald. He had broken the story on the Malawi scandals, and his reports helped guide my reforms. He pleaded with *Roll Call*'s editors not to negate that effort. They ignored him in order to achieve a cheap bit of propaganda.[6]

We also saw the irony in these personal attacks. Starting in February, the signature authority for ministerial acts had been transferred from the clerk to me. Every week, Dorsey would arrive with up to fifty legal binders, relating to members and staff, for me to sign on behalf of the House. These included bankruptcies, garnishment of wages, and court orders relating to nonpayment of alimony and child support. All of these were confidential and all came across my desk. Any one of these documents could end a career. It would be a treasure trove for blackmail in the hands of a lesser person.

Even my critics considered *Roll Call*'s last attack as over the top. Letters of support for me poured into the Speaker's office. Every one of my former bosses, except Otto, wrote the Speaker. Many of my Crosby colleagues and my Peace Corps volunteers wrote to say that the attacks were all false and that, if anything, I was modest about what I had accomplished in life. Sue reviewed my three-ringed binder filled with documents that point-by-point rebutted the last article and declared the matter closed.

I had weathered four months of being under the "proctoscope" and survived, but Linder didn't speak to me for the rest of my tenure.

CYBER-CONGRESS

The summer of 1995 included the sad duty of removing three of the A Ring. I chose not to confront Wadel or the Speaker on these forced removals. The *Roll Call* and Livingston battles removed any leverage I might have had. Each of my loyal deputies was informed of his fate.

Mutersbaugh would be the first to go. He took the news with class. We worked out the details, down to a farewell luncheon and a certificate thanking him for his work on the reforms.

I wanted Rick Endres to remain on as an adviser to the new head of HIR for a few months. He couldn't believe that Ehlers backstabbed him. He assumed they had a working relationship.

Sweetland took the news in stride. He asked only that he remain on board through the year so as not to jeopardize his reemployed annuitant status. I explained the situation to Sue Wadel, and she made sure Thomas understood the situation. There was plenty to do. I had Paul work with Lusby on the postal moves and renovations.

The summer also saw further additions to the CAO team. One of the happiest was Don Rice's joining Anfinson's finance team. Don had been one of my most successful Peace Corps volunteers in Malawi. As the CFO for Air Malawi, the government-owned airline, he revolutionized their operations and made it one of the few profitable air carriers in Africa.

Another set of hires and reassignments related to the cyber-Congress initiative. Netscape had rolled out its Web browser in early 1995, and the world of the Internet changed forever. The closed culture of university and government "gophers" exploded into the information age. Two young and gifted professionals became our bridge to this new world. John Atkinson joined my staff as the in-house "techie" to school the CAO team on Web-based applications. Trent Coleman was the embodiment of the new CAO culture. He had been managing mailing lists for the House post office. He was far too talented and creative to just check zip codes. I promoted him to Atkinson's team to build the House's first intranet and the first Web portal. To round out my technology brain trust, I brought in Chad Mosley, a brilliant software developer whom I had worked with in the late 1980s. He would guide the Capability Maturity Model and ISO 9000 certifications for the House's computer systems.

The cyber-Congress needed a dynamic new leader whom I could "launder" through Ehlers. I met with one of my FMI business partners, Ramon Barquin, to brainstorm about people. He recommended Ken Miller.

Ken had all the right credentials and experience. He had been a top manager at IBM for twenty-two years, building a reputation as a motivator and innovator. He had also been in on the ground floor of the early Internet, having worked on the Community Learning Information Network (CLIN) and America Tomorrow, the Chamber of Commerce's visioning effort for the information age. Ken was also an idealist, serving on the boards of the Urban League and the Red Cross. This combination of futurist, idealist, and proven executive would be invaluable.

The three of us met on June 28 to orchestrate Ken's appointment. I took great pains to downplay any link to Ken. I could honestly say that I consulted industry leaders and had not known Ken prior to meeting him on June 28. Ehlers met with Ken, one-on-one, on June 30 and was impressed. His first day at the helm of HIR was July 17.

Ken's primary task was to create a strategic plan for moving the House, in one giant leap, from the nineteenth century to the forefront of the information age. There were many problems, one of which was that several congressional task forces had used faulty assumptions and the old HIS mindset to develop ill-conceived and obsolete approaches. Endres had written a detailed critique of this minefield. His insights helped us anticipate Ehlers's arguments.[7]

Ken and I met over lunch at the Ford Building on August 3. Anfinson had projected a huge budget surplus for the end of the fiscal year. We could reprogram some of that money for building the cyber-Congress, instead of letting it all go back to the Treasury. Such an audacious move could create the information infrastructure in months instead of years.

"What I need is a bond issue," I began. "Just as school districts go to the voters with a plan for new schools and entrepreneurs go to investors with a prospectus. I need a detailed plan for the cyber-Congress that I can sell to Newt, complete with a cost-benefit analysis of what would happen if we didn't do it this way."

Ken nodded in agreement and proceeded, with the help of Endres, the brain trust, and many other key people throughout the CAO, to develop a masterful and visionary document:

- Five miles of fiber optics and thirty miles of T-1 lines, with all servers and switches installed through the entire campus.
- A Pentium computer in each member, committee, and leadership office. This would allow for paperless transactions, from "Dear Colleague" letters to whip operations to financial record keeping, purchasing, and work orders.
- All the service contracts, equipment, training, and support to immediately make the entire system operational.
- Moving all operational documents and databases onto a compatible digital database.
- A distributed architecture of secure servers, with sufficient firewalls to allow for Internet access, a local area network, and intranet operations, even to district offices, without fear of hacking or other security breaches.
- A unified e-mail system.
- Enough server power and memory to support a 310 percent increase in electronic-based communications in the House in the first year, doubling each year for ten years.

- A decision support center allowing for virtual caucuses, virtual committee meetings, and strategic-planning meetings accessing distant users.
- A complete upgrade of CAO support based on information-age technology. This will include all financial data, human-resources data, and personal-property inventory data being available electronically. It also will allow for desktop procurement and other forms of electronic commerce.[8]

The "bond issue" document was complete, with individual approvals for each item. Kiko's team developed the purchase orders for off-the-shelf items, short lists of approved vendors, and RFPs for everything else. I reviewed the final package with Ken's team and sent it on to the CHO. To be safe, I also sent copies to Wadel, Nussle, Packard, Blankley, and Meyers.

The "bond issue" reached Gingrich's desk just as the confrontation with the Clinton administration over the fiscal year 1996 budget was igniting. Thomas was furious. He mustered his opposition forces. Fortunately, Miller had also worked the "bond issue" through Ehlers, finally persuading him to embrace distributed architecture. I had worked it through friendly members who were "techies," including Shays, Hoekstra, Chrysler, and Stockman. I also alerted DeLay. The forces for and against the "bond" collided in the Speaker's office on Friday, September 29.

Gingrich called a meeting at noon in his office. Thomas was pacing back and forth like a caged lion. Dan Meyer was pensive. "Let me get this straight," Newt started. "We can get everything we need to create the cyber-Congress with this one action?"

"That is correct," I asserted.

"And how much money are we talking about?'

"$36 million."

"And that's for everything?"

"Yes." He then turned to Thomas.

"Bill, how much money are we going to return to the Treasury?"

"About $105 million."

"So, we can still say we saved money and get the cyber-Congress?"

Bill saw where this was going and was not happy. He exploded into a tirade about the coming battle with the White House and the need to show frugality. Gingrich turned back to me. "What happens if we don't do this?"

"We fund some of it in fiscal year '96 and some in fiscal year '97, but it will be piecemeal at best."

"Why didn't we fund it all in the fiscal year '96 bill?"

"This is a one-time general-fund expenditure that gives equipment and services to each member office. There was no place to put such a project in the legislative appropriations as they are structured. This one-time reprogramming of surplus funds will let us do the project without altering the accounts."

"Then do it."

Thomas threw up his hands. He shot a look at me and then smiled at the Speaker. "As you wish, but we will not be able to claim this as savings."

"I realize that," said Newt, and the meeting was over.

I spent the balance of that Friday and all day Saturday signing purchase orders and contracts. Kiko and Miller filed into my office with additional documents, including policies and Dear Colleague letters. The cyber-Congress was born.

CEMENTING THE SANDCASTLE

January 18, 1996

It was as if some magician had made the entire Capitol disappear. Only when you neared the Grant Monument did the fog clear enough to see the lower portions of the west front.

Phil Crosby was on the telephone from Orlando. All flights into the Washington area had been canceled, and he could not keynote the CAO graduation ceremony.

This was to be the culmination of the new culture. Over the previous five months, all members of the CAO team had participated in a series of workshops, learning the principles and skills of customer service and continuous improvement. The Cannon Caucus Room had been reserved, along with an honor guard and the Air Force quartet, for the mass graduation.

I huddled with Davison to discuss options. Thanks to the House's technology upgrade, we could link Crosby via satellite. Within hours, Crosby was at an Orlando studio, and the Caucus Room was lined with large televisions on elevated stands. I would later write in the CAO newsletter,

> The mark of success for any organization is its ability to respond to rapidly changing events while maintaining its excellence. Graduation day delivered a clear message that our organization is reaching this high standard of world-class service delivery. The cooperation, initiative, and "can-do"

attitude displayed by everyone involved on that wild morning is what Building a Quality Culture is all about.[1]

The graduation ceremony was one of the high points of my life. All members of the CAO team received a graduation certificate on parchment. Each came forward to receive his or her "diploma" and had photos taken, along with family members who were in attendance. There were many poignant moments, including when stevedores, dressed in business suits, stepped forward with tears in their eyes. "I never graduated from high school. This is my first graduation." We were all visibly moved. We knew this would be a defining moment in the cultural revolution, but none of us realized how life changing it would be for all involved.

Changing the culture was one of the keys to institutionalizing the reforms. Each cycle of party dominance in the Congress and the White House leads to governing activity. Executive orders, regulations, memoranda, legislation, and hearings occur with much fanfare. Yet when the other party wins control, most of what occurred can be reversed. Worse, public laws and regulations can die in someone's in-box. A law is only as good as its enforcement. Therefore, most governing remains on the "beach" and can be eroded or swept away with the next tide. To create a lasting transformation, you must find ways to preserve what you are building. Only by "cementing the sandcastle" can you achieve lasting change and gains.

We mixed cement into every aspect of the House reforms. We changed the chart of accounts, we changed all the systems and processes, we got rid of furniture and equipment, we got rid of physical space, we altered physical space, we, literally and figuratively, rewired the entire complex. The final coat of cement was changing the culture. You cannot erase knowledge once it is acquired. Once all members of the CAO team were trained, and allowed to apply these new skills, there was no going back.

We had come a long way since the summer of 1995. The first rumors of the reforms panicked many of the "careerists." They called members, leaked what they could to the media, and even held prayer vigils for their jobs.[2] The A Ring reached out, one person at a time. Then small groups were involved in problem-solving and measurement workshops. Little by little, the new CAO organization, and its work culture, took shape.

There were three major elements to reshaping the culture. The first was serving as role models and conducting outreach. Everyone in the A Ring was expected to "walk the talk" and display, in every action and communication, the new culture. We knew that the new CAO organization would be composed of mostly "careerists." Ultimately, more than 400 "holdovers" became part of the 630-member CAO team. The balance was new hires. Many of the 700 who were downsized ended up working for our vendors. They also needed to understand the new work culture while they were in transition.

Many of the employees we inherited were skilled professionals with years of knowledge. I openly mused that "I do not know all the answers nor do I know all the questions." I forged an alliance with those who truly knew the process. The benefits of this leveled playing field were immediate and numerous, ranging from insights on the unique needs of member offices to shortcuts through the tunnels. The furnishings staff suggested that only the contents of desks and bookshelves be moved instead of all the furniture. Moving thousands of pieces of identical furniture was always a major task, resulting in major damage. This saved millions of dollars in repairing and replacing furniture during the transition to the 105th Congress.

I repeatedly said that "anyone can speak to anyone about anything" and modeled this behavior by seeing any CAO employee whenever someone asked. I also repeated that, although there was an organizational chart for accounting and legislative purposes, there was no organizational chart in terms of operations and communications. "My only organizational chart is my speed-dial list, and that changes as the projects change." Cross-functional teams and multilevel teams were emphasized. On any given day, a "stevedore" and a "techie" might be sitting in my office along with one of the A Ring to assess solutions for a service issue.

When we did use an organizational chart, we aligned it with the new customer-focused culture. In this model (see figure) the customer was the main focus of everything we did. Frontline "customer service" delivered service through direct interaction with customers. "Customer support" was composed of managers and others who made sure the frontline had everything they needed to be successful in serving their customers.

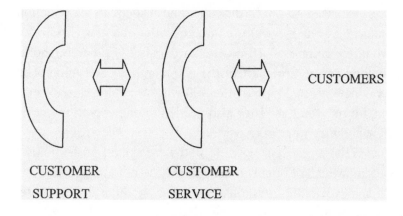

CUSTOMER   CUSTOMER
SUPPORT   SERVICE

The chart served to "hardwire" everyone into thinking about process, not hierarchy. The associate administrators, and other managers, were viewed by all employees as resources and facilitators—not as bosses. This allowed interactions to be among equals with common goals and opened up communication channels for ideas, feedback, and guidance.

As the months progressed, the cultural change could be seen and felt. When I first became CAO, the stevedores would bow their heads and remain silent if we shared an elevator. Later they would say hello but still call me "sir." By December 1995, they would smile, greet me with "Hi Scot," and we would discuss how their day was going and their improvement ideas.

Another "reality check" for implementing the new culture was winning over our in-house skeptics. Skeptics are solid professionals who need more proof before committing to the new order of things. They perform a useful role in keeping change managers "honest." Leaders of transformation and their "early-adopter" allies may cut corners in their zeal to achieve change. Skeptics ask the awkward questions that ground the effort. They are different from those who fight the change and from those who subvert change through "malicious compliance."

Joe Simpson was a skeptic. He led the Office of Printing Services, which printed and distributed legislative documents. This was the last unit to be transferred from the clerk's office to the CAO. There were arguments both for and against moving the office. The transition team and I argued that the transfer allowed for the seamless flow of information and the rapid digitalization of that information. The clerk fought every effort to improve the flow of information, especially to the public, and fought the digital revolution. Joe liked what we were doing but had institutional loyalty to having all legislative information housed under the clerk.

For most of 1995, Joe challenged every action, questioning its intent. However, he was a top performer and was an excellent manager of a loyal team. As the year progressed, he saw what was happening in the CAO operation and what was not happening in the clerk's office. During a management-simulation workshop, he walked up to me to admit that he had been wrong, that he now fully understood the revolution, and that he was ready to embrace it. It was another moving moment for me, as I had won over the last skeptic. He went on to be one of the most valued members of my executive team.

The second element was training. There had never been an effort to improve the skills of any of the CAO personnel. Wendy Younk, Gloria Wright-Simmonds, and Bill Sturdevant developed a set of core skills, a curriculum, and training modules. To emphasize its importance to the new culture, I personally conducted all the kick-off sessions. In these sessions, I would explain the new organization, review the credo and the Contract with Congress, and preview the skill modules that everyone would attend. I also conducted a shortened version of this presentation for each group of new hires in my office. Our goal was to show that the new culture was important and that everyone would gain the skills they needed to achieve excellence.

I personally trained the now forty-member CAO team in a series of two-day quality-principles workshops. "Careerist" and A Ring members sat side by side to work through how to apply quality to daily operations. Lainhart and his top lieutenants attended to better understand our cultural revolution. This achieved a common frame of reference and common terminology, which aided the implementation of internal controls.

By May 1996, each CAO employee had a performance agreement. This "contract" bound each manager and employee to mutually work at making each a success. Part of this "contract" was an "individual development plan" (IDP). These IDPs guided educational experiences so that each CAO employee could become a high-performance service professional.

The third element was recognition. We made sure that "thank you" was said often. We also made sure that everyone, at every level, asked, "Is there anything I may do to assist you?" as part of any work-related discussion. Kay Ford, Bern Beidel, and representatives from each unit met regularly to develop recognition processes and awards for excellence. They worked closely with Gloria, Bill, and Wendy to make sure employee recognition was compatible with training and cultural change. They kept me informed, and I would share "best practices" from the wealth of case studies on quality management. Our most successful recognition was obtaining tickets to all the free holiday concerts, plays, and programs, including the tour of Christmas decorations in the White House. Many were only available to Hill staff, and others could only be obtained using insider knowledge or persistence. Hundreds of tickets were acquired and then handed out to all nonsupervisory CAO employees so that they and their families could enjoy the holiday season as never before. We wanted to make it clear that everyone was special in the new culture.

Every few weeks, Vicki and I would join Gloria at her apartment for incredible Jamaican food and to review the cultural change in detail. Gloria was a no-nonsense person. Over jerk chicken and a shepherd's pie to die for, she would scold me if I had missed an opportunity or praise me if I was on track. I valued her guidance. All members of the A Ring had an open door to bring challenges and opportunities to my attention. Only Gloria turned this into true coaching.

CHANNEL 25

One of our most powerful tools for outreach and training was a new in-house television channel. The House has a unique and challenging audience. Its nearly ten thousand employees not only work highly pressured and unusual hours, but a third of them work part- or full-time outside Washington, D.C. These factors severely limited the effectiveness of traditional methods, such as scheduled briefings, for imparting information and conducting compliance training.

It was especially important to reach this audience as the compliance program became a reality. Luckily, Jim Stephens, one of the new members of the independent Compliance Office, was an "Inchon" member and longtime friend. Along with Dorsey, we worked with the entire Compliance Office team to codify House compliance regulations and procedures. We also used compliance as a tool for improvement. Joan McEnery tracked overtime and discovered ways to reorganize various work processes to reduce these payments.

We obtained training videos from the various federal regulatory agencies to show to all House staff members. It was an important part of compliance, and necessary for preventing violations.

Channel 25 was authorized on June 14, 1995. The intent of the resolution was for the CAO to develop programs, for the CHO to approve the programs, and for the CAO to then broadcast them. This operational partnership ended the moment Channel 25 went "live."

On the first day, Otto twice called the architect of the Capitol to stop the broadcast, in mid-program, because he had "changed his mind" about some of the content. These sudden calls for justification, sometimes in mid-program, continued for months. All the programs had previously been previewed and approved, in writing, by Otto.

Otto then began requesting detailed program schedules and justifications for the showing of CHO-authorized tapes, even though it had been decided that audience feedback would determine frequency and scheduling. When the Compliance Office began to complain, Otto focused on delaying approval of informational briefings relating to administrative services or personnel benefits because they had CAO personnel in them, usually Younk, Ford, or Sturdevant.

Fortunately, other communications were outside the jurisdiction, or beyond the comprehension, of the CHO. We began a monthly employee newsletter to promote the new culture. The name "CAO Connection" was chosen from employee suggestions. There was a "chart of the month" to show how important measurement was to achieving excellence. I wrote an article providing homilies about quality and service. The balance of the newsletter was composed of employee news and submissions by CAO employees. *Roll Call* made fun of the newsletter, branding my homilies as hokum or mindless cheerleading about improving carpet fibers.

The CAO intranet was our ultimate achievement. Everything that was in print was eventually placed online. Atkinson and Coleman became our webmasters. They kept us on the cutting edge of digital technology and website design. We watched as the "hit rates" for the intranet grew from a few a day to thousands a day. It served as the test bed for our ultimate goal, a House Web portal that made everything public. This would not become a reality until November 1996.

ROAD SHOW

Tony Blankley was determined not to repeat the debacle of the Price Waterhouse report. We sat in his office to discuss how to make sure the American public knew that at least one part of the "Contract with America" had become a reality. Tony reviewed all the key players. In each case, the members most associated with the reforms, Representatives DeLay, Packard, Nussle, Boehner, Dunn, Ney, Shays, and Hoekstra, were either too partisan or too involved in policy matters to barnstorm audiences on management issues. "You are the only one who can go out to business audiences and make them understand what has been accomplished," said Tony.

"Oh God," I began. "Thomas and Livingston will enjoy branding me as a glory seeker."

"Let me run interference. I'll get Newt's and leadership's sign-off. This story must be told."

A week later, we sat down again. "Everyone likes the idea of a road show. Let me set up some initial interviews and speaking engagements. It will snowball from there. I also want you to tap some of your contacts." And so it began.

On September 13, 1995, the American Society for Quality Control (ASQC) held their board meeting on Capitol Hill. I arranged for various reform members to present, and I acted as overall host. It was a great event as Packard, Nussle, Hoekstra, Chrysler, and former representative Don Ritter (R-PA), the "father" of the House's quality revolution, all presented to the board. As a way to accommodate the rotation of speakers and to further symbolize the new culture, I arranged for the ASQC board members to sit in the members' seats on the dais in a subcommittee room. The members then sat and presented at the witness table. Everyone enjoyed the reversal.

From this "curtain-raising" event, I took the show on the road. I either keynoted or was the featured speaker at an alphabet soup of business and professional association meetings. There were also presentations at the Kennedy School of Government and various Republican events. The Harvard trip was memorable. It fell during the time that Colin Powell announced he would not run for president in 1996. Many at the Kennedy School seemed to be in mourning as Powell's announcement was broadcast on the giant-screen television in their commons.

Vicki and I stayed in John F. Kennedy's dorm room, the VIP guest quarters. The room included a large guestbook for everyone to sign. The book contained signatures and comments by Mikhail Gorbachev, Nelson Mandela, and many other world figures dating back many years. I tried to think of what I could add to such a stellar list. At Vicki's suggestion, I wrote, "The truth is out there" in homage to the *X-Files*, our favorite show, and signed my name.

On April 2, 1996, I was to speak at the national meeting of the Human Resource Planning Society, in Palm Springs, California. Vicki and I flew out early to visit my relatives and John Garbett and his family. John had just returned from New Zealand. He was amazed at what we had accomplished. We enjoyed the film *Fargo* and discussed his time "down under."

Vicki contacted her old friend, John Barletta, who headed Ronald Reagan's Secret Service detail. Reagan was suffering from Alzheimer's disease, and rarely saw visitors. We remained on standby until an hour before our meeting. The former president was having a "good day." Barletta had briefed him on who we were. Vicki and I were told not to bring up current events and to follow Reagan's lead on what was to be discussed. The former president was robust and chipper when we entered his office. We reminisced about the 1980 campaign and his time in the White House. "What are you doing now?" he asked.

"I am bringing your revolution to the Congress." I replied. He asked several questions about what the reforms were about. I presented him with a piece of the east front stairs of the Capitol, and he gave me one of his "It can be done" leather desk ornaments. After forty-five minutes, a photographer arrived to take our photo, and President Reagan wished Vicki and me adieu. It was the last time we were together. This was the man who shaped so much of my life, from first hearing him on the eve of the 1964 elections to first meeting him in 1975 to working for him in 1976 and 1980, and then serving him throughout his presidency. Vicki and I were overwhelmed with emotion for many hours afterward. Later that day, we joined my relatives for a VIP tour of the Reagan Library. It is a moment we will vividly remember to our dying day.

Throughout this period, Tony arranged for various interviews and guest appearances with the national media. Jim Davison also linked me up with C-SPAN. There were times when C-SPAN needed "color commentary" about legislation. A House member would appear in a box, or just as a voice-over, during a vote to explain the parliamentary situation. The stand-up for the cameras would be in either Statuary Hall or the corridor nearby. My knowledge of House procedures and the fact that my office was just downstairs made me the "pinch hitter" of choice when a member was not available. Jim would call me, state the bill, and ask, "Can you be upstairs in five minutes?" I would turn on the floor feed and quickly call up the leadership recordings to determine what was happening and then be on my way.

My short and succinct "sound bites" turned into a catch phrase for Jim, Terri Hasdorff, and Vicki. Whenever I got verbose at a hearing, in an interview, or in a meeting, they would pass a note or whisper, "C-SPAN mode" to remind me to stay focused and short-winded.

THE COLD WAR

As the reforms progressed, Thomas, Otto, and Stacy probed for weaknesses and launched their own end runs around the CAO operation. They excluded CAO team members from briefing CHO members and their staffs on selected reform initiatives. We just continued our one-on-

one meetings. CHO agendas and requests for witnesses were often not communicated until the day of the meeting. Witnesses were denied the ability to correct and certify their remarks. Hearing transcripts were only available in the CHO offices. Photocopying was forbidden.

Thomas issued his own set of "Dear Colleague" letters without coordinating with relevant CAO offices. I would have to issue a clarifying "Memorandum for Members, Committees, and Staffs." In one instance, the CHO issued a "Dear Colleague" on travel reimbursement that outlined direct-billing services for travel. The inspector general, the CAO's Finance and Internal Control Offices, and Price Waterhouse were not consulted or informed of this arrangement. It actually contradicted a number of recommendations in the House audit.

The CHO staff continued to act like the old Committee on House Administration, creating their own "member services" unit to expedite various services. They immediately began playing favorites, helping only Republican members. Worse, they would call into the CAO operation, demanding expedited handling. This caused confusion within the CAO, since frontline "careerist" staff did not know whom to follow. These issues arose because some offices were not following the new procedures. When a bill was not paid because of incomplete paperwork, they blamed the CAO's operations for not being responsive. The CHO staff exploited this transitional turbulence by not alerting the CAO team to these issues. They severed vital feedback loops in the hopes of blinding the CAO operation.

Joan DeCain formed a customer liaison office, called "ONECall." This office was designed as a "one stop shop" to handle cross-functional service requests. The office included Edith "Edie" Vivian, John Hitzel, the director of Food Services, and Barbara Hanrahan, a former Member's spouse who provided insights into family needs. The office also conducted customer satisfaction surveys and handled various unique issues, such as disaster assistance to district offices. Joan's efforts, as well as Jane Bennett's and Debbie Hansen's roving among the member offices, uncovered most of these issues before they festered, but the CHO did all it could to communicate the old culture and frustrate the new culture. "They worry about who gets the credit, while we worry about if it gets done," Jane complained.

We proceeded with implementing the reforms, doing the best we could to fend off attempts by Otto and Stacy to micromanage the process. Dorsey's team created a searchable CD-ROM of the U.S. Code, thus eliminating the need for costly leather-bound volumes and quarterly supplements. The outsourcing of postal operations took center stage. Kiko and his team did an excellent job at making sure there was full and fair competition. A review panel was set up. They created a detailed set of selection criteria and then rated each submission. I joined the panel as they visited the three finalists to review their operations. One finalist sent a huge stretch limo to take us to their local site. "We are going to the prom!" I mused to Kay Ford.

Pitney Bowes won the competition. Their $23 million contract was approved by the CHO on December 13 and signed on December 15. I met with Dan Meyer on December 7 to complain about the "cold war" and asked him to run interference to make sure Thomas didn't sabotage the postal contract. Thanks to his intervention, we proceeded with this historic contract, but we still faced a far greater threat.

The issue rested on the most basic of questions—should officers be able to manage their internal human resources? While in the opposition, Thomas wrote to then minority leader Michel and then minority whip Gingrich:

"As you know, Chairman Rose's signature is required on all official forms of the director . . . payroll changes have languished since June, and the director has a virtual stack-up of other changes. . . . At the August 4, 1993, Oversight Committee meeting, I strongly advocated a policy in which the director would have the authority, under an approved structure, to take any personnel actions he believes necessary, including selection, appointment, assignment, transfer and termination, without exception."[3]

Thomas's worldview changed when he became chairman of the CHO. On June 14, 1995, the CHO unanimously approved 275 positions for the new HIR organization. Existing personnel were allowed to compete into these new approved positions, but fifty vacancies remained to be filled. Otto told Endres, and later Ken Miller, to delay the personnel paperwork to fill these fifty vacancies. He required detailed explanations of why all fifty positions needed filling, even though both the CHO and the Appropriations subcommittee approved all 275 positions.

Service began to degrade because of this staff shortage. Thomas sent a memo outlining, in minute detail, what must be done before any candidates for these vacancies would be approved. A heated exchange of letters between Thomas, Otto, and me continued through the Christmas recess.

This blockage of new HIR staff came as we were making the final decision on which e-mail system would be the universal platform for the House. On January 14, 1996, the CHO issued a "Dear Colleague" letter on "Computer Messaging Proof of Concept Update," which outlined progress on the cyber-Congress initiative and announced a series of meetings to provide customer feedback for the final messaging decision. Reynolds Schweickhardt, the CHO's "techie," was named as the staff contact. HIR had already initiated its own series of customer focus groups and test offices. Miller appealed to me to resolve these issues and allow him to hire his additional staff.

I appealed to Wadel and Meyers.[4] They flat out stated that Newt was still immersed in "damage control" from his budget battle with President Clinton. I was on my own on this one. I turned to Dorsey. We crafted a letter to the House parliamentarian requesting a clarification of House Rules pertaining to CHO-CAO jurisdiction relating to personnel. Within a day, I received a terse call from Stacy. "The chairman wants to meet with you right now!"

Thomas's hideaway was a two-room suite (H-163 and H-164) looking out on the Mall. We had had a number of cordial meetings in the suite, discussing the reforms and munching on huge bowls of pistachios, which were grown in his district. This was not to be one of those cordial sessions. Otto and Stacy were already in the room. I brought Dorsey and Hasdorff as witnesses.

We exchanged awkward pleasantries. Then Thomas and Boehner entered the room. They were in the middle of a roll-call vote. We took our seats around a conference table and John got right to the point. "This is a serious matter. I cannot stay here for very long, but leadership wants the two of you to resolve this issue," Boehner began.

We each laid out our perspectives. Thomas took issue with my going behind his back to the parliamentarian. He then stood by Otto and his concerns that HIR might not need fifty additional staff positions. I stated that I had the authority to implement actions approved by the CHO without further interference.

"I want the two of you to work this out and report back to me." Boehner pointed at each of us. The second set of bells rang, and he departed. As the door closed, Bill looked across the table at me, his eyes narrowing.

"Okay, you asshole, what the hell do you think you're doing?" he exploded.

I calmly explained the personnel issue and reminded him of his own words about managerial discretion.

"You're not going to get away with this! I have already spoken with the parliamentarian, and he agreed to step aside on this issue. You are going to have to deal with me! The Speaker is not going to save your ass on this one!"

"I still think I am right in asserting managerial discretion and will appeal to the CHO."

Thomas's face flushed red. He leaned over the table, violently stabbing at me with his index finger. "Listen, you little shit! I am going to crush you, if that takes tearing down every brick of this institution! I will do it, because I will be the only one left standing!"

★ FULL AWARENESS ★

August 3, 1996 (Wroxton Abbey, Oxfordshire, England)

What wonderful irony, I thought, that the discussion about revolutionary reform in the U.S. Congress was being held in Lord North's old house. After all, it was Lord North's policies on taxation and representation during the 1770s that led to the American Revolution.

Wroxton was a magnificent estate, now Wroxton College. The cellar still had remnants of the eighth-century abbey. Parts of the house dated to the time of Henry VIII. Luckily, Vicki and I had a room in the main house. This allowed us to explore the wonderful Tudor drawing rooms and sit alone in the paneled great hall, communing with the spirits of the past.

The delegates for the Second Workshop of Parliamentary Scholars and Parliamentarians had arrayed themselves about the cavernous meeting hall. Thirty nations were represented. Dr. Larry Longley was the cochair of the international forum. Our joint paper "Changing the System: Institutional Change (and Inertia) in the U.S. House of Representatives" had received much advance interest.[1] Our paper suggested that political scientists change their scholarship and their curriculum to address the business and management theories driving the wave of reinvention at all levels of government.

Early that morning, Vicki and I strolled with Longley and his wife through the magnificent grounds of Wroxton Abbey.

"So Scot, what's next, now that you have conquered Congress?" asked Longley jovially.

"We are going to New Zealand!" Vicki blurted.

"Oh? I would think you'd be ready for another term," Longley reacted quizzically.

"Not if I can help it!" Vicki continued. "He might be able to put up with those idiots for another two years, but I will be dead."

I related examples of how personal animosity had permeated the reform struggle. Vicki launched into her take on the matter. "You just can't imagine what we have been through. Scot comes home and some nights it would be hours before he calms down about what they did to him that day! It has been draining on both of us. Scot has done everything they wanted, and all Newt does is sit back and let Thomas and the opposition shit on him. They don't deserve him!"

Longley looked puzzled. "I thought matters were well in hand."

"They are, for now. The meeting that happened before the break was great. Thomas really got his wings clipped." I reviewed the confrontation that took place on July 26. "However, he has been swearing to destroy me since January."

"And bring every brick of the institution down if that's what it takes!" inserted Vicki.

"Vicki!" I chastened. "We don't need to go over that now."

"Yes, we should!" Vicki responded emphatically. "Larry, you just can't imagine what Bill Thomas has said to Scot over this last year. He has been against the reforms from the start. He and Newt have fought each other for years, and now Scot is in the middle, and Newt wouldn't even lift a finger to help him."

"Thomas is a powerful leader among the moderates. Newt needs Thomas's votes for legislative battles," I offered.

"It's worse than that! I still think Thomas has Polaroids of Newt in some compromising position when they were roommates. I think Newt is afraid of Thomas," asserted Vicki.

I wondered what Longley, who was a member of the Democratic National Committee, was thinking of this airing of Republican dirty laundry. He had been my professor, adviser, and mentor since 1971. I was uncomfortable serving up GOP dirt to the Democratic Party's inner circle just three months before an election.

I diverted the conversation. "The whole reform fight is complex and worthy of a book. I will probably write one once I am out of there." Longley then imparted helpful advice on publishing political science books as we made our way back to the manor house.

COLLISION COURSE

It had been an eventful six months since that fateful meeting with Thomas. Following the confrontation, I met with DeLay, Boehner, Dunn, and Hoyer. They all agreed that I was in the right and pledged to muster votes for a showdown at the next CHO meeting. I had Ken Miller whip Ehlers into a frenzy on protecting the independence of HIR. "Okay, you got our attention," ceded Sue when we next met. The House was in recess. In the days since January 25, I had lined up as many as eight votes against Thomas. Only Fazio and Roberts balked at a showdown. "We can't have anything that looks like a no-confidence vote. Even if you lose, it will be a huge embarrassment."

"I am not going to lose," I retorted. Everyone I spoke with was tired of Thomas's antics.

Sue took a deep breath. "All right. I will make sure Thomas signs off on the HIR positions. I also want you to write a paper for the Speaker outlining the problems you have had with Thomas and the committee staff. Include recommended actions."

"So we will finally sort this all out?" I queried.

"Yes, but in return, stop fighting Thomas. You've won. Let me sort this all out."

During the Presidents' Day weekend, I worked on the "Operational Review of Administrative Services in the U.S. House of Representatives." This nineteen-page, single-spaced document outlined the battles between the CAO and Thomas, and laid out sixteen recommended actions.[2] It was a devastating critique of Thomas's reign of terror and detailed how he had systematically undermined and delayed the reforms. It outlined a set of operating procedures, including deadlines for CHO action. Thomas, Otto, and Stacy would have to go on record rejecting

CAO actions, which could then be appealed to the full CHO. Things would no longer go into the "ether," and they would not be allowed to "pocket veto" actions without accountability.

Sue read the document. She commented on how damning the document was, as it put everything into perspective and fully documented how Thomas and his staff went "rogue." "This will take some time; please be patient." I told her I understood.

There was plenty of activity to keep the CAO team and me busy. To help "cement the sandcastle," I had Sturdevant, Wright-Simmonds, and Younk oversee a strategic-planning process for fiscal year 1997 and beyond. Up until this point, the strategic direction had been driven by the transition team report and my vision of the CAO. Now that we had completed the first round of training, it was time to open the "floodgates" for all employees to provide input into the future of the organization. We wanted to build a sense of ownership that spurred action and innovation.

Sturdevant's team grew into a cross-functional core group. Members of this group held visioning workshops, conducted focus groups, and reached out to our customers for their input on what else they needed to feel fully supported by the CAO operation.

The postal outsourcing moved forward. "Must consider" was written into every outsourcing contract. This meant each vendor had to interview each employee in the outsourced service before they made their final hiring decisions. This "get acquainted" provision allowed dozens of House employees to find jobs with the private contractors. Kay Ford's shop helped these employees with drafting résumés and improving their interview skills. Ultimately, 88 of the House's 107 postal employees were offered employment. Lusby and Kiko led the implementation of this vast and diverse enterprise, including the dry runs.

The CHO's delay in approving the Pitney Bowes contract created a major time bind. Otto and Stacy refused to let us implement any part of the postal outsourcing contract until the CHO had voted, however, the Congressional Accountability Act (PL-104-1), which ended the House's exemption from eleven federal labor and employment laws, was scheduled to take affect on January 23. One of these laws was the Worker Adjustment and Retraining Notification (WARN) Act. Under the WARN Act, workers must receive written notice no later than sixty days before being displaced. This protection was intended for plant closures. We wanted to allow Pitney Bowes to conduct their interviews and make their rehiring decisions before sending WARN Act letters. When the CHO delayed the vote until December 13, we were faced with moving forward with WARN letters before January 22 or delaying the entire postal changeover until the Easter recess.

Kiko, Ford, and Dorsey huddled with the compliance staff. Kay Ford sent out a general notification to all employees immediately after the CHO vote, explaining that a selection process would commence, ending sometime in January. Pitney Bowes completed their selection process on January 19, 1996. Kay and her staff finalized and distributed the nineteen termination letters in record time. Their terminations were effective on February 12, a full sixty days after the CHO vote and in the "spirit" of the WARN Act. Everyone was comfortable that we were complying with requirements that had yet to take effect.

That was not how Thomas saw it. He pounced on us for issuing letters one day before the Accountability Compliance Act went into effect. They conveniently ignored Ford's December 13 letter and fixated on the January 22 communications. We were portrayed as conspiring to duck the WARN Act by Thomas, several Democratic members, and of course, *Roll Call*.[3]

There was "transitional turbulence" in everything we did. The Pitney Bowes contract was no different. Some mail was delayed or delivered to the wrong office. *Roll Call* pounced on every glitch, and "Ottograms" flooded my e-mail. However, an array of feedback and measurement systems allowed us to prevent most problems before they happened, or we were able to alert Pitney Bowes to resolve the problem before there was any real harm. The first major restructuring of House postal operations since 1800 went far better than anyone expected.

Simon and Anfinson had moved the financial system to the next level. They were beta testing a monthly online financial system that projected future expenditures for each office and provided a running balance of unspent funds for the fiscal year. Anfinson was a master at finding ways to reduce costs. Each week, we would review operational measures and look for inefficiencies. He also managed cash flow to the point where the House did not have to suspend any operations during the government shutdown.

Debbie Hansen was working on the 1997 inaugural. The House and Senate actually run the inauguration, since it happens in and around the Capitol. The military handles the parade. Therefore, planning starts a year in advance, without any input from either candidate. The invitations for the parade units go out just as they do for the Rose Parade and the Macy's Thanksgiving Day Parade. Each state sends a unit. The only adjustment for an incoming president is prominently placing the president's home state unit in the parade. The House shops were supplying new bunting. We worked closely with the architect, who oversaw construction of the ceremonial rostrum and seating.

Each reform was chronicled on the CAO intranet. Trent Coleman enjoyed posting digital photos of the various renovations. Ken Miller and his team met regularly to roll out the cyber-Congress. We worked with the architect's office to wire more than thirteen million square feet of office space. We were able to use the old chimneys in the Capitol to thread wire between floors to minimize any structural impact. Borcherdling and Bennett mobilized trainers and technical support to guide each office into the information age. Davison and I worked with the media galleries to make sure they were among the first to have the new equipment. My member "road shows" expanded to more and more offices to champion the cyber-Congress.

Some of these road shows uncovered pockets of resistance. On May 28, I spoke to a breakfast meeting of the House's Administrative Assistants Association. These were the chiefs of staff for member offices and some of the most powerful and senior staffers in Congress. After some brief remarks, I opened the floor for questions. Everyone in the room, including colleagues I had known for nearly twenty years, unloaded. "Why are you making us obsolete?" was their outcry. They were most concerned about HouseSmart and the CAO intranet. "You realize that when everything is online, all our years on the Hill will be meaningless!" they protested.

I also focused on reshaping the CAO operation. There had been many personnel moves since the beginning of 1996. Back in November, I convinced Sue Wadel that I needed to fill the "Garbett slot." Sweetland had made plans to retire, so I turned to Bill Crain, another Crosby colleague.

Bill had been an executive with General Motors before heading PCA's Midwest region. He had also served in special operations in the military. Bill had mentored me during my first year with Crosby. He oversaw my training sessions with EDS and other Dallas-area clients. Carole Kordich departed on May 1, 1996, to care full-time for her ailing husband.

Susan Marone had moved to Kay Ford's shop. She had wanted a new challenge. My front office was too much like what she did for Nixon. She wanted to break out of that rut. Vicki recommended Gail Henkin, a longtime friend of hers. Gail had managed the financing, sales, and operations of commercial real estate. Earlier in her career, Gail had worked for a political consulting company. She was eager to move to Washington and join my team.

Two other additions filled out the inner circle. Carol Kresge moved from Ritter's operation to help Simon, and Donna Wiesner joined my personal staff to serve as deputy chief of staff. Donna was a major force in conservative personnel circles. Her "personnel pods" had taken the "Inchon" and the Conservative Network personnel networks to a higher level of sophistication and effectiveness. She had headed the executive secretariat at the Department of Education. It was her attention to detail and document flows that I needed. Jackie Aamot had served in this capacity for a year, but was swamped with compliance issues. I needed my own "final filter."

I also had to make adjustments to changes around me. Coggins had left for the private sector and Packard had selected the officious Ray Mock as his replacement. The fiscal year 1997 appropriations cycle was more time and paper intensive. Although Mock never approached Otto's micromanagement, his constant demands for more detail drove Anfinson and me to distraction.

Each week I would have breakfast with the "AAs"—Anfinson, Crain, Ford, Kiko, Miller—to discuss operations and make sure everyone knew what everyone else was doing. This inner circle supplemented the large Monday staff meetings that now included all forty supervisors.

As the year progressed, Thomas and Otto explored new ways to harass the reforms. "Ottograms" peppered the A Ring with increasing frequency. By late March, many of the delays that had led to the January confrontation had seeped back. The AAs were restive, openly wondering if anything had been done with my February 16 memo. Wadel had forwarded my memo to Stacy for her comments. She rejected everything. I invited Sue Wadel to join the "Breakfast Club" on March 26 to explain the situation. She assured everyone that Gingrich was reviewing the memo and that "good news" would be forthcoming. Many felt she was too vague to be credible.

Seventeen months of being in "overdrive" and constant warfare was taking its toll on the A Ring. Some wanted us to ease back and allow the reforms to soak in. We had implemented almost every reform we proposed, so why not pause for a moment? Others worked outside normal channels to seek peace with the CHO or possibly a separate peace. Several in the A Ring had ties to Otto and others that dated back to the Reagan-Bush campaign. There were also skirmishes among the A Ring members. Tom Simon leveraged his relationship with the inspector general's team in an attempt to assume more control of financial operations.[4] This attempt failed, but soured his relationship with Anfinson.

Vicki had been extending her influence in my office since Gail and Donna joined the inner circle. Just as Nancy grew more protective of President Reagan after the assassination attempt, so had Vicki grown more protective of my well-being after Thomas's confrontation. She would annotate my daily schedule with checklists to make sure Terri, Gail, and Donna followed up on various actions. She also made sure I was not overscheduled. Dorsey and Simon were the most critical of her role, leading to several arguments. Edith Vivian wrote me about this situation.[5]

I met with various members of the A Ring to seek their guidance on how to break out of the "horse latitudes" in which we were foundering. My introspection was relieved by moments of levity. Each nice day, I would walk to work. In the early morning, high school bands would be practicing for their lunchtime concerts at the Capitol. One day, a band was playing the theme song to *The Simpsons* as I walked up the western stairs. It seemed appropriate music for my world.

There was a steady stream of visitors. Foreign delegations kept arriving, as did old friends. Gene Hedberg joined me several times for lunch to share his ideas and insights. Senator Byrd and I arranged for a photo session in the Capitol's chapel for Brad Nash and his new wife, Ginny. John Garbett asked me to help Tim Burton and his production team with permits for filming *Mars Attacks!* David Letterman's producers wanted to film their "mailroom intern" helping out. I jumped at the chance, since I am a big Letterman fan and thought a sketch could highlight our reforms in a nontraditional venue. Tony Blankley vetoed the idea. "Newt detests Letterman."

I returned to Harvard for the orientation of new members to the Russian Duma. Senator Tom Harkin (D-IA) and I covered parliamentary processes and constituent services. At the end of orientation, Oleg Finko, the chairman of the Communist Party of the Russian Federation, rose to thank me. "We are very impressed with your knowledge. If Mr. Gingrich is ever finished with you, would you consider coming to Russia and being the general secretary of the Communist Caucus?" The participants broke into laughter. "I will have to consult with Speaker Gingrich on that," I responded to more laughter.

RED-HANDED

I met with Dan Meyer on April 18 to find out what was happening with the CHO issue. Otto was holding up a growing backlog of procurement actions, including service-contract renewals. Meyer assured me that progress was imminent.

Starting on May 7, I worked with Sue on the next wave of reforms, including refinements in the HIR structure and the cyber-Congress. I also proposed adding explanatory notes to clarify transactions in the public financial reports.

At one of the regular meetings between the CHO and CAO staff, Otto rejected all the reforms out of hand. I blew up at him, stating that I was tired of his "circle jerk" and deserved more professional treatment. Wadel came to my office, very upset with my outburst. "This is not productive. Let me work these things out." Later that month, Meyer, Nussle, and Boehner met with Thomas, demanding that he "back off." This seemed to have some effect, but Thomas found another avenue of attack.

My relationship with Lainhart had deteriorated since he attended the quality sessions. During 1996, he and his staff became more assertive in second-guessing the reforms. Some of this arose from his bias for internal control over management. Many of his recommendations assumed that measurement, alone, would ensure integrity. I assumed that people could "game" any measurement system. Therefore, cultural change had to precede and follow measurement and accountability. "It's incredible, but people come into my office and just lie to my face," complained the secretary of agriculture (and former congressman), Dan Glickman, while we visited before a joint meeting of Congress. I witnessed similar gaming at the GSA. In one instance, we measured "work in progress" (WIP) to track how fast our warehouse personnel were processing agency supply orders. In the first two months, WIP fell from forty-five days to nine days. We were impressed until we discovered that warehouse managers had unilaterally redefined WIP to meet our goal.

Lainhart directly challenged Chad Mosley on certifying the House's data systems and network, including Chad's use of the National Institute of Standards and Technology (NIST) guidelines for software development life cycle (SDLC). Lainhart was adamant that Mosley use the SDLC approach developed for the Federal Aviation Administration (FAA), even though both the FAA and the GAO had found numerous problems with this "homegrown" approach. Lainhart held his ground, and we held ours, which resulted in a series of blistering reports by the inspector general's technology team.[6]

Lainhart's more aggressive tone and approach concerned all of us. We had contracted with Ernst & Young to "shadow" Lainhart's and Price Waterhouse's auditors. Up until a day before the draft audit's release, everyone verified we had a "clean opinion." However, at the last minute, Thomas rejected our revisions of the CHO's mass-mailing authorization policy and procedures. This appeared as a "material weakness" in the audit, leading to a "qualified opinion," even though no federal funds were at risk. House Rules required members to reimburse the House from personal funds if there were any overpayments. Both Simon and Anfinson considered it a "screw job." We were all furious that CHO inaction, and Lainhart's interpretation, could deprive us of a fully "clean" audit. We considered it an act of sabotage.

We worked on rebuttals through most of July. We disagreed or "non-concurred" with a majority of the findings and recommendations. We thought we had a good working relationship with Tom Craren and his team and did not understand what had happened.

"Scot, you need to hear this," said Anfinson, entering my office with Craren late on Monday, July 22. They looked serious and got right to the point. Craren did most of the talking. He explained that Bill Thomas had been intervening in his team's operations since February. Thomas had made "strong suggestions" on what the audit should find and recommend. In the last few weeks, Thomas had personally met with Craren, demanding he amend the audit with a criticism of my management style. When Craren refused, Thomas had threatened him with cancellation of their contract.

"Scot, you and your team have been one of the most cooperative organizations we have ever worked with," Craren concluded. "What you have done is nothing short of a miracle."

We discussed what needed to happen next. Craren was willing to meet with Gingrich to document "Thomas's unethical and possibly illegal actions." Gail called upstairs. She reported that Gingrich was not available at that time. Craren gave me his various contact numbers, including his home number. "I have never been confronted with such wanton abuse of power. Please help me with this situation," Craren pleaded as he departed.

I swung into action. I decided to bypass Wadel and send a memo directly to Gingrich requesting a meeting. Dan Meyer called me moments later. "Do you really want to meet with Newt or can we discuss the matter?"

"I must meet with the Speaker on an urgent personal matter," I explained.

At nine o'clock the next morning, I met with Meyer and Gingrich. I related my conversation with Craren. The Speaker was visibly shaken. "I need all of Craren's numbers. Rest assured, I will speak with him immediately."

I then related Thomas's threat to "tear down every brick of the institution."

"Would you please repeat what he said?" asked the Speaker. When I repeated Thomas's threat, Gingrich was shocked. Gingrich then asked how things could have gotten so out of hand. "Haven't you seen my memo?" I asked. "What memo?" he responded.

I handed him my February 16 report. The room was silent as he studied the document for several minutes. His brow furrowed and he looked sternly at Dan. "Why have I not been told about any of this?" Dan looked down, averting his eyes. Gingrich hung his head and murmured, "I should have been told."

Gingrich then looked at me. "What proof do you have?"

"There were three staffers in the room when Thomas made the threat," I explained.

"This situation must end. It may take your leaving, it may take Thomas leaving, or both of you leaving, but it will end," said Gingrich grimly. "We need a meeting on this immediately!"

Craren contacted me later that week, reporting that Gingrich called him at home and that he had related all his experiences with the inspector general, Thomas, and the CHO staff. The Speaker now had all that he needed to take decisive action.

At 11:15 a.m. on Friday, July 26, Gingrich, Nussle, Boehner, Thomas, Meyer, Stacy, Otto, Wadel, Blankley, and I were arrayed around the "T-Rex Room."

"I had the naive notion that we could all work together if the goals were big enough," Gingrich began. He proceeded to "read the riot act" to Thomas in front of all of us. He also looked over at Stacy. "The Oversight staff certainly shares the blame for this breakdown."

He ended this amazing thirty-minute meeting by saying, "I want all of you to find a way to get this behind us and move forward. I do not want to hear about anything like this again."

After lunch, Wadel came to my office, upset that I went around her. I challenged her on not forwarding the memo. "You have lied to me since February."

"Scot, I was trying to work this matter out without making it into a major issue. By taking this to Newt, you may have put yourself and the reforms in jeopardy."

"They are already in jeopardy," I countered. "Thomas will push until someone bigger than him pushes back."

"Still, we shouldn't have to have meetings like the one this morning."

"I agree. If Thomas and his staff stopped turning back the clock and followed what the transition and leadership have been saying for the last eighteen months, this wouldn't be happening."

Sue nodded as if lost in thought and departed. I was completely burned out and called Vicki. We drove toward Harpers Ferry, stopping for Mexican food at Guapo's and losing ourselves in movies.

On Wednesday, July 31, Wadel convened a "peace conference" in 1309 LHOB with Otto, Stacy, and me. Stacy teared up. "The Speaker has never looked at me like that before. It was as if he had discovered I was the enemy!"

I hid my disgust at her attempt to "play victim" and tried to sound conciliatory. "We should get on with the end of the 104th and look for ways to shape expectations when the new members arrive after the election. The transition can start things off with a clean slate. The new members just want their offices operational; they could care less who does it."

"That is exactly my point!" Stacy exclaimed. "If you have a bunch of low-level staff taking care of all of the members' needs, then we will never be able to give credit to members! Services will have no impact! You might as well do away with our committee!" There was a very pregnant silence. I looked at Wadel with a "now you understand what I am up against" look. Stacy proceeded to sail the rest of the way off the cliff. She leaned toward Wadel.

"In fact, that is just what you were really proposing in March! If we had agreed to any of your suggestions, we would have stripped the Oversight Committee of any power it had. We must make sure that members know who is providing the services! We must make sure that the committee is active in administration!"

There was another very pregnant pause.

I broke the silence. "That is why it is important that we sort out who does what for the 105th Congress. Let the transition set the tone and the turf for the future. The 104th is effectively over. Let's just try to get through this Congress."

EVERY BRICK OF
THE INSTITUTION

April 5, 1997 (Cape Palliser, New Zealand)

"I need more film!" I waved at Vicki as she began to make her way along the knife-edge. The cold winds from the Antarctic buffeted us as we hung on to the ridge of basalt jutting into the sea. Just eight feet away, two more seal pups had joined three colleagues, forming a small audience looking over at my camera and me.

A young Maori boy had directed us to the seal colony. The bone-shaking ride along the coast had been worth it. The fishing village of Ngawi was picturesque, and the lighthouse at Cape Palliser was dramatic. This was a moment of a lifetime.

The seals were all around us, some diving into the icy waters, while others basked in the sun. They covered the peninsula. Further into the ocean, the peninsula broke into a series of ridges rising ten feet out of the water. Between each edge were water-filled gaps. The pups had climbed to the top of one such edge; Vicki and I now sat along the facing one.

We were dressed in black sweaters and pants. The seals probably assumed we were just another set of marine mammals. They frolicked with each other, stopped and looked over at us, then returned to frolicking. One of the large female seals kept a watchful eye from another ridge about twenty feet to our right. Her presence reminded us that we were vulnerable to parental attack. We remained wary as we clung to the rocks.

We were taking a much-needed break from working in Wellington. The musings of 1996 had become the reality of 1997; we were working in New Zealand. The Australia and New Zealand (ANZ) Bank was going through massive reengineering. I led the change-management effort. The scope was daunting: $100 billion in assets and forty thousand employees spread across forty-three countries.

We had moved into an apartment within walking distance from ANZ's Wellington office. Our full-time base was in Melbourne, Australia. It had become a dream come true. We made our escape from Washington—a fifteen-thousand-mile escape. It reminded me of a similar break in 1984, when I traveled to Malawi, Africa, to head the Peace Corps. There is nothing more cleansing for the mind than to be in a part of the world where there is little, if any, news from the United States. It is liberating to discover that treaties are signed, heads of state meet, and people go about their lives without American involvement or input from the egos inside the Washington Beltway.

Thomas and Lainhart were searching for us. An odd array of colleagues, many of whom had not talked to us in years, left messages and asked my parents our whereabouts.

Our A Ring allies regularly reported to us. They described the various searches being conducted and how upset our enemies were that we had managed to move on with our lives. Rumors had us in New York, in Canada, and in Europe. Each rumor helped erase our trail. We savored the prospect of healing half a world away from our enemies and their vendettas.

PARALLEL UNIVERSES

The autumn of 1996 saw the formation of two parallel universes. In the Thomas universe, *Roll Call* branded me an enemy of the state. In my universe, Tony Blankley launched another road show and media effort. In this universe, *USA Today*, the *New York Times*, and numerous other news outlets hailed the reforms. Also in this universe, management awards, including one from the Ford Foundation's Excellence in Government program, were bestowed.

In Thomas's universe, the transition to the 105th Congress would be a traditional affair. Incoming freshmen members would be cloistered in a suite of rooms in Rayburn and schooled in the old ways by CHO staff.

In my universe, the freshmen would be treated as if they entered a college campus. They would be free to roam about, be given an orientation "book," and be welcomed by hundreds of willing support staff.

The genesis of the CAO orientation came from John Atkinson. He reported that our databases could be made interactive. A series of meetings with Bennett, Hansen, and DeCain's team brought the initiative into focus. We would develop a full intranet portal that would allow every member to access all CAO information and services online.

The CHO unknowingly gave us the mechanism. They requested that we find a way to hand out laptops to each incoming member that would allow secure e-mail messages from leadership. The laptops should include the searchable databases of the U.S. Code and House Rules, which Dorsey had developed, plus a link to the Library of Congress's Thomas system.

Ken Miller worked with the techies at the National Security Council to acquire state-of-the-art encryption technology linked to a secure server. Each member would have a digital card that changed the PIN every ten seconds. Once this card was inserted into the laptop, a user could access House databases via the secure server. The entire process was vetted through the National Security Agency (NSA). We shared this with Bill Livingood and the Speaker's office as a system that could ensure the continuity of government during any emergency.

HIR loaded each laptop with the CHO-mandated information and links. We then took it to a new level. Thanks to Carole Kordich's "HouseSmart," we had already published information on House services. I now asked each part of the CAO to make "HouseSmart" fully interactive. The major breakthrough came in furnishings. That group came up with an interactive "fabric board" that allowed office staff to mix and match drapes, rugs, paint, and upholstery, and then place work orders directly with the CAO and architect teams. This was years ahead of its time. The entire furnishings catalog and the ordering of items were also placed online, with guidelines on how many items were allowed per office.

Atkinson and Coleman worked with each office on developing their sections of the intranet. It was an amazing example of how things should always be. Stevedores and Web designers, postal clerks and accountants, public employees and private vendors, all worked together to create a revolution in online service. Each week, the associate administrators and I would have an office present its section of the intranet. Bennett, Hansen, and DeCain's team would help us critique each beta site for completeness, accuracy, clarity, and visual impact.

The next phase was beta testing with actual users. Earlier, we had worked closely with Representative Hoekstra and his team to create a "decision support center" available for all House leaders. This was a space, carved out of the old Longworth mailroom, filled with laptops loaded with the latest decision software. A Georgetown-based firm provided the software and the trainers. People could create affinity diagrams, conduct weighted voting, and explore other collaboration and consensus-building tools.

Once Congress went into recess for the 1996 campaigns, we took over the room. Under Bennett's leadership, we brought in various focus groups to "test-drive" the intranet. Besides asking participants to critique each part for completeness, accuracy, clarity, and visual impact, we gave each a "scavenger hunt" list of facts they had to find on the site. We tracked how many mouse clicks it took them to find each item. We then adjusted icons, and navigation, to make sure each item could be found easily and quickly. Bennett even conducted a focus group with retiring members and members who were going to win by default.

Two other components completed this revolutionary orientation. I personally conducted tours of the House floor for groups of CAO employees. I had been appalled that most CAO employees had never been on the floor and didn't know basic facts about the Capitol. Knowledge is not only power, it is pride. The better they understood their role in making the House operate, the more their efforts were "ennobled" and placed into context. I worked with Bud Brown to have docents conduct special tours of the Capitol and had Hasdorff take groups up in the dome. By late October, everyone who wanted to participate was schooled in the history and art of the Capitol. It made every CAO employee a roving ambassador fully ready and able to assist new members and staff when they arrived for the 105th Congress.

The other component was the overall theme and approach to this revolutionary "welcome wagon." Davison and Lynn Borkon, his new team member, brainstormed with me about what could be done. We decided to use the actor William Summerfield to portray George Washington in a welcome video and on flyers and posters. Summerfield regularly portrayed Washington at Mount Vernon and Harpers Ferry. He jumped at the chance. Davison and I drafted a script drawn from Washington's own words about public service and the Congress. We felt that Washington was the only nonpartisan national figure and would be better than welcoming remarks by Gingrich and Gephardt.

On October 29, 1996, we turned the ornate House Reception Room (H-207, off the House floor), or Rayburn Room, into a movie studio. Summerfield's Washington created an amazing juxtaposition of a historical figure logging onto a laptop. It honored the past while embracing the future.[1] Davison produced huge posters that featured Summerfield, with the heading "Let's make history together!" along with addresses to both the CAO intranet and the orientation sites. Jim was so excited that he took one of the first runs to Blankley, who ushered him into see Gingrich. "This is what the cyber-Congress is all about!" beamed the Speaker as he placed the poster over his office's fireplace mantel.

Davison, Borkon, Atkinson, and I arranged for large monitors, with the welcome videos on loop mode, to be stationed at each major location within Longworth, including the office supply and gift shops. Bennett created "How may I help you?" buttons, which also read "Welcome to the 105th Congress." These were distributed to all 630 CAO employees.

The morning of Monday, November 18, was the first workday for new members and their staffs. It dawned to an explosion of the future. I spent two hours on C-SPAN walking through the entire website, showing the whole world what transparency could be like. Staff wearing "How may I help you?" buttons flooded the office buildings. The videos began playing. Within the first twelve hours, the intranet had more than three thousand visits, which quickly climbed to a steady forty thousand hits a day. "You proved to us it could be done. You gave us what we always dreamed should happen!" exclaimed Nussle when we last spoke.

"Stop it! Stop it all this instant!" thundered Otto over the telephone. He invoked Thomas, the CHO, and invectives to no avail. "We should have been in charge of this!"

"Sorry Otto, the Speaker and leadership know about it, and they love it," I responded. He slammed the phone down. We would speak only one more time in our lives.

"DO THE MATH"

One of the major priorities set by the transition was to bring the finances of the House up to generally accepted accounting principles (GAAP). We "triaged" this activity by first "stopping the bleeding," thus preventing the undocumented disappearance of hundreds of thousands of dollars. We then created a temporary alternative system to ensure the integrity of ongoing financial operations. In the third phase, we developed procedures and technology that would achieve ongoing financial integrity, full transparency, and ensure compliance with GAAP.

This final phase was to be a common platform not only for the House but also for the Library of Congress, the Congressional Budget Office, and the GAO.[2] The Senate, which remained forever mired in the past, did not show any interest in any of the reform initiatives.

The American Management Systems, Inc. (AMS) "Federal Financial System" (FFS) had been used by twenty federal agencies, including the Departments of State, Veterans Affairs, and the Interior. We were introduced to the system when we temporarily ran payroll through the U.S. Geological Survey (USGS). After gaining CHO approval, Anfinson and his team proceeded to make FFS work by expanding the USGS system into the Congress.

There were multiple phases and many reviews, including reviews conducted by the other congressional entities using the common platform, by Lainhart's team, and by the Price Waterhouse audit team. Every step was vetted, beta tested, and certified before being brought online. Kiko's team worked closely with Anfinson's team to bring "Procurement Desktop" into this system. This was a real-time seamless procurement system that triggered electronic transfers of funds and automatic reporting once the appropriate clearances were logged in.

By September 20, 1996, the first two phases of FFS were complete. Phase 3 took longer than expected. As usual, this was because Otto refused to sign off on various changes in policy and procedures. On May 28, I attended one of the FFS coordination meetings at the urging of Simon and Anfinson. They wanted me to "see Otto in action." It was a dreadful display of capricious and arbitrary intervention. I made sure FFS was on the agenda when things came to a head in July 1996. In June, Anfinson developed a beta test for online searchable financials of all member and House accounts. To force the issue, we had C-SPAN feature the site, showing how the public would soon have access to accurate and timely information on public spending.

Anfinson and I also knew that even an online system using GAAP would be confusing to nonaccountants. We began drafting explanatory notes to be included both online and as part of the printed financial report of the House. Otto vetoed both as "too much information." I then proposed an "editorial board" composed of representatives from leading government watchdog organizations to advise on the clarity of public disclosure. I personally discussed this concept with the heads of Common Cause and the National Taxpayers Union, and was scheduled to meet with Ralph Nader's CongressWatch, when the plug was pulled. A concept paper had been floated among leadership. Representative Boehner dropped by my office to discuss it. "Scot, we all understand what you are trying to do, but this is too public," John began. "Most members are just not ready for this kind of transparency."

FFS was a powerful tool for ensuring financial integrity because of its various "fail-safe" systems. A payment voucher or purchase order could not enter the system without proper documentation. Once in the system, a payment would not be processed if the office had exceeded its authorized balance.[3]

A year into using FFS, there were still glitches. Most member staffs did not have anyone with even basic accounting skills. Anfinson's office included "financial counselors" to train each office on the new system and to help them properly submit payment information. In our "universe," offices would report any vendor who was not getting paid in a timely manner to their financial counselors. In the "universe" of Thomas and the CHO staff, members were to come to them to report payment problems. We worked through the intranet and staff organizations. Thomas worked the House floor, cloakroom, and Republican Conference. Confusion was inevitable, as many members of both parties were still used to the old days when the Committee on House Administration dispensed waivers and favors.

This confusion became public when Representative Ron Klink (D-PA) began having problems paying his telephone bills through FFS. Klink approached Thomas on the floor to complain about his situation. Thomas was dismissive. Klink asked why the CHO was ignoring the needs of Democrats. Thomas retorted, "You do the math."

Klink held a press conference on Tuesday, July 30, to assail FFS and late payment of his long-distance telephone bills. National news stories appeared about the House's financial problems. Klink launched an ongoing series of attacks on the failure of FFS.

I immediately put Jane Bennett on the trail. She met with Klink and his staff. His chief of staff expressed frustration with the CHO. He thought his financial counselor was just part of the CHO staff, and therefore Klink spoke directly to Thomas. When Thomas stonewalled, Klink went to the microphones.[4] This public uproar spurred Lainhart to expand his oversight of FFS. Anfinson and Simon's teams ultimately spent 8,306 staff-hours responding to various inspector-general requests instead of implementing and managing the new system.[5]

When fiscal 1996 ended, we once again returned money to the Treasury to prove Republican frugality, especially in an election year. Thanks to the reforms, we had saved an additional $79,246,004 over projected spending.[6] Before returning funds, we had to set aside enough money to cover expenditures incurred before the end of the fiscal year. Invoices had not arrived, but we knew from our projections that they would arrive in the next billing cycle.

Thomas, *Roll Call*, and many Democrats pounced on this as proof that FFS was not working. The $4.5 million carryover was far less than previous years. It was actually based on solid accounting principles and projections, not the "funny money" games of the past.

Election-year politics sometimes worked in our favor. On Thursday, September 11, Speaker Gingrich made a one-minute speech on the House floor. He held up an ice bucket and boasted about the reforms and their savings. He brandished the ice bucket on *Meet the Press*.

STORM WARNINGS

The shift to election-year politics should have relieved us from the incessant warfare with the CHO. That was not to be the case. Soon after Thomas was caught tampering with the Price Waterhouse audit, Lainhart announced that KPMG had been hired to conduct "performance audits" of the three House officers.

These audits were "intended to review the operations of the three House officers." I had a feeling that this was going to be Thomas's counterattack. My fears were confirmed when John Hummel, Thomas Skibe, and Kevin McFadden arrived at my office. They looked like extras out of *Goodfellas* and acted more like prosecutors than auditors. They also announced that they had originally planned to devote equal time to each officer but that after talks with Lainhart, they would be "beefing up" their review of the CAO.

I alerted both Meyer and Wadel to my concerns. I also raised the concern that the KPMG team had stated that they hoped to release their report in November, "in time for review by leadership before the next Congress." Both Sue and Dan thought that I was being paranoid.

Donna Wiesner became my liaison with KPMG. Simon was pressing me to make him deputy CAO so that he could have more authority in the next Congress. I was concerned that Tom would steer KPMG to recommend such a position.

The KPMG audit could not have come at a worse time. There was disarray within the old A Ring. Some thought I was going to bail out. Others worried that Thomas was going to "get" me. They all feared for their jobs. My assurances did not settle matters. Some worried that I was planning to "refresh" the inner circle with people more willing to launch another round of reforms. I had temporarily stopped the "Breakfast Club" because of the intense work on the transition. There were also signs that some A Ring members were leaking information or cutting deals to insulate themselves from whatever fate awaited me.

The campaign season emptied out the Capitol. I felt alone. Packard was leaving the Legislative Branch Subcommittee to chair the Military Construction Subcommittee. Except for the July 26 meeting, I had not met with Nussle since February. Many nights, I would knock on his hideaway door when I saw lights or heard noises from inside. No one ever answered. Then one day Jane Bennett announced, "Jim has a girlfriend," as she waved newspaper clippings about his impending divorce.[7] A few weeks later Jane dropped by again. "Newt has a lady friend." She described Callista Bisek, who worked on the House Agriculture Committee. "Does everyone up here have zipper problems?" I exploded in exasperation. This was the greatest opportunity for Republicans in two generations. Couldn't they keep their priorities straight?

I kept up appearances. Gloria and I had begun a lecture series in which business and international leaders spoke to all CAO employees. On October 7, Maurice McTigue, a member of the New Zealand Parliament who had led reform in that institution, addressed all employees in the Cannon Caucus Room. It was thrilling to hear insightful and intelligent questions asked by people who had been written off as "the dregs" by the previous regime.

The election of November 5, 1996, resulted in Republican defeat. Dole had been expected to lose, but the GOP lost a net of eight House seats while gaining two in the Senate. It was a mediocre sequel to 1994. Members began filtering back to the Capitol. So did alarming intelligence.

A fax arrived from California. A businessman I knew had attended a rally where Bill Thomas spoke. He overheard Thomas boasting to supporters and sent this report: "Thomas plans to remove you from office. Your departure will clear the way for ousting Gingrich."[8]

I made copies of the fax and shared them with Dan Meyer and Representative Gerry Solomon (R-NY). Gerry and I had been meeting on a regular basis to refine the House Rules for the 105th Congress. Both dismissed the fax as "crazy." Gerry turned to reviewing the orientation website. "This is the single most important thing you have done in the Congress," he declared. "We should send this to every civics class in America."

A colleague of the California businessman called me. "I was swamped but wanted to share what we learned as soon as possible." He proceeded to explain Thomas's plans in more detail. As we compared notes, he speculated that Thomas must have something on Gingrich.

"There are rumors that Newt has a girlfriend," I commented.[9]

"That must be it!" exclaimed my source.

"I would think there is a balance of terror, as Thomas may also have a girlfriend."[10]

"Gingrich wants to be president. Exposing his affair would be devastating. Thomas has the upper hand. You need to be careful. Let's meet when [XX] is in town." My source rang off.

The formal orientation for new members was set for Saturday, November 16. The Republican Conference to finalize rules and officers was scheduled for Thursday, November 20. The CHO-versus-CAO conflict was about to be resolved one way or the other.

THE PURGE

The first meeting of Republican leaders went well. Late on Wednesday, November 13, I began receiving congratulatory calls. They had endorsed me for a second term, and Thomas's version of House Rules had been rejected. I would still report to the Speaker.

Thomas was definitely in a foul mood during the CHO orientation on Saturday. The CHO orientation book was riddled with errors, including dozens of typos. Thomas was darting around, yelling at Stacy and Otto about a variety of miscues. At one point, he stood by a stack of boxes filled with CHO briefing materials. They were supposed to have been on a table for members to pick up as they entered the Cannon Caucus Room. He looked over at two Capitol police officers who were providing security and ordered them to distribute the materials. When they refused, Thomas exploded. "Don't you know who I am? I am important!"

I rolled my eyes and looked over at Henkin, Hasdorff, Bennett, and Davison. We were not to be part of the proceedings but thought it best to come and see what Thomas and his staff had to say. Boehner opened the session and graciously introduced the officers. Tom Simon joined us. He reported on his FFS meeting and then mentioned the performance audit.

"The KPMG guys are really going after you," he commented, relating some of the discussion he overheard. "I should have been your liaison. Donna really alienated them."

I was miffed at his criticism of Wiesner. Tom continued, "What will you do if the audit attacks you?"

"It depends," I began matter-of-factly. "If they launch a bunch of cheap shots, I may have to seek legal counsel. I am not going to allow them to slander me or the reforms."

I left the orientation and returned to my office. Despite Thomas's mood, there were too many unsettling factors in play. I called Vicki and asked her to meet me in my office. We spent the day archiving, packing, and removing all my personal work files for the 104th Congress. This was a planned part of my records management. However, I chose to do it sooner rather than later because of the uncertainty. I had always planned to take the boxes to Harpers Ferry for safekeeping. I have been in politics too long to trust the integrity of the public record. If things "went south," Thomas and Otto would destroy my files. They contained too many "awkward realities" that contradicted their worldview.

Gingrich and the Republican leaders reconvened late Saturday to complete their work on the rules for the 105th Congress. Disturbing rumors were rippling through the Capitol as I finished my C-SPAN program. DeLay wanted to see me.

I called Wadel to see what she knew. The reporting relationships had been "clarified." All House officers would be directly under the CHO. The Speaker was completely taken out of the loop! Sue tried to calm me down. "We need to get through the leadership elections. We will take this one step at a time. Just let things happen. We will revisit the matter in the new year."

DeLay was heading out the door for a meeting. We met outside my escape door. Tom was furious about the rule change. "I can't believe they are rewarding Thomas after all he has done to stop the reforms!"

Tom related what happened on Saturday. The draft of the House Rules Solomon and I had prepared was "revisited." Thomas took control of the proceedings. Gingrich was very passive. When DeLay and Armey raised objections to Thomas's wording, Newt announced he had reconsidered his position and now thought it best to consolidate reporting relationships under Thomas.

"Scot, the revolution is over!" exclaimed DeLay as we walked toward his car. "Newt has sold us out to Thomas. You need to save yourself!"

I walked back to my office, visibly shaken. Hasdorff and Henkin asked what I had heard. I shook my head and waved them off.

A few hours later, Anfinson called. He had just met with Lainhart regarding FFS. He related that, in the course of their conversation, Lainhart complained how he and his team had had to work all weekend on the CAO management audit. Thomas had demanded that a draft be ready before the Republican Conference on November 20. "I think you know what that means," Tom began with a note of worry in his voice. "Thomas wants to use the Lainhart draft to derail your reappointment."

We discussed how this was déjà vu from the July Price Waterhouse report. "I can't believe Thomas thinks he can get away with it," I commented.

"You should call Lainhart and explain what is happening," offered Anfinson.

"Don't you think he may be in on it?" I countered.

"It can't hurt to hear him out. Maybe something can be done." Anfinson rang off.

I called Vicki. She was very upset about DeLay's news. We weighed options. Life under the CHO would be pure hell. Otto would be the de facto CAO. "It is clear that Thomas wants to be the de facto Speaker," observed Vicki.

We reviewed what should be done next. We decided to avoid Wadel but to try to get with Meyer. A call to Lainhart might flesh out details to guide our countermoves. So I called him.

Lainhart sounded frazzled. He complained about the long weekend trying to meet the new deadline. "You understand," I began, "that this is all about politics and not about management. You are independent. You should do a thorough, professional job, not just a hurry-up one for Thomas." I could hear Lainhart take a deep breath on the other end of the line. He hurriedly ended the call.

On Tuesday, I drafted a note to Meyer about the call and my concerns that Thomas was using KPMG the way he had tried to use Price Waterhouse. These days were filled with good-bye meetings with retiring members, including old friends Bob Walker and Toby Roth. I also met with Representative Bob Ney (R-OH) to brief him on the CAO orientation website. All were jovial and assured me that the current setback on rules could be worked out.

Vicki arrived with our granddaughter, Amanda. We took her to the House floor. The chamber was empty. Amanda played her own version of one-person "hide and seek," running and ducking among the rows of seats. Vicki and I surveyed the "representatives' retiring rooms," which, along with the hallway, was also known as the Speaker's lobby (H-212–H-214). This was technically the clerk's domain. Joan DeCain had found a way to work directly with the parliamentarian and the architect of the Capitol to clean up and modernize the space. She wanted us to assess what could be done. It was a mess. It looked like a seedy men's club. I wrote down a long list of ideas, and then Vicki and I enjoyed the solitude of the chamber.

On Wednesday, I went up to the Speaker's corridor to deliver my memo to Meyer. Gingrich's stepfather had just died, so everyone was in a somber mood. A meeting had just adjourned in the T-Rex Room. I waved at Fred Fielding. Fred walked up to me, smiled, put his hand on my shoulder, and without saying a word, walked into Tony Blankley's office.

I watched as Gingrich walked out of the meeting room and down the hall to the private bathroom. I decided not to give the Speaker a copy of the memo, given his stepfather's passing. I watched as he walked alone back from the bathroom, head down. I briefly gave him my condolences. He looked up grimly and thanked me, and then we parted.

Later, I dropped in on Blankley. I gave him a copy of my memo raising issues about the independence of the inspector general.[11] "You might want to stick your head into Dan's office. I think he wants to see you," Tony said gravely.

I went next door and said hello to Dan. He looked up from his telephone and told me he would be a few minutes, and to wait outside. Within minutes both Sue Wadel and Arnie Christiansen, the deputy chief of staff, entered the room. Sue turned to me. "We'll be just a minute."

A few minutes later, Sue ushered me into Dan's office. She gestured toward a large wing chair. "Not the comfy chair!" I protested, thinking I would lighten the mood with a Monty Python reference. It didn't work. Dan began.

"Scot, did you call the inspector general on Monday?"

"Yes."

Dan hung his head. "Then it is over."

"Huh?" I queried. Dan handed me a memo from Lainhart. In it, Lainhart said I had threatened him and tried to derail the audit. "This is all lies. I never said anything like this."

"Well, no matter what was said, Thomas is demanding you resign," continued Meyer.

We went back and forth about what had or had not happened. "Why did you call him at all?" Dan asked.

"Anfinson and Vicki thought it would be a good idea, and I agreed."

"You should have come to me," Wadel said, leaning forward.

"Sue, you have lied to me for more than eight months. I wanted to see for myself."

"Scot, this is going to cost you your job." Dan then proceeded with details of the "endgame." I would "disappear," feigning illness, until other details were decided. My suggestion that Dorsey be acting CAO was deemed "unacceptable to Thomas." Dan sighed and concluded, "At least we don't have to tell many people. The conference has been postponed."

I returned to my office and called Vicki. She immediately came to my office. Henkin and Hasdorff had left for the day. I called Nussle.

"I feel ashamed that I didn't call you first," Nussle began. "I just can't believe this is happening." We reviewed the series of unfortunate and inexplicable events. Nussle lightened the mood by commenting on the welcome wagon and intranet. "I will always remain amazed at all you have accomplished."

DIASPORA

The first decision was to complete the removal of important items from my office. Washington protocol defines memorabilia as personal property, so Vicki and I concentrated on removing all personal working documents to make sure the history of the CAO was preserved.

The second decision was whether to disappear or do something else. Things went so bad so fast; I wanted to do something unconventional. If I just disappeared, whatever had been set in motion and whoever set things in motion could cover their tracks and the full truth would never be known. My reappearance might throw the cover-up into disarray. I also weighed the possibility that Thomas wouldn't honor any deal anyway.

On Thursday, November 21, I came into the office as normal. Terri Hasdorff and Gail Henkin asked about my late-night meetings. I shrugged, saying they related to the rule changes. Phil Kiko came by for his scheduled meeting on procurement matters, and then we walked together over to the CHO office for the scheduled meeting with Otto.

As I walked in, Dorsey looked at me quizzically. Simon looked as if he had seen a ghost. He was speechless for several minutes and seemed very distracted. Otto poked his head in, scowled, and then left. It was ten minutes before he came back into the room. A moment later, Sue Wadel knocked on the hallway door and asked to see me.

As I cleared the door, Sue violently grabbed my arm and spun me around. "What the hell do you think you are doing?" she screamed. I saw terror, not anger, in her eyes. I explained that I wanted to attend this one meeting and then depart as per the agreement.

"There is no more agreement! You are out as of now!" She began to escort me to the elevators with the intent of walking me back to my office. When we rounded the corner, the elevators were full, and we proceeded to the next set.

"Sue," I began in a conversational tone. "What is this really about?"

She stopped and handed me a memo. It was from Tom Simon to Lainhart, dated November 19. "I must warn you that Scot Faulkner will take legal action if you criticize his management of the CAO," the memo began. It went on for several more paragraphs, stating that I was seeking Lainhart's removal and that I had to be stopped.

It all started to make sense. If Simon aspired to be deputy CAO, why not go for CAO? Poisoning the strained relationship between Lainhart and me was underhanded but obviously effective. I related Simon's machinations to Sue. "He has to go," she announced.

We walked back to my office, and I wrote a "resignation" letter. Basically, I just took my reappointment request letter, which outlined the accomplishments of the 104th, and changed the last line from "I look forward to serving you" to "I am informing you that I will not seek reappointment." I chose not to formally resign, leaving options open. I told Hasdorff and Henkin a short version of what had happened. They were shocked and appalled. We worked on various broadcast announcements to inform the CAO team, and then I left.

Back in Harpers Ferry, I began collecting my thoughts, pursuing employment options, and ensuring an orderly retreat. I called Blankley to discuss Thomas, my inspector-general memo, and what might happen to Newt. I called Davison to work on media strategy for the anticipated *Roll Call* attacks. *Roll Call* was gleeful in my downfall. Their editorial cheered the news that Thomas would run the CAO. They portrayed my tenure as one long series of mistakes and screwups. They concluded by embracing their parallel universe: "The truth is that Faulkner seems to have been hired as much for his political dependability as his management expertise. We trust that House leaders won't make the same mistake again."[12]

On Monday, November 25, Jeff Trandahl was named acting CAO. He immediately agreed to move the Office of Publications back to the clerk's office. Joe Simpson was then punished for his loyalty to me and eventually fired in a wanton act of retribution.[13] Carle's reign of terror and personal abuse of her office led to her removal during the 105th Congress.[14]

Vicki worked with my personal staff to retrieve all my books and memorabilia. Harkening back to military history, we made sure Hasdorff "saved the colors." My House flag, complete with all the "battle ribbons" heralding each reform victory, arrived in Harpers Ferry.

Trandahl may have been acting CAO, but Dorsey worked closely with Otto on how best to "cleanse" the CAO office. On Tuesday, December 3, the A Ring loyalists received their terminations. Anfinson, Wright-Simmonds, Henkin, Hasdorff, Hansen, Bennett, McEnery, and Wiesner were all fired. Simon got his walking papers at the same time.

I released statements decrying the "Christmas purges" to various friendly media contacts. The Speaker's office was flooded with telephone calls, faxes, and letters from my supporters both within the CAO offices and among the public. People began to realize what was really happening and were incensed.

Just before Christmas, I met with the people who sent me the fax from California. They went into more details about what was overheard and what they had learned since. Thomas's plan was straightforward. He would neutralize Gingrich with the threat of exposing his mistress. He would eliminate me and resurrect the CHA, thus regaining the power once held by Charlie Rose. Using that reconstituted power, he would exploit the disarray resulting from aborting the revolution and elevate Livingston to Speaker. I passed this new information on to Blankley and other allies, and then turned my attention to personal issues.

Brad Nash died on January 1, 1997, at age ninety-six. I was saddened to lose a good friend and mentor. Two days later, the 105th Congress opened with the Thomas rules being adopted. Trandahl was CAO, reporting directly to the newly resurrected Committee on House Administration. Stacy Carlson and Sue Wadel departed for the private sector. Otto was now in control. His first two acts were to dismantle the CAO intranet and Channel 25.

Vicki and I moved in a new direction. We were quietly married by Reverend James Ford, the House chaplain, in Henry Clay's old Speaker's office in the Capitol (HB-25) on Valentine's Day. My parents, Justin Logsdon, and Terri Hasdorff attended the ceremony. A week later, Vicki and I departed to live in Australia and New Zealand.

That should have been the end of the story. But Thomas was not satisfied with victory. He wanted a victory like that of Rome over Carthage. He proceeded to "salt the earth."

Lainhart and the KPMG team began a new "investigative" report on my tenure. This time they brought CAO employees before an inquisition. Employees were threatened that if they did not provide sufficient "dirt" on me, they would be fired and prevented from being employed anywhere in the legislative branch.

Calls, faxes, and e-mails from my allies chronicled this horrific abuse of power. Ken Miller wrote, "The Inspector General is doing the bidding of Oversight. They know Oversight was the fly in the ointment. They stopped everything we tried to do. Now they want to blame anybody but themselves." Several wrote to Gingrich, exposing the inquisition in detail and documenting how they were pressured to attack my tenure. Ben Lusby wrote, "The House is determined to paint Faulkner's performance as grossly inadequate." Bill Crain and Jim Davison submitted a joint letter stating, "We are concerned that the Office of the Inspector General is receiving directions and/or assistance from Otto Wolff and the Committee on House Oversight. This puts the independence and objectivity of the Office of the Inspector General into question."[15] Nothing was done to stop it.

I had some solace in May 1997. Journalist Ron Kessler had interviewed me during the media road show of 1996. His book, *Inside Congress*, portrayed me as one of the few who tried to clean up Congress.[16] The chapter featuring my reforms was reprinted in the *Washington Post*.[17] This positive coverage in the "real world" enraged Thomas. He expanded his effort to track me down and force me to come before their inquisition.

While visiting the outback in Australia, I sent Lainhart a postcard stating that "I was geographically unable to testify," and affixed a stamp featuring a cattle inspection station. "That should confuse them," I mused.

The July 1997 report by the inspector general was an amazing work of fiction. It went well beyond the December report. It made Vicki its centerpiece. Lainhart accused her of being an unpaid chief of staff and running things behind the scenes. Besides the report being totally false, I found it ironic that the inspector general would overlook all the paid sinecures that members created for wives, relatives, and mistresses, while attacking Vicki for occasionally volunteering to help me. The report also claimed that I had cost the House millions of dollars by delaying the reforms. They concluded that the reforms finally happened because of the leadership of Bill Thomas.

The draft report, with many names and unfounded allegations, was leaked to the media. A less damning report was made part of the official file months later. To this day, political enemies anonymously send copies of Lainhart's reports to my clients and colleagues in the hopes of tripping up my career. They will never forgive me for making the reforms happen and exposing their misdeeds.

The remaining House revolutionaries tried one more time to reverse things. On July 16, 1997, a small band of "true believers," along with De-Lay and Armey, mounted a revolt against Gingrich. This ill-fated "palace coup" weakened both the plotters and the Speaker. Gingrich's mounting ethics problems made his last months like a virtual "house arrest."[18] His power diminished with each passing day. In December 1998, Bill Thomas played his final card. Representative Bob Livingston (R-LA) prepared to ascend to the Speakership. Only Livingston's own "zipper problem" foiled Thomas's plan.

After the failure of the "palace coup," the Republican revolution was deemed officially over. As the 106th Congress began, Gingrich was gone. Livingston was gone. Walker and Solomon were both gone. Except for a dwindling band of "true believers," most House Republicans succumbed to the enticements of power, prestige, and money. Their embrace of the "dark side" would lead to individual and collective ruin. Bill Thomas, with his vision of old-style power, remained the only person left standing.

★ INTO THE ABYSS ★

May 25, 1999 (Brussels, Belgium)

"Gares du Midi, s'il vous plaît."

"Eurostar, monsieur?"

"Oui."

The taxi pulled away from Management Centre Europe on rue de l'Aqueduc.

I was midway through my quarterly meetings in Europe. My Brussels team continued their planning for conferences in Reykjavik and Nice, while I headed to London for the International Quality and Productivity Center's conference on shared services at the Dorchester.

The entire world was finding new ways to improve services and operations while cutting costs and improving profits. The dawning of the twenty-first century promised a true global economy, linked by the Internet, in which everyone could compete on a fair and level playing field. In a few years, this would be chronicled in Tom Friedman's seminal work, *The World is Flat*.[1]

"Every place in the world except Washington, D.C.," I mused to myself as the Eurostar silently dipped under the English Channel. If there is a trailing edge for management, it is the federal government.

It was, therefore, a major disappointment that, even at its zenith, the Republican congressional revolution did not fulfill its most basic goal—to improve the operation of government. Throughout the 104th Congress, the Appropriations Committee and the various authorizing committees failed to launch meaningful reviews of government operations.

This lack of "indictments" resulted in the public not understanding the budget battles of 1995 and 1996.[2] During this time, the government was shut down in a major standoff with the Clinton administration. The result was a stalemate and the perception of a Republican defeat.

Still smarting from this sequence of events, the status quo-oriented Republicans in Congress chose a safer path. They would be content with minor victories, tactically scaling back Clinton budget proposals, but shying away from major reforms. The budget "hawks" and reformers were eclipsed by the "cardinals" of the House Appropriations Committee. It did not take long for Republicans to realize that being "Santa Claus" was preferable to being "Scrooge." By 1997, they were well on their way to embracing earmarks and spending increases, along with their Democratic colleagues. In the process, oversight efforts dramatically shrank, as Republicans did not want to anger potential allies within the bureaucracy and jeopardize pet projects. After the July 1997 palace coup failed, it was all downhill until their defeat in 2006.

METAMORPHOSIS

The odyssey of the Republican Party from the party of reform and smaller government to the party of abuse and big government began many years earlier.

In 1978, several pro-life organizers who had run Jimmy Carter's Iowa caucus campaign arrived in Virginia to discuss "payback." They were still stung by Jody Powell's remarks after Carter had won the Iowa Democratic caucuses. In a postcaucus meeting, Powell backed off Carter's pro-life pledge. When challenged for reneging on a promise, Powell dismissed the pro-lifers with several flippant comments about moving on. These grassroots leaders now wanted to redirect their legions of supporters toward helping the Republicans defeat Carter. Their first show of force would be on behalf of Richard Obenshain's 1978 Senate race in Virginia.[3]

Their fervor and tireless efforts paid off. Obenshain shocked the national Republican establishment by defeating a better-financed John Warner for the nomination. A few weeks later, Obenshain was killed in an airplane crash. The pro-life forces proceeded to help Warner become Senator.

In the run-up to the 1980 presidential campaign, the conservative movement reached out to the pro-lifers as well as to groups describing themselves as pro-family and Christian. I was part of the coordination group for this new element within the conservative movement. It was called "Library Court" and met every Thursday at Paul Weyrich's office. There emerged natural alignments between these newcomers and the traditional conservative activists. This included opposition to the Carter administration's aggressive funding of ultra-left groups. Howard Phillips launched his "Defund the Left" movement to help Reagan's landslide in 1980.

However, there were also troubling signs that this coalition challenged many conservative principles. The first was the pro-lifers' liberal Democratic Party roots and their unwillingness to focus on issues they viewed as irrelevant to overturning *Roe v. Wade*. "If Castro landed in Miami, and took the pro-life pledge, they would make him the president," mused one activist.

This uneasy alliance raised basic issues about conservatism during the Reagan administration. The "Christian Right" wanted to take control of government and redirect its resources and powers to further their agenda. The "traditional Right" wanted to dramatically reduce the role and size of government, harkening back to its libertarian roots.

The Christian Right grew rapidly in power. During the 1980s, it methodically took control of state Republican Party organizations. These takeovers occurred in many caucus-based states where the Christian Right could outvote the smaller cadres of traditional party activists. The balance tipped further as many of the "Cold War" or "anti-Communist" Republicans retired, died, or became less active after victory was achieved over the Soviet Union.

The biggest schism happened in 1989. George H. W. Bush was now president, in large part because he framed his candidacy as "Reagan's third term." It did not take long for Bush to implement his real agenda, which was that of the old Rockefeller 1964, Ford 1976, and Bush 1980 moderates. By the end of March 1989, Secretary of Transportation John Skinner fired all Reagan "holdovers" in his department. He proudly announced that he was the first to "cleanse" his department of Reaganites. This was met by cheers from the other Bush cabinet members. As the purges spread through the Bush administration, conservatives vowed revenge. Their ire was fueled by Bush's reversal of his "no new taxes" pledge and dramatic increases in government spending and regulation. The conservatives paid Bush back for these betrayals by voting for Ross Perot in 1992. "Bush fired us. We fired Bush!" they declared on election night.

The 2000 presidential election marked many turning points. A symbolic one was the media literally changing the colors of the electoral map. During the twentieth century, the media portrayed Republican states as blue and Democratic-held states as red. This echoed the colors used throughout Europe for conservative and right-wing parties versus labor or socialist parties. This is why old video of the 1980 and 1984 presidential election coverage shows the United States all blue for the Reagan landslides and why "Blue Dog" Democrats were congressmen from "blue" or Republican states who supported Reagan.

That color shift was also symbolic of the changes happening inside the Republican Party. More and more, Republican rhetoric reflected the themes of the Christian Right. Even though the Republican congressional landslide of 1994 was based largely on traditional conservative themes of strong national defense, law and order, and reducing the size of government, many congressional races were won because individual candidates added pro-life, pro-family, social conservative values, or Christian issues, to their platforms.

As the Republican congressional revolution was playing out in House operations, an increasing number of members were seeking ways not to shrink government but to turn government "around." "Social" legislation and spending became more important than government reform.

The failure of the budget battles during the 104th Congress led to Republicans *using* government instead of *cutting* government. Although traditional conservatives like Representative John Kasich (R-OH) made great strides in passing budget resolutions that outlined a bold change agenda, the "third party" in the House, the Appropriations Committee, remained the primary engine for expanding government spending. The budget resolutions were nonbinding and were ultimately ignored. Just as in earlier Democratic Congresses, the budget resolutions became empty "press release" efforts while appropriators "kowtowed" to parochial interests.[4]

More and more Republicans behaved like Democrats as they embraced the concept that spending and earmarking federal funds ensured reelection more than holding the line on spending and conducting oversight. The Democrats had been the past masters of earmarks, driving such spending to $10 billion spread over 1,439 pet projects. The Republicans proved even better spenders. After a one-year dip in earmarks for fiscal year 1996, the Republicans simply took over the "pork" process. By fiscal year 2005, they had nearly tripled the Democrats' record, with $27.3 billion spread over 13,997 local projects.[5] By 2006, even budget hawks were supporting record expenditures and deficits,[6] and Bush was signing every budget-busting bill into law.

The Republican Party and the conservative movement were morphing in other ways. The conservative movement had proud historical and intellectual roots dating to the Founding Fathers' embrace of inalienable rights, basic freedoms, and the concept of government arising from the will of the governed. During this period, Adam Smith wrote *The Wealth of Nations*, giving the world its first comprehensive manifesto on free trade and economic liberty.

For more than 220 years, conservatives measured their candidates and their agendas against these time-honored principles. By the mid-1990s, conservatives were abandoning these timeless guidelines. They were replaced by cults of personality and partisanship. As the sexual exploits of President Clinton permeated the national psyche, increasing numbers of conservatives and Republicans grew to view anything associated with Clinton and the Democratic Party as wrong and evil.

Conversely, when George W. Bush became president, these same activists, columnists, and elected officials then viewed everything Bush did as good for the country. The definitions of "conservative" and "Republican" became defined by what Bush did or didn't do, not by timeless guidelines. One of the most bizarre episodes in the metamorphosis occurred at the Conservative Political Action Conference (CPAC). In a debate between former Judiciary Committee member Representative Bob Barr (R-GA) and Viet Dinh, one of the authors of the Patriot Act, Dinh "urged the CPAC faithful to carve out a Bush exception to their ideological principle of limited government."[7]

Many of these "morphing" Republicans began to view all policies and programs through this lens of Bush and Republican infallibility. They suspended their disbelief and checked their skepticism at the door. They also sank further into blind partisanship, in the process missing numerous opportunities for achieving common political ground and for adopting best practices from across the political spectrum. The principles and practices that led conservatives and Republicans out of oblivion and into power were cut free of their moorings and cast adrift.

The morphing Republicans in Congress took their own actions to cut loose from the shackles of principle. Republicans cut the budget of the GAO by a quarter and eliminated a third of its positions. A party that was once the main watchdog of government spending sliced the GAO to its lowest level since before World War II.[8] Congress abandoned its oversight of the executive branch.[9] Even when Congress did conduct oversight, many times it furthered parochial interests.[10] Republicans in Congress became apologists for George W. Bush and his fiascoes, from Katrina relief to Iraqi reconstruction. Even when Bush's ill-fated appointment of Harriet Miers to the Supreme Court showed that he valued cronyism over ideology, they persisted in asserting that "Bush can do no wrong."

The morphing Republicans and conservatives borrowed heavily from the Democrats to justify expanding the role of government. They began to nationalize local, state, and even private issues. The Terri Schiavo matter, though a heart-wrenching family tragedy, did not justify shredding the Tenth Amendment and lowering the threshold for federal intervention. Gay marriage was another issue that did not warrant usurpation of a state function.

As the morphing Republicans and conservatives drifted ever further from their core beliefs, they drew fire from "true believers" who could not understand why government was growing, spending was spiraling out of control, and government was ever more dysfunctional.

As the Bush fiascoes mounted, it became clear that his administration was less "Reagan-esque" and more an incompetent sequel to the moderate Republicanism of his father. Yet most Republican and conservative leaders failed to raise the alarm. Worse, the politics of 9/11 allowed some to cry "traitor," "un-American," or "You are helping the terrorists" whenever a rational voice, even on the Right, rose up to point out the insanity of it all. Once again, the naked emperors continued their parade, while opposing voices in the crowd were silenced.

This abandonment of principle raised growing concern among the "faithful." A growing chorus of Republicans tried to calm their followers. They first used the "Bush defines what is right" argument. When that failed, they used the old "if you knew what we knew you would understand" argument. Their final line of defense was "We are the only moral ones."

As the 2006 midterm elections loomed, personal behavior became more important than ideas and deeds. Ideally, voters will elect good moral people who then proceed to enact just laws and oversee the implementation of enlightened programs and policies. Reality is more about trade-offs. Flawed people can rise to greatness. Decent people can create disastrous policy.

The moral argument is always risky. Republicans are just as moral, or immoral, as Democrats. Corruption is a function of opportunity, not ideology. There are just as many adulterers and addicts among the Republicans as among the Democrats. Playing the morality card became the Republicans' last line of defense and their leap into the abyss.

EVANS'S LAW

The first signs of the abyss became visible when the Justice Department began investigating the activities of Jack Abramoff in November 2002. Congressional hearings and additional federal probes followed. It was the beginning of a full-scale review of the close association between lobbyists and Congress. By the time the dust settled, two House members (Bob Ney and Duke Cunningham) would be heading to jail and many Washington careers would be ending.

Lobbying has been a fundamental part of government since the beginning of human civilization. It has been around since the first person needed a favor from someone else with more power and influence. This activity did not get its name until favor-seekers began hanging out in the lobby of the Willard Hotel in Washington to accost government officials who stayed at the hotel or came there to eat. Thus, food and lobbying have remained inseparable.

The governance culture of Washington made lobbying a fine art. Two of the great travesties of Washington are "public information" and "public processes." Like the Native Americans of the Arctic who have numerous words for describing snow, so too do the natives of Washington have many different ways of defining what is public. A "public hearing" means allowing a hundred people, mostly Washington lobbyists, to sit in a room to observe a committee, but it rarely means televising or webcasting. A "public document" means printing a few copies and sending them to colleagues, but it rarely means putting the document on the Internet.

Most Washington lobbyists and attorneys make their living by being paid amazing fees to locate public information that should be readily available to the public. To sustain this world of public information that is not really "public," an entire culture has arisen. This culture builds mystical legends and rituals around how basic information and democratic processes are really special and must be handled differently from the way they are handled in the rest of the world.

Lobbyists also act as filters of the public will. All members spend time "hearing" from constituents, either in their districts or through countless letters and e-mails. But most members really only "listen" to lobbyists. This distilling of public input through entrenched and highly paid elites has undermined representative democracy since its inception.

Prior to 1994, the Democrats dominated this bizarre world. They ran every major corporate office, law firm, and lobbying firm in Washington. This made sense in that each special interest wanted to be welcomed by those in power. As long as those in power were Democrats, it stood to reason that Democrats were the preferred lobbyists. Occasionally, Republicans would be hired when there was a need to form bipartisan coalitions to pass legislation.

There has always been a cozy relationship between Congress and lobbyists. Prior to 1994, Democratic members and key Democratic staffers knew that they could ultimately leave Congress to become part of the lobby establishment.[11] There are countless stories of staffers placing overly complex provisions into House and Senate bills so that they could later parlay their knowledge of these provisions into lucrative lobbying positions related to that legislation.

There has also been a long history of family members cashing in on their family ties to Congress. The most famous in recent years was Linda Daschle's rise to become one of Washington's major lobbyists, thanks to being the wife of Senator majority leader Tom Daschle (D-SD). The son and son-in-law of Senator Harry Reid (D-NV), the current Senate majority leader, have also built successful careers aided by their family ties.[12]

Media interest in the relationship between Congress and lobbyists rose as Republicans finally gained control of this last citadel of the Washington establishment. The Republican lobbyist success led to a major realignment of political resources and influence, but it also led to a new array of abuses. Some of these expanded to epic proportions. The sheer scope of lobbying was cause for concern. The total number of registered Washington lobbyists had steadily risen from around 10,000 in 1982 to more than 17,000 by 2001, and then jumped to 34,750 by 2005.[13]

Jack Abramoff's amazing audacity launched countless media stories and books.[14] His shameless exploitation of clients and his unethical largess to members, staff, and leading conservatives stimulated calls for lobbying reform. Except for Abramoff's over-the-top illegalities and antics, Republican-era lobbyists conducted themselves like all their predecessors since the Grant administration. Phil Nicolaides once mused, "Behind every double standard is a single standard." It is worth wondering why the incestuous relationship between Congress and lobbyists did not become newsworthy until the Republicans dominated K Street.

There certainly was illegal and unethical lobbying activity occurring on the Republican "watch." "True believers" were also horrified that the takeover of K Street had resulted in more government, more spending, and more abuses of power. This was the exact opposite of their expectations. The Republicans' fall from grace became the latest proof of "Evans's Law."

M. Stanton Evans was an early "wunderkind" of the conservative movement in the 1950s. He became one of its thinkers and leaders, coining a wonderfully insightful concept of Washington political life. "Evans's Law" states: "By the time one of our people gets to where they can do us [the conservative movement] some good, they stop being one of our people."

No matter what actions were taken, most conservatives seemed to stray from the "faith" or go "squishy" in direct correlation to their acquisition of power. Over the years, numerous efforts were mounted to inspire conservatives to "keep the faith." However, after decades of failure, the maxim of "Evans's Law" remained the reality of Washington.

The lure of power for power's sake always trumped achieving power to further the conservative agenda. Like moths to a flame, conservatives and Republicans alike flew into the brightness of Republican hegemony and exploited it for personal wealth and ambition.[15]

The Republicans had abandoned their principles and their constituency, and now were abandoning their political instincts. In the wake of the lobbying scandals, the Republicans could have trimmed their sails, distancing themselves from those going down in disgrace. The Republicans could also have embraced lobbying reform, turning a negative into a positive by making long-overdue changes in the way Washington worked. They did neither.

During the spring and summer of 2006, the congressional Republicans shied away from meaningful or even superficial lobbying reform. They also further absented themselves from governance. They would log the lowest number of days in session since the Truman administration. The number of committee meetings held was less than half the number held in the 1990s.[16] They had virtually ceded the field to the Democrats.

Thus, by mid-2006, the same dynamics that led to the downfall of George H. W. Bush in 1992 were in motion. The conservatives and Republicans had "morphed" into abominations of themselves, and their traditional base was completely alienated and angry.[17] Worse, Republican rule was being labeled "corrupt" because of their lobbying abuses.

On top of all that, Republicans were also labeled "incompetent" because of Katrina, Iraq, and countless other fiascoes. This was indeed ironic. Prior to George W. Bush's becoming president, Republicans were considered the "adults" running things. This had been particularly true when the Reagan administration took over from Carter. Commentators from across the political spectrum breathed a sigh of relief that Washington was back under "adult supervision." The initial phase of the 1994 Republican takeover of the Congress echoed similar themes of professionalism. But the failure of that revolution and the Republican unwillingness to conduct oversight to the point of being seen as Bush apologists erased their credibility with the electorate. By mid-2006, many Republicans and conservatives openly hoped for Republican defeat in order to cleanse the movement of all the incompetence, corruption, and general dysfunction that had tarnished Republican rule. But things got far worse.

FREE FALL

Even with the scandals and the worsening situation in Iraq, Republicans still had hope. Public trust in Congress had sunk to 1994 levels, down to only 16 percent,[18] but 73 percent of voters still saw no difference between the parties when it came to ethics.[19]

The Republicans still believed that their Christian and social-values voter base would hold. In one test, Speaker Hastert sought to block the FBI search of Representative William Jefferson's (D-LA), offices. Jefferson had been caught stashing $90,000 in bribes in his freezer.[20] The Christian base remained oblivious to Hastert's embracing institutionalism over the rule of law.

That all changed on Friday, September 29, 2006. Representative Mark Foley (R-FL) was a relatively obscure member. ABC News was digging into allegations of inappropriate contact between Foley and House pages, including extensive evidence of sordid e-mails, instant messages, and drunken visits to the page dorm. It seemed that Foley used pages as a "farm team" for selecting gay sexual partners once they turned eighteen years of age. As ABC's investigation neared airtime, Foley resigned. It was just thirty-nine days before the election.

Three trap doors swung open, and the Republican Party plummeted out of power.

Trap Door #1. Unlike the lobbyist scandals, the page scandal was instantly understood by every voter. Protecting young people is practically part of our genetic code. Recent coverage of sexual crimes, including the *Dateline NBC* "To Catch a Predator" series on pedophiles, had increased public awareness of online sexual predators. Many new federal and state laws, including one ironically sponsored by Foley, had been signed into law to expand protection for young people and to increase the penalties for sex offenders. The page scandal was a major breach of trust. If Congress cannot even protect those entrusted to them, where else are they negligent?

Trap Door #2. The Republican response was not horror but parsing. On Monday, October 2, Speaker Hastert made the biggest mistake of the campaign by saying that Foley's e-mails were not as bad as his "IMs" and therefore had not triggered any concern. Vicki and I, as the guardians of our fourteen-year-old granddaughter, were appalled by his remarks. Any caring parent would have been outraged had an adult sent his or her child an e-mail like that. Hastert's parsing showed how out of touch he was with basic parental concerns. His efforts, and those of other Republicans, to turn the issue into a hunt for the Democrat who had leaked the information, further alienated the heart of the Republican constituency.

Trap Door #3. Gays have been part of the modern Republican Party and the conservative movement since Whittaker Chambers exposed Alger Hiss as a Communist spy and Roy Cohn assisted Senator Joe McCarthy's investigation of communism. The role of gays was never brandished, but never denied. When the Republicans morphed and morality became the primary focus, a major disconnect occurred. The morphed Republicans and conservatives would oppose gay rights and make banning gay marriage a national issue, but remain silent on how many gays were in key positions of leadership. Various articles on this dichotomy periodically surfaced but failed to resonate with the general public.[21]

The fact that Foley, who served on the page board, and the clerk of the House, who oversaw the page program, were both gay raised major concerns among the Christian Right. They saw Republicans as betraying their core beliefs. The general public and the media raised the issue of hypocrisy. Were the Republicans trying to have it both ways? Did Republicans really think that they could sustain their official antigay stance while allowing gays to run many of their political operations? Did Republicans think that they could avoid reconciling these two realities?

In the final weeks of the 2006 campaign, the collision of these parallel universes destroyed any hope for the Republicans. Columnist George F. Will invoked the hypocrisy of the fictitious Reverend Elmer Gantry to explain the implosion of the Republican core.[22]

Former majority leader Dick Armey called on Republicans to stop vivisecting their beliefs and to return to some semblance of principle: "We must avoid the temptation to use the power of government to perfect our society and its citizens. That is the same urge that drives the Left and the socialists, and I can assure you that every program or power we give government today in the name of our values can be turned against us when the day comes where a majority of Congress is hostile to us."[23]

Conversely, the Democrats began sounding like a breath of fresh air and like the 1994 Republicans. Representative Tim Ryan (D-OH) declared:

> We have to squeeze this huge, huge monster, where the government loses $9 billion in Iraq and nobody blinks an eye. . . . There are billions of dollars in the Pentagon that go unaccounted for. Programs aren't working. There is going to be a lot of accountability because Democrats have learned a hard lesson: just writing a bigger check doesn't solve the problem. The old Democratic Party of big government is just not going to happen.[24]

The power elite of Washington, now dominated by Republicans, began sounding like the Democrats of 1994. As one story reported, "This focus on oversight 'is going to tie everyone in knots,' says one Washington business lobbyist. 'It will be all oversight all the time with more oversight hearings about more departments every week. It's all bad and it's all going to move in the wrong direction.'"[25]

The results on November 7, 2006, surprised only a few. The Republican era had ended not with a bang but with a whimper.[26]

★ FULL CIRCLE ★

November 15, 2006 (Cumberland, Maryland)

Jack Abramoff arrived early Wednesday morning at the Federal Correctional Institution (FCI). It was the first day of his prison sentence of five years and ten months for defrauding banks of $23 million in his purchase of a Florida casino cruise line in 2000. Additional sentences for fraud, tax evasion, and conspiracy to bribe public officials, weighed against his cooperation with federal prosecutors, still lay ahead.

Before becoming inmate number 27593-112, Jack sent off a final e-mail to friends and colleagues reflecting on his impending incarceration: "I have learned more lessons in the past three years than I have my whole life."[1]

A day later and 130 miles away in Washington, D.C., the Democratic Party took its first steps to reclaim leadership of the House of Representatives. They were mostly missteps that proved very little had been learned from the previous sixteen years.

Within days of the November 7 election sweep, Democratic Speaker-designate Nancy Pelosi backed Representative John Murtha (D-PA) for majority leader. She wished to reward him for taking the lead in galvanizing opposition to the Iraq War. She seemed willing to overlook Murtha's history of skirting ethics issues.

THROUGH THE LOOKING GLASS

In the late 1970s, FBI agents posed as wealthy Arab businessmen offering Congressmen cash and investments in exchange for favors. Murtha was one of the thirty-one public officials targeted in the sting operation. Eventually, one senator and five House members were convicted of bribery and conspiracy.[2]

In a fifty-four-minute FBI videotape, Mr. Murtha meets with the "Arab businessmen" and offers to provide names of businesses and banks in his district where money could be legally invested. They offer to pay him $50,000 to assist their efforts. He responded, "You know, you made an offer. It might be that I might change my mind someday." Later, he explained how that might happen: "I want to deal with you guys awhile before I make any transactions at all, period," he told the fake sheiks. "After we've done some business, well, then I might change my mind. I'm going to tell you this. If anybody can do it—I am not BS-ing you fellows—I can get it done my way. There's no question about it."[3]

Walking away from the bribe helped Murtha avoid the fate of his colleagues. However, this was not the only time Murtha bumped up against ethical issues. In 1997, Murtha joined with Representative Billy Tauzin (R-LA) in blocking outside groups and private citizens from filing complaints directly with the House ethics committee. More recently, his brother Robert "Kit" Murtha, along with Carmen Scialabba, a former aide from Representative Murtha's office, became a senior partner at KSA Consulting, a Rockville-based lobbying firm specializing in appropriations and government contracting.[4] Kit Murtha assisted at least sixteen defense manufacturers with business before the Appropriations Committee, including earmarks supported by his brother John.[5]

On November 14, Murtha then broke with reform-minded Democrats by commenting on proposed ethics legislation in a caucus meeting, "Even though I think it's total crap, I'll vote for it and pass it because that's what Nancy wants."[6]

This was enough to hand Representative Steny Hoyer (D-MD) the majority leader's post on Wednesday afternoon. Hoyer's 149–86 victory showed that most Democrats realized the 2006 election was about more than just Iraq. Pelosi's myopia about Murtha was the first in a series of moves that rewarded loyalists, no matter what their ethical record.[7]

As the Democrats settled into running Congress, oversight returned to pre-Bush levels.[8] Lobby reform superficially went forward, then was circumvented, then died. There was no more talk of a "culture of corruption." While the FBI continued its probes of Abramoff's and Cunningham's colleagues, there were no congressional investigations of member ties to lobbyists. The Democratic Party had benefited from demonizing Republican lobbyists; now they benefited from cozying up to Democratic ones. Political action committees tilted back to the Democratic Party.[9]

The pre-1994 Democratic hegemony returned. Even appropriations earmarks, so reviled during the 2006 elections, quickly rebounded.[10] Bill Livingood was retained as sergeant at arms, and a professional manager became CAO. Thus, the new management culture remained intact, while the Republican era vanished like footprints along a beach in a rising tide.[11]

The cycle of Washington, therefore, began anew.

The day before the fateful November 16 leadership votes, former Speaker Newt Gingrich signaled his interest in running for president in 2008. In an e-mail to various Republican and conservative lists, including *Human Events*, Gingrich announced a new "Twenty-first Century Contract with America," stating, "It is essential that we spend time now thinking about the lessons of 2006 and what has to be done. If we do this, we can accept 2006 as a corrective but necessary interruption in our pursuit of a governing majoritarian party."[12]

REVOLUTION

It is the story of American politics in the twenty-first century—the same players, constantly recycled. Gingrich, the architect of the 1994 Republican revolution, was also the primary architect of its demise. Now he reemerges to reclaim the leadership of the Republicans once again in opposition.

Just as in science fiction, a dead character arises in a new form for a sequel. As America readies for the 2008 elections, everything has come full circle; nothing has really changed.

America would be a much better place if everyone learned lessons not only from the implosion of the Republican Party but also from the multiple mistakes made by both political parties in the Congress over the past twenty-six years. First, the Democrats became arrogant and discon-nected. They became nearly comatose as their colleagues robbed the place blind. Then, in 1994, the Republicans brilliantly swept the compla-cent Democrats from office, only to turn a blind eye to the larceny and foibles of their own colleagues.

On the night of November 7, 2006, the bottom fell out on the Repub-licans in Congress. I watched the end of the Republican era from Avanti's Restaurant in Charles Town, West Virginia. Since returning from Australia, Vicki and I had embraced the old Earth Day motto: "Think Globally, Act Locally." We consulted with clients around the world, but channeled our political energies into local candidates in Jef-ferson County, West Virginia. In the course of nine years, we had com-piled a 24–3 record in helping county and municipal candidates.

These candidates were all part of a reform coalition pushing for open government, slow growth, historic preservation, and environmental pro-tection. They ran in mostly nonpartisan races. Vicki and I ended up sup-porting equal numbers of Republicans and Democrats in the partisan elections. Our coalition was an amalgam of Christian homeschoolers, atheist vegans, Democrats, Republicans, and everything in between. All of the candidates were first-timers. Our greatest feeling of fulfillment was helping these normal citizens who wanted to make a difference be-come successful candidates.

So on November 7, I was pulling an all-nighter helping a Democrat win her closely, contested county commission race. I put the partisan whoops of triumph into the back of my mind as I shuttled between the restaurant and the courthouse across the street. Those of us in the cam-paign's inner circle were immersed in counting votes and keeping a care-ful watch on the new optical-reader technology to ensure an accurate vote count.

My time spent in local coalition politics proved a major truism that I learned early in life—neither party can lay sole claim to upholding the rule of law and honest government. Over the years, I have watched officeholders from both political parties break the law and watched as reform-minded leaders from both parties stepped forward to tangibly improve government.

What holds our democracy together is the "20 percent." No matter what level of government is considered, around 20 percent of those in power meet or exceed our expectations. The balance disappoints. Unfortunately, I had a front-row seat to watch as the Republicans in Congress disappointed me and further validated this "20 percent" rule.

Is there any way Americans can improve this percentage? Are we destined to be disappointed in our elected officials and to be disenchanted with the entire system of representative democracy? Are we damned to watch the same set of flawed players recycle and repackage themselves to then lead us through yet another round of disappointment and disillusionment?

If American democracy is going to last into the twenty-first century, we need to rethink what it means in the context of this century. Just as in the old *The Six Million Dollar Man* television show it was said, "We have the technology—we can rebuild him," so too can we rebuild democracy.

The first step in rebuilding American democracy is to get over denial. For much of the twentieth century, our national government has actually been an oligarchy. A small elite has run our nation. If we are going to rekindle democracy, we must first understand that oligarchy is not the best form of government. As long as a small group of highly-networked professionals rotate between governing and lobbying in Washington, D.C., true democracy will be a fiction.

Some pundits cynically argue that America can never be a true democracy. They like to point out that more people know who is competing on *American Idol* than for public office. The elites of Washington devote lifetimes to mastering issues that would bore most Americans. The pundits recoil from high voter turnouts and ask, "Do we really want all those ignorant and apathetic couch potatoes deciding our future?" Many advocates of democracy promote only the selective participation of their political allies and special-interest voters.

In this worldview there is no way we can ever break the 20 percent barrier. The system, the culture, and the oligarchs work against change, accountability, and democracy.

The oligarchs can easily cope with and absorb new infusions of House members and staffs because they know most will succumb to the temptations of political office (remember "Evans's Law"). Their other line of defense is keeping everything they do from the public. They know that the "mere mortals" among the citizenry lack the time and resources to pry open the system and find out what is really going on. Ignorance and apathy are their greatest allies.

Various efforts to rein in the oligarchy have been tried and they have all failed. Bipartisan gerrymandering prevents true competition in all but fifty or so districts out of 435. Term limits have been shot down in the courts and ignored by most who espoused them. Even if they did work, term limits would toss out the productive 20 percent along with the rest, depriving Americans of the dedicated public servants who keep things from falling apart. If Americans wish to improve their government, they need to consider changing the "rules of the game."

GET RID OF THE MONEY

The Washington oligarchy is fueled by money. The congressional schedule is altered to make way for fund-raisers, even if doing so holds up important legislation. The "Tuesday–Thursday" House schedule was designed for fund-raising and campaigning. Even with ethics and campaign rules, most congressional staffers spend time helping raise campaign funds. Congressmen realize they must raise more than $10,000 a week, every week, to be ready for the next election. That obsession poisons everything. The Washington elite is capable of creatively avoiding every campaign reform and financial disclosure. There is always a way to beat the system.

It is time to federally fund congressional campaigns. The British have been publicly funding campaigns for decades, and the world hasn't ended. American presidential campaigns have been publicly financed for years, and no one thinks that has hurt democracy. Although public financing might strengthen the roles of political parties, at least a member and his or her staff would be able to opt out of the money treadmill. Other reforms would be needed to keep the political parties and "independent" expenditures from end-running this arrangement, but there would be a fundamental shift in the way congressional business is conducted. No more "silver bullets" from lobbyists to swap donations for votes. No more juggling of the legislative schedule so that members can attend private fund-raisers. The people's business would finally become the main business of Congress.

LIMIT THE DAMAGE

The main problem with the current oligarchy is that it is so relevant in our daily lives. Government has grown, even under the Republicans. The Bush dogma shredded the Tenth Amendment of the Bill of Rights, which reserves many powers and prerogatives for the states. Federalism has given way to nationalism. We are still nowhere near France's strict national-government structure, but we are passing the British, who, themselves, are moving toward more local control. The so-called war on terror has expanded the federal government's involvement in private matters. Christian moralists and security alarmists seek to limit our privacy even further.

If you look at places like Australia and New Zealand, their national governments are generally irrelevant. People go about their daily lives in freedom, prosperity, and security without needing to worry about what is going on in the capitals of Canberra and Wellington. Major newspapers cover business and view elected officials as comic relief or as a sideshow to the main events of life and commerce. If only our national budget, debt, and tax burden could be reduced so that the oligarchy's impact on our lives shrank back to manageable levels.

Limiting the reach of the federal government is fraught with ideological land mines. Everyone has a special interest they feel should be addressed at the national level. Rolling back the reach of government may be viewed less as a redressing of imbalance and more as an insidious effort to deprive a group or issue of the protection and resources it deserves.

Therefore, it is time to limit government at the structural level. Limit federal spending to a fixed percentage of the previous year's GNP. Only a two-thirds vote of both houses of Congress could permit the government to exceed that limit. Using the previous year's GNP means no one can play budget-projection games. The number is the number.

Within this framework everything is on the table and competing for resources. Unlike previous budget limitations, this one starts with a real number, and no one can game the figures. It would force Congress to make real decisions and cope with real consequences and trade-offs.

MOVE THE CAPITAL

It is time to change all the ground rules of Congress and evolve from "representative" democracy to "direct" democracy.

One of the main reasons democracy worked in America is that the Constitutional Convention, in 1787, decided that it was important that the new nation have a completely new capital. The Founding Fathers feared the mayhem that arises from governing within a major existing city and then proposed and passed Article I, Section 8 of the Constitution, which established a federal district outside of any state.[13]

Locating America's capital in a malaria-ridden swamp meant that it took decades for the existing power elite and entrenched interests to gravitate permanently to Washington, D.C. By the time the federal government eradicated malaria and air-conditioned its buildings, America had enjoyed nearly 150 years of a fresh start.

Many other countries saw the wisdom of locating capitals in obscure and undeveloped areas. Canada chose the little fur-trading village of Ottawa in 1857. Australia moved its government to Canberra in 1927. Brazil started carving Brasília out of the jungle in 1960.

If America wants to free itself of the shackles of oligarchy, it is time to once again relocate the capital. This does not mean moving everything to Fargo, North Dakota. We need to use current and emerging technology to move government away from its current power center, break open the current system, and reallocate power back to the people.

If "representative" democracy has ceased to be representative, save for the oligarchs, then we should explore returning to the roots of "direct" democracy. In the fourth and fifth centuries BC, all those effected by the government of Athens met to decide policy. In the twenty-first century, a collective meeting of 300 million Americans can only occur using technology. It would not be practical to turn everyone into perpetual parliamentarians, but there are ways to introduce the concept of "direct" democracy into key elements of our government in order to eradicate the most wanton abuses of power.

The foundation for citizens having direct input in their government was laid down in the Magna Carta. In 1215, the right to due process and the right to a jury trial became codified in Western law. In a jury trial, normal citizens interact with officers of the court to decide cases. For nearly eight hundred years, this most direct of democratic actions has proved that citizens take their duty seriously and that this mix of public and private input clearly and equitably enforces the law far more often than not. Why not add new ways for citizens to interact with their government?

DIRECT DEMOCRACY IN BUDGETING

April 15 is an ominous day for most Americans. Tax day is the one day we all feel the impact of the federal government. Imagine if tax day also became budget day. The Internal Revenue Service could provide everyone with a form that listed all major federal programs. Each taxpayer would be given a hypothetical $100,000 to allocate for these programs. Details about minimum allocations and how expansive the program list should be would need to be worked out. The budget forms would be submitted with the tax returns. In essence, there would be a nationwide plebiscite on spending every April 15.

The allocations would be totaled, and the percentages of that total would be applied to the actual federal budget moving through the Congress. For the first few years, this plebiscite would be only advisory. As the kinks were worked out and people became savvier about how to allocate their $100,000, the advisory plebiscite could evolve into actually directing the spending priorities of the federal government. For example, we could require a two-thirds vote of both houses of Congress to allocate more or less funding than was allocated by the plebiscite for a particular line item. National disaster assistance and declared wars could be exempted.

Over time, the April 15 spending plebiscite would become as important as Election Day. Instead of spending their time swaying 435 House and 100 Senate members, the special interests and federal agencies would have to persuade the 172 million people who file tax returns (as individuals or jointly). No longer would secret budget deals be made among the oligarchs.

DIRECT DEMOCRACY IN SPENDING

In June 1995, my CAO team put the finances of the House of Representatives online. We then began working on making them fully searchable and ensuring that they were updated on a monthly basis. The Republicans stopped our prototype website, saying, "We never meant for our spending to be *that* public." In October 1996, the GOP also stopped the formation of an outside editorial board with members from Common Cause, CongressWatch, and the National Taxpayers Union. My intent was to develop reporting formats and explanatory notes understandable by everyone. Once we proved that one billion dollars in congressional spending could be accurately and clearly reported, monthly, we could congressionally mandate that all nonclassified federal spending be placed online. This was considered too radical in 1996, but its time has come.

In recent years, a number of public-interest groups have begun placing public information on their websites and making these databases searchable. However, this is the modern version of private citizens having to track down public information. True "transparency" will occur only when all public information is placed directly on the Web, in real time, by the government.

Imagine if anyone with access to the Internet could search and review the entire federal budget. Imagine if the accounting systems of the federal government were up to private-sector standards, meaning direct and automatic data capture of all transactions and the real-time or monthly updated display of those transactions in meaningful and understandable formats. Imagine if the government could finally agree on a standard definition of waste.[14] No more funny money, accounting games, or hidden boondoggles.

Such a system is possible; it is only the oligarchs who are refusing to do it. Think of what would happen if everyone became his or her own Government Accountability Office. Conservatives would pore over welfare and regulatory spending. Liberals would pore over defense spending. The media, the blogs, and the Congress would have hundreds of millions of "deputy sheriffs" and investigative reporters demanding the enforcement of legislative mandates and exposing waste, fraud, and abuse. There would be a revolution in the way government operates, for people would be appalled at how public funds are squandered with impunity.

DIRECT DEMOCRACY IN PUBLIC ACCESS

It is time to put *all* House and Senate meetings online. It is cheap and easy to permanently install digital cameras in every committee and subcommittee room—one facing the rostrum and another facing the witness table. Every meeting could then be webcast and podcast to everyone. Public hearings and meetings would become truly public. Currently, "public hearings" are just attended by lobbyists, federal officials, and a few tourists. Occasionally, some topic is deemed worthy of news coverage, but most of the forty-plus daily meetings of the Congress go unreported. The transcripts of these meetings are approved months after actions are taken, and the transcripts are altered under the general provision to "revise and extend remarks." I proposed an early version of this recording system to the GOP in February 1995. They rejected it with exclamations of "Not *that* public!"

This quantum expansion of public information will erode the power of K Street and the oligarchs, because lobbyists use "insider" information from these meetings to justify their fees. If everyone can see the same thing, much of that "I know something you don't know" arrogance will evaporate. Imagine what kinds of oversight hearings could be conducted to investigate the executive branch with web- and podcasting making sure Americans could watch the hearings in their entirety without the risk of news producers filtering the proceedings.

Over time, selected oversight hearings could change their rules to allow regular citizens to submit questions for the witnesses via e-mail or fax. They could even set up blogs to air issues and provide input. If citizens have full access to government-spending records, some of these questions could be quite pointed and expose major issues. Committee staff could reserve the right to ignore "boxers or briefs"–type questions.

Some might raise the question, "What kinds of people would seek public office if all the prestige and power are taken away?" America is fortunate to have many people, spanning the political spectrum, who would want to serve in such an environment. They would see their role as making sure there was no erosion of direct democracy. They would explore additional ways to keep the public informed and involved. They would use their staffs to better define and focus issues and to ensure that public decisions were diligently and fully implemented. They would propose new ideas and approaches through public forums to address current and future issues facing the nation. In short, they would do what elected representatives should be doing already.

This book outlined many of the actions and issues that played out over time and caused America's current crisis of confidence. It will take many changes and new ideas, implemented over time, to rebuild confidence in our government. This effort should include a major national effort to teach civics to young people. In addition, all institutions, public and private, need to rethink their role in defining and fostering our civic culture.

These are the first steps toward reshaping government in positive ways to serve all Americans. Implementing full and complete public access to spending data and public meetings is already long overdue. These reforms would improve democracy, rebuild trust, and allow America to continue to be a beacon of freedom and democracy for generations to come.

★ APPENDIX ★

List of House Reforms—104th Congress

INFORMATION DISSEMINATION
Abolish in-house printers
Abolish folding room
Eliminate House post office—USPS partnership
Privatize internal postal operations
Move postal operations to Ford Building—include security-screening unit
Establish off-site security-screening facility
Eliminate Joint Committee on Printing
Electronic document room
CD-ROM of searchable U.S. Code and Code of Federal Regulations
Franking reforms
Distribution of *Congressional Record* reform
Establish charges for in-house distribution of publications
House Intranet/Internet—Office 2000
Reform and realign House Information Resources—professionalize
Eliminate proprietary and in-house software development and use
Renegotiate and improve vendor and service contracts
Improve visitor maps and signage throughout campus
Visitor kiosks and interactive displays *(rejected)*
Channel 25—full informational program schedule

LEGISLATIVE SUPPORT FACILITIES

Camera policy for House floor
Additional cameras and microphones in House
Use of wireless technology—including simultaneous translation
Internet/scanners in committee rooms
Direct satellite links
Periodical/press Internet system
Press gallery renovation
Robotic cameras in committee rooms *(rejected)*
Improve satellite path from recording studio
Digitalize all House broadcasts—upgrade equipment
Outsource photography and recording studios *(rejected)*

MEMBER SERVICES

Abolish Western Union office
Eliminate House bank—allow private ATMs
Privatize beauty- and barbershops
Privatize shoeshine and shoe-repair shops
Privatize travel office
Outsource supply and gift stores *(rejected)*
Eliminate legislative service organizations
Bring other private-service vendors onto campus
Eliminate ice delivery
Revise flag-distribution policy
Parking reform—public lot
Parking reform—end leased lots
Customer-service guide—HouseSmart
Customer-service center—ONECall
Customer-service teams
Customer feedback and performance tracking
Photo and broadcast locations for members
Consolidate member allowances
Cardholders responsible for payments
Generally accepted accounting principles (GAAP) for House finances—
  clean audit

House financial statement revisions—accuracy, clarity, completeness, explanatory notes

House financial statements online—private editorial board *(rejected)*

Eliminate all petty-cash accounts

Real-time tracking and modeling of financial operations and member accounts—monthly reports

Charge market rates for members purchasing furnishings

Paperless systems

Restructure photography and studio fees

End free U.S. Code distribution

End free Capitol Historical Society calendars

ADMINISTRATIVE FUNCTIONS

Establish personal property management system

Dispose of all excess personal property

Eliminate in-house equipment repair—abolish typewriter unit

Eliminate leased warehouse

Eliminate one office building *(rejected)*

Remove and rebuild new O'Neill House Office Building *(rejected)*

Build secure page dormitory *(completed later)*

Consolidate freight facility *(rejected)*

Prohibit names on CAO stationery

Prohibit use of official funds for executive-level business cards and stationery

Create and distribute customer-service cards to all employees

Establish professional development program and core skills for all CAO employees

Provide secure remote access to systems

HIR cross-servicing and outside revenue generation

Consolidate human-resources functions

Position descriptions for all jobs

End patronage hiring

Restructure and professionalize House Placement Office

Flextime and flexplace policies

Procurement reform

Ministerial signature authority consolidated to CAO

House regulatory compliance with all federal laws—drug-free workplace

Establish EEO, employee-relations, and employee-assistance functions

Conduct OSHA and environmental inspections

Balanced scorecard and performance measurements for all CAO functions

OTHER FUNCTIONS

Architect of the Capitol—new elevators, renovate Longworth, space consolidation—CAO

Architect of the Capitol—realign functions—CAO

Capitol Historical Society—coordination of visitor services—CAO

Government Printing Office—realign functions—digital document distribution—CAO

Library of Congress—support for emerging democracies—CAO

Library of Congress—Thomas system—Congressional Internet portal—CAO and clerk

★ NOTES ★

INTRODUCTION

1. Congressional Research Service, analysis, and demographics of House Membership, 104th Congress.

PROLOGUE

1. Philip Crosby Associates, "Quality Improvement Process Management College," course leader notes.

2. Grand Old Party Action Committee pamphlet, 1991.

3. Philip B.Crosby, *Quality Without Tears* (New York: McGraw-Hill, 1984).

4. Representative Newt Gingrich, *A Process for a Successful America*, 102nd Cong., 1st sess., *Congressional Record* 137 (daily ed. April 24, 1991): H2513.

5. *Congressional Record* 137 (daily ed. April 24, 1991): H2515–H2520.

CHAPTER 1

1. Representative Jim Nussle, remarks on House floor, 102nd Cong., 1st sess., *Congressional Record* 137 (daily ed. October 1, 1991): H7120.

2. Jane Hook, "What Did Foley Know?" *Congressional Quarterly*, March 21, 1992, 700.

3. Jane Hook, "What Did Foley Know?" *Congressional Quarterly*, March 21, 1992, 700.

4. Some of the details are drawn from Representative Jim Nussle's transition report. Representative Jim Nussle, memorandum to Representative Newt Gingrich, "The GOP's Open House: A Proposed Restructuring of the Functions and Operations of the U.S. House of Representatives," November 28, 1994.

5. "Each of the three times the bank came up short, the House appropriated public funds to make up the loss—a fact not noted by the House Administration panel's report." Phil Kuntz, "History of the House Bank," *Congressional Quarterly*, February 8, 1992, 283.

6. Phil Kuntz, "Uproar over Bank Scandal Goads House to Cut Perks," *Congressional Quarterly*, October 5, 1991, 2843–2844.

7. Phil Kuntz, "Uproar over Bank Scandal Goads House to Cut Perks," *Congressional Quarterly*, October 5, 1991, 2843–2844.

8. William Safire, "Cleaning Housegate," *New York Times*, September 30, 1991.

9. Nancy Gibbs, "Washington Perk City," *Time*, October 14, 1991, 18–20.

10. *U.S. News & World Report*, October 14, 1991, 32–35.

11. Janet Hook, *Congressional Quarterly*, April 18, 1992, 991.

12. Phil Kuntz, "22 Cited for Abuse of Bank," *Congressional Quarterly*, April 4, 1992, 859.

13. Some of the details are drawn from Ronald Kessler, *Inside Congress* (New York: Pocket Books, 1997), 52–53.

14. Phil Kuntz, "House Agrees to Hand Over Records of Its Bank," *Congressional Quarterly*, May 2, 1992, 1130.

15. Phil Kuntz, "House Agrees to Hand Over Records of Its Bank," *Congressional Quarterly*, May 2, 1992, 1130.

16. Kenneth J. Cooper, "House Bank Crusaders Feel the Heat," *Washington Post*, October 28, 1992, A14.

17. Details are drawn from Representative Nussle's transition report (see note 4 above).

18. Some of the details are drawn from the excellent overview of the House scandals prepared by the Congressional Research Service, *House of Representatives' Management: Background and Current Issues*, by Paul S. Rundquist, April 17, 1992.

19. The Gallup Organization, *Washington Post*–ABC News poll; and *Washington Post*, November 16, 1994, A23.

20. News Digest, *Time*, August 2, 1993; and "Selective Ethics," editorial, *New York Times*, August 4, 1993.

21. Robert Pear, "Audit of House Post Office Finds Inadequate Controls over Money," *New York Times*, April 1, 1992, A23.

22. Phil Kuntz, *Congressional Quarterly*, March 14, 1992, 599.

23. Dane Kaplan & Charles Mehtesian, "Election's Wave of Diversity Spares Many Incumbents," *Congressional Quarterly*, November 7, 1992, 3570.

24. Phil Kuntz, "Rostenkowski on Trial: Assessing the Charges," *Congressional Quarterly*, June 4, 1994, 1442–1443.

25. Joe Davidson, "Rostenkowski Reimbursed Government $82,000 for Purchases of House Supplies," *Wall Street Journal*, February 11, 1994.

26. Paul Rodriguez, "House Leaders Want Rostenkowski Probe," *Washington Times*, February 12, 1994, A-1.

27. John Harwood & Viveca Novak, "Embarrassed Leadership Plans Changes in Operation of House Stationery Store," *Wall Street Journal*, July 18, 1994, B6C.

28. Representative Rod Grams, remarks on House floor, 103rd Cong., 1st sess., *Congressional Record* 139 (daily ed. July 21, 1993): H4865.

29. Representative John Boehner, remarks on House floor, 103rd Cong., 1st sess., *Congressional Record* 139 (daily ed. July 22, 1993): H4995.

30. Representative Joel Hefley, remarks on House floor, 103rd Cong., 2nd sess., *Congressional Record* 140 (daily ed. September 27, 1994): H9768.

31. Janet Hook & David S. Cloud, "A Republican-Designed House Won't Please All Occupants," *Congressional Quarterly*, December 3, 1994, 3434.

CHAPTER 2

1. Representative Robert Walker, remarks on House floor, 103rd Cong., 2nd sess., *Congressional Record* 140 (daily ed. February 1, 1994): H87.

2. Leonard Wishart, letter to Speaker Foley, July 23, 1993.

3. Janet Hook, "Approval of Administrator Creates More Rancor," *Congressional Quarterly*, April 11, 1992, 929.

4. Janet Hook, *Congressional Quarterly*, April 11, 1992, 929.

5. Phil Kuntz, "Post Office Patronage Worker Ties Members to Stamp Scam," *Congressional Quarterly*, May 23, 1992, 1419.

6. Phil Kuntz, "Post Office Patronage Worker Ties Members to Stamp Scam," *Congressional Quarterly*, May 23, 1992, 1419.

7. Phil Kuntz, "Post Office Patronage Worker Ties Members to Stamp Scam," *Congressional Quarterly*, May 23, 1992, 1415.

8. Phil Kuntz, "Members Lose Perks, Respect in Wake of Bank Scandal," *Congressional Quarterly*, October 12, 1991, 2935.

9. Phil Kuntz, "Parties Trade Bitter Charges over Post Office Inquiry," *Congressional Quarterly*, February 8, 1992, 289.

10. Janet Hook, "The Buck Stops with Foley," *Congressional Quarterly*, March 14, 1992, 600.

11. Ronald Elving, "The Titanic Disaster and the House Bank," *Congressional Quarterly*, April 25, 1992, 1118.

12. Ronald Elving, "The Titanic Disaster and the House Bank," *Congressional Quarterly*, April 25, 1992, 1118.

13. Janet Hook, "The Bank Stops with Foley," *Congressional Quarterly*, March 14, 1992, 600.

14. Beth Donovan, "Privileges Under Scrutiny: More Talk Than Action," *Congressional Quarterly*, March 28, 1992, 785.

15. Beth Donovan, "Privileges Under Scrutiny: More Talk than Action," *Congressional Quarterly*, March 28, 1992, 785.

16. Beth Donovan, "Privileges Under Scrutiny: More Talk than Action," *Congressional Quarterly*, March 28, 1992, 786.

17. Beth Donovan, "Privileges Under Scrutiny: More Talk than Action," *Congressional Quarterly*, March 28, 1992, 786.

18. Janet Hook, "Leaders May Seek an Administrator," *Congressional Quarterly*, March 7, 1992, 516.

19. Beth Donovan, "Privileges Under Scrutiny: More Talk than Action," *Congressional Quarterly*, March 28, 1992, 785.

20. Janet Hook, "Leaders May Seek an Administrator," *Congressional Quarterly*, March 7, 1992, 516.

21. Beth Donovan, "Privileges Under Scrutiny: More Talk than Action," *Congressional Quarterly*, March 28, 1992, 785.

22. Beth Donovan, "Privileges Under Scrutiny: More Talk than Action," *Congressional Quarterly*, March 28, 1992, 787.

23. Representative Richard Gephardt, speaking regarding the House Administrative Reform Resolution of 1992, 102nd Cong., 2nd sess., *Congressional Record* 138 (daily ed. April 9, 1992): H2548.

24. Janet Hook, "Approval of Administrator Creates More Rancor," *Congressional Quarterly*, April 11, 1992, 929.

25. Janet Hook, "Approval of Administrator Creates More Rancor," *Congressional Quarterly*, April 11, 1992, 930.

26. Janet Hook, "Approval of Administrator Creates More Rancor," *Congressional Quarterly*, April 11, 1992, 930.

27. Phil Kuntz, "Retired Army General Hired to Clean House, but How?" "Retired Army General Hired to Clean House, but How?" *Congressional Quarterly*, October 31, 1992, 3491.

28. Phil Kuntz, "Retired Army General Hired to Clean House, but How?" *Congressional Quarterly*, October 31, 1992, 3491.

29. Phil Kuntz, "Retired Army General Hired to Clean House, but How?" *Congressional Quarterly*, October 31, 1992, 3491.

30. Phil Kuntz, "Retired Army General Hired to Clean House, but How?" *Congressional Quarterly*, October 31, 1992, 3491.

31. Phil Kuntz, "Retired Army General Hired to Clean House, but How?" *Congressional Quarterly*, October 31, 1992, 3491.

32. *Constitution, Jefferson's Manual, and Rules of the House of Representatives*, 103rd Cong., 1st sess., 1993, H. Doc. 102-405.

33. William L. Riordon, *Plunkitt of Tammany Hall* (New York: Dutton, 1963), 13.

34. Details extracted from the profile of Bill Thomas in *Congressional Quarterly's Politics in America 1990*, ed. Phil Duncan (Washington, D.C.: CQ Press 1989), 154–156.

35. Michael Barone and Grant Ujifusa, *The Almanac of American Politics 1990* (Washington, D.C.: National Journal Group, 1989), 129.

36. Barone and Ujifusa, *Almanac of American Politics 1990*, 129.

37. Barone and Ujifusa, *Almanac of American Politics 1990*, 129.

38. Phil Duncan, ed., *Congressional Quarterly's Politics in America 1994* (Washington, D.C.: CQ Press, 1993), 166.

39. Duncan, *Politics in America 1994*, 154.

40. "The History of the House Bank: Scandal Waiting to Happen," *Congressional Quarterly,* February 8, 1992, 290.

41. "Voters Will Render Judgments on Members' Checking Habits," *Congressional Quarterly*, April 18, 1992, 992.

42. Duncan, *Politics in America 1994*, 166.

43. Paul Rodriguez, "House Leaders Want Rostenkowski Probe," *Washington Times*, February 12, 1994, A1.

44. John Harwood and Viveca Novak, "Embarrassed Leadership Plans Changes in Operation of House Stationery Store," *Wall Street Journal*, July 18, 1994, B6C.

45. Committee on House Oversight Republican Staff, memorandum for transition team, "Summary of Transfers," November 14, 1994.

46. Committee on House Administration Republican Staff, memorandum, "Fundamental Issues with Bipartisan Oversight Structure," July 26, 1994.

47. Phil Kuntz, "Rostenkowski Case Exposes Ambiguous Expense Rules," *Congressional Quarterly,* July 30, 1994, 2109.

48. Leonard Wishart, letter to Representatives Charlie Rose and Bill Thomas, June 9, 1993.

49. Leonard Wishart, letter to Robert Shea, July 13, 1993.

50. Leonard Wishart, letter to Speaker Tom Foley, July 23, 1993.

51. Leonard Wishart, letter to Speaker Tom Foley, July 23, 1993.

52. Representative Bill Thomas, letter to Representatives Bob Michel and Newt Gingrich, November 24, 1993, 3.

53. Committee on House Administration Republican Staff, memorandum, July 26, 1994.

54. Thomas, letter to Michel and Gingrich, November 24, 1993.

55. Representative Jim Istook, remarks on the House floor, 103rd Cong., 1st sess., *Congressional Record* 139 (daily ed. October 13, 1993): H7714.

56. Leonard Wishart, letter to Representatives Charlie Rose and Bill Thomas, January 5, 1994.

57. Leonard Wishart, letter to Speaker Tom Foley, January 10, 1994.

58. Representatives Bill Thomas and Bill Barrett, letter to Chairman Charlie Rose, June 13, 1994.

59. Committee on House Administration Staff, memorandum, November 14, 1994, 4.

60. "Charlie's Ploy," editorial, *Roll Call,* March 14, 1994, 4.

61. Representative Bill Thomas, letter to Charles Bowsher, August 18, 1994, 1.

62. Thomas, letter to Bowsher, 3–4.

63. Thomas, letter to Bowsher, 5–6.

64. Thomas, letter to Bowsher, 6.

65. Thomas, letter to Bowsher, 6.

66. Congressional Research Service, *House of Representatives' Management: Background and Current Issues*, by Paul S. Rundquist, April 17, 1992, 39–40.

67. Biographical material drawn from *Congressional Staff Directory*, Spring 1996, 1043.

68. Committee on House Administration Staff, memorandum, November 14, 1994, 6.

CHAPTER 3

1. Newt Gingrich and others, *Contract with America* (New York: Times Books, 1994), 7.

2. Details drawn from Dick Armey, *The Freedom Revolution* (Washington, D.C.: Regnery Publishing, 1995), 135–136.

3. Gingrich and others, *Contract with America*, 15–16.

4. Gingrich and others, *Contract with America*, 16.

5. Phil Duncan, ed., *Congressional Quarterly's Politics in America 1990* (Washington, D.C.: CQ Press, 1989), 267.

6. Duncan, *Politics in America 1990*, 267.

7. Richard Sammon, "Focus on Reform Effort Shifts to Ending Hill Exemptions," *Congressional Quarterly*, July 9, 1994, 1856.

8. Richard Sammon, "Focus on Reform Effort Shifts to Ending Hill Exemptions," *Congressional Quarterly*, July 9, 1994, 1856.

9. Richard Sammon, "House Strongly Backs Bill to End Hill's Exemptions," *Congressional Quarterly*, August 13, 1994, 2314.

10. Stephen Gettinger, "New Procedural Proposals Are Weak, Says GOP," *Congressional Quarterly*, August 6, 1994, 2219.

11. Richard Sammon, "House Strongly Backs Bill to End Hill's Exemptions," *Congressional Quarterly*, August 13, 2314.

12. Richard Sammon, "House Strongly Backs Bill to End Hill's Exemptions," *Congressional Quarterly*, August 13, 2314.

13. Richard Sammon, "House Strongly Backs Bill to End Hill's Exemptions," *Congressional Quarterly*, August 13, 1994, 2113.

14. Richard Sammon, "Senate Demurs on Labor Rules, But House Acts on Its Own," *Congressional Quarterly*, October 8, 1994, 2855.

15. Jeffrey Katz, "Republicans Dust Off Blue Prints for Changing House Operations," *Congressional Quarterly*, November 12, 1994, 3220.

16. Jon Healey, "Jubilant GOP Strives to Keep Legislative Feet on Ground," *Congressional Quarterly*, November 12, 1994, 3210.

17. Keith Glover, "Legislative Spending Bill Squeaks Through House," *Congressional Quarterly*, May 28, 1994, 1370.

18. Gingrich and others, *Contract with America*, 184.

19. Gingrich and others, *Contract with America*, 186.

20. Gingrich and others, *Contract with America*, 188.

21. Gingrich and others, *Contract with America*, 194.

22. House Republican Conference, "GOP OPEN HOUSE REFORMS"; news release, December 1, 1994.

23. Jim Nussle's transition report has been previously referenced in Chapter 1. Representative Jim Nussle, memorandum to Representative Newt Gingrich, "The GOP's Open House: A Proposed Restructuring of the Functions and Operations of the U.S. House of Representatives," November 28, 1994, 1 (hereafter cited as Nussle, transition report).

24. Nussle, transition report, 5.

25. Nussle, transition report, 6–7.

26. Congressional Research Service, *House of Representatives' Management: Background and Current Issues*, by Paul S. Rundquist, April 17, 1992, 33, 37.

27. David Cloud, "GOP's House-Cleaning Sweep Changes Rules, Cuts Groups," *Congressional Quarterly*, December 10, 1994, 3487.

28. David S. Cloud, "GOP's House-Cleaning Sweep Changes Rules, Cuts Groups," *Congressional Quarterly*, December 10, 1994, 3487.

29. David S. Cloud, "GOP's House-Cleaning Sweep Changes Rules, Cuts Groups," *Congressional Quarterly*, December 10, 1994, 3487.

30. *Constitution, Jefferson's Manual, and Rules of the House of Representatives*, 104th Cong., 1st sess., 1995, H. Doc. 103-342, 346 (hereafter cited as *House Rules and Manual*, 104th Cong.).

31. *House Rules and Manual*, 104th Cong., 427.

32. *House Rules and Manual*, 104th Cong., 337–347.

CHAPTER 4

1. Thomas S. Kuhn, *The Structure of Scientific Revolutions*, 2nd ed. (Chicago: University of Chicago Press, 1970), 92.

2. "A System in Disarray," *Washington Post*, March 22, 2007, A8. The chart shows that only 15 of the 126 appropriations bills have been passed into law since fiscal year 1998.

3. Good background on these individuals can be found in "Bauman & Co.: House Guerrilla Fighters," *Congressional Quarterly*, July 7, 1979, 1342–1343.

4. William L. Sturdevant, obituary, *Washington Post*, February 19, 1997, B4.

CHAPTER 5

1. Jim Nussle's transition report has been previously referenced in Chapters 1 and 3. Representative Jim Nussle, memorandum to Representative Newt Gingrich, "The GOP's Open House: A Proposed Restructuring of the Functions and Operations of the U.S. House of Representatives," November 28, 1994, 15 (organizational chart).

2. Stephen R. Covey, *The Seven Habits of Highly Effective People* (New York: Simon & Schuster, 1990), 151.

3. Scot Faulkner, meeting notes, December 10, 1994.

4. Faulkner, meeting notes, December 10, 1994. All subsequent descriptions of meetings are drawn from notes taken during or immediately after the stated meeting.

5. See *Wikipedia*, s.v. "Debategate," http://en.wikipedia.org/wiki/Debategate; and Stephen Jendraszak, "Debategate: The Scandal of July 1983," http://www.bsu.edu/web/shjendraszak/classes/text/debategate.txt.

6. Kenneth J. Cooper, "House Republican Proposals Are Topic A All Over the Hill," *Washington Post*, December 14, 1994, A4.

7. Five members were injured: Clifford Davis, Ben Jensen, Alvin Bentley, George Fallon, Kenneth Roberts. See *Wikipedia*, s.v. "U.S. Capitol shooting incident (1954)," http://en.wikipedia.org/wiki/U.S._Capitol_shooting_incident_%281954%29.

8. Scot Faulkner, prepared remarks to House Republican Conference, December 16, 1994.

CHAPTER 6

1. Richard M. Nixon, *RN: The Memoirs of Richard Nixon*. (New York: Grosset & Dunlap, 1978), 315–352, 355–356.

2. House Committee on Standards of Official Conduct, letter to Representative Deborah Pryce, November 22, 1994.

3. House Committee on Standards of Official Conduct, letter to Representative Jim Nussle, December 14, 1994.

4. Draft letters to employees, December 15, 1994.

5. Michigan Governor's Office, confidential memorandum on Vernon Ehlers, December 22, 1994, 1.

6. Michigan Governor's Office, confidential memorandum on Ehlers.

7. [author], transition report on House Information Systems, December 10, 1994.

8. Michigan Governor's Office, confidential memorandum on Ehlers.

9. Mary Jacoby, "Chief Officer Has Very Partisan Past," *Roll Call*, December 19, 1994, 1.

10. Price Pritchett and Ron Pound, *High-Velocity Culture Change* (Dallas, Tex.: Pritchett Publishing, 1993).

CHAPTER 7

1. *Constitution, Jefferson's Manual, and Rules of the House of Representatives*, 104th Cong., 1st sess., 1995, H. Doc. 103-342, 336.

2. A recent guidebook proudly proclaims the removal of the Capitol chandelier. It can be seen in the Sam Rayburn Library in Bonham, Texas, population 7,023. *Texas 1998 State Travel Guide* (Austin, Tex.: Texas Department of Transportation), 36–37.

CHAPTER 8

1. House Resolution 1 passed on January 4, 1995, attested to by Robin Carle, clerk.

2. "Lobby Control," editorial, *Roll Call*, May 27, 1995; and Jim Drinkard, "House GOP to Stop Giving Lobbyists After-Hours Access to Capitol," Associated Press, May 25, 1995.

3. *Roll Call*, March 9, 1995, 1 (photograph).

CHAPTER 9

1. Scot Faulkner, "Chief Administrative Officer Management Philosophy," Chief Administrative Officer.

2. Excerpts from February 3, 1995 "listening points."

3. *Wikipedia*, s.v. "Ron Packard," http://en.wikipedia.org/wiki/Ron_Packard.

4. Patrick M. Reynolds, "The $8-a-Day Artist," Flashbacks, *Washington Post*, August 12, 2005, Comics, sec. 2; and Barbara A. Wolanin, "Getting Established in the New World," in *Constantino Brumidi: Artist of the Capitol* (Washington, D.C.: Government Printing Office, 1998), 49, http://www.access.gpo.gov/congress/senate/brumidi/Brumidi_5.pdf.

5. Heredity Society Community, "History of the Society of the Cincinnati," http://www.hereditary.us/cin_history.htm.

6. Rep. Jim Nussle, prepared remarks, testimony before the Committee on House Oversight, February 8, 1995.

7. Cindy Loose, "Changes Pose Downer for Hill Picker-Upper: 12-Year Elevator Operator Fears GOP Job Cuts," *Washington Post*, December 11, 1994, B-1, B-7.

8. U.S. General Accounting Office, testimony before the Subcommittee on Post Office and Civil Service, Committee on Governmental Affairs, U.S. Senate, *Personnel Practices: An Overview of Ramspeck Act Appointments* (prepared statement of Nancy R. Kingsbury, director, federal human resource management issues), http://archive.gao.gov/t2pbat1/154204.pdf.

CHAPTER 10

1. Timothy Burger, "On Chief Administrator's Wish List: Closing Folding Room, Open Parking," *Roll Call*, March 6, 1995, 1.

2. Tom Craren, letter to John Lainhart, March 7, 1995.

3. Approval request for personnel actions, March 1, 1995.

4. Starting on February 1, 1995, I had a printed daily schedule on which my staff and I took detailed notes relating to the various meetings. Much of the detail in this book is drawn from these documents.

5. "Announcement of the Establishment and Membership of the Cabinet Council on Management and Administration," news release, September 22, 1982, http://www.presidency.ucsb.edu/ws/index.php?pid=43028.

6. President's Private Sector Survey (Grace Commission), *President's Private Sector Survey on Cost Control: A Report to the President*, http://www.uhuh.com/taxstuff/gracecom.htm.

7. Alice Love, "Squawk Boxes Headed for Hill," *Roll Call*, May 15, 1995, 1.

8. Timothy Burger "Thomas Memo Blasting Faulkner Signals Tension between House Oversight, CAO," *Roll Call*, May 15, 1995, 1, 27.

CHAPTER 11

1. Timothy Burger, "Growing Impatient, Appropriations May Upstage House Oversight on Reforms," *Roll Call*, May 22, 1995.

2. Timothy Burger, "Packard Scores House Reforms," *Roll Call*, May 29, 1995.

3. Stacy Carlson, memorandum to Scot Faulkner regarding House Information Resources personnel reform, June 6, 1995.

4. Timothy Burger, "House Clears Spending Bill (& OTA Money)," *Roll Call*, June 26, 1995, 1, 30.

5. Matt Schundel, obituary, "Pamela Ahearn, 52, First Protocol Chief for U.S. House," *Washington Post*, April 9, 2007, B6.

CHAPTER 12

1. Carole Kordich, auction report, September 28, 1995.

2. Terri Hasdorff, e-mail to Scot Faulkner and Jim Davison with meeting transcript, July 14, 1995.

3. "House Broken," editorial, *Wall Street Journal*, July 18, 1995.

4. Representative Bob Livingston, letter to Scot Faulkner, July 11, 1995.

5. Timothy Burger, telephone interview of Scot Faulkner, July 26, 1995, transcript.

6. Juliet Eilperin, "Faulkner's Nine Months of Sound and Fury as CAO," *Roll Call*, September 18, 1995, 1, 20, 21.

7. Rick Endres, "Office 2000 and Computer & Information Services Working Group: A Discussion Paper," June 29, 1995.

8. Scot Faulkner, report to Bill Thomas, "Request to Procure Communications Infrastructure Upgrades," September 7, 1995.

CHAPTER 13

1. "A Note from Scot Faulkner," *CAO Connection*, January 1996, 1.

2. "Praying for your job," flyer, March 23, 1995.

3. Representative Bill Thomas, letter to Minority Leader Bob Michel and Minority Whip Newt Gingrich, November 24, 1993.

4. Scot Faulkner, letter to Dan Meyer, December 27, 1995. Calls and meetings also took place.

CHAPTER 14

1. Scot M. Faulkner and Lawrence D. Longley, "Changing the System: Institutional Change (and Inertia) in the U.S. House of Representatives" (paper presented at the Second Workshop of Parliamentary Scholars and Parliamentarians, Wroxton College, Oxfordshire, U.K., August 3–4, 1996).

2. Scot Faulkner, memorandum to Speaker Newt Gingrich, "Operational Review of Administrative Services in the U.S. House of Representatives," February 16, 1996.

3. Juliet Eilperin, "CAO's Handling of Post Office Layoffs Draws Fire from Oversight Chairman," *Roll Call*, February 5, 1996, 3.

4. Tom Anfinson, memorandum to Scot Faulkner, January 16, 1996.

5. Edith Vivian, memorandum to Scot Faulkner, March 15, 1996.

6. David Berran, memorandum to Chad Mosley, November 19, 1996; and Chad Mosley, memorandum to Scot Faulkner, November 21, 1996.

CHAPTER 15

1. Eric Schmitt, "New House Members Get Online Aid," *New York Times*, November 10, 1996, 1.

2. Office of the Chief Administrative Officer, report, "Federal Financial System (FFS); Implementation Status," September 20, 1996.

3. Office of the Chief Administrative Officer, report, September 20, 1996.

4. Jane Bennett, memorandum regarding Representative Ron Klink, November 6, 1996.

5. Tom Simon, e-mail regarding staff hours spent on audits, November 14, 1996.

6. "Saving Taxpayer Money by Cleaning Our Own House: 104th Congress Republican Majority Reforms," Fact Sheet issued by House Republican Conference, November 1, 1996. House Republican Conference, November 1, 1996.

7. David Lynch, "Rumors of Infidelities Frustrate Nussle," *Iowa Gazette*, August 2, 1996.

8. Confidential fax to Scot Faulkner, November 6, 1996.

9. Amy Reiter, "In the Eye of the Newt Storm: Thar She Blows!" *Salon People*, August 17, 1999.

10. Debbie Schussel, "Sleeping with the Enemy: Bush Health Care Advisor, Congressman are GOP's Monica and Bill," *Jewish World Review*, July 11, 2000; and confidential fax and e-mail to Scot Faulkner.

11. Scot Faulkner, confidential memorandum regarding the inspector general audit of the CAO, November 19, 1996.

12. "TQMismanagement," editorial, *Roll Call*, November 23, 1996, 4.

13. S. Joseph Simpson v. Office of the Clerk; Office of Compliance Case No. 98-HS-20, January 20, 1999.

14. "House Clerk Resigns Under Fire," Associated Press; *Washington Post*, December 22, 1998, A8 also Jock Friedly, "Five House aides fired by GOP claim bias," The Hill, January 21, 1998, 1.

15. William Crain and James Davison, letter to Speaker Newt Gingrich, November 22, 1996.

16. Ronald Kessler, *Inside Congress* (New York: Pocket Books, 1997).

17. Ronald Kessler, "Membership Has Its Privileges," *Washington Post Sunday Magazine*, May 16, 1997, 16–18, 35–36.

18. See transcript of interview conducted by Jim Lehrer with Reps. Porter Goss and Ben Cardin, "Judgment Day—Gingrich Ethics Vote"; *Online NewsHour*, January 21, 1997; http://www.pbs.org/newshour/bb/congress/january97/reprimand_1-21.html; and John Yang, "Speaker Gingrich Admits House Ethics Violation," *Washington Post*,

December 22, 1996, A1. For more information on the coup and Gingrich's last days see: Tracy Connor, "Power Crazed Newt had a Bawl While He Fought Coup," New York Post, February 12, 1998; Guy Gugliotta and Juliet Eilperin, "Gingrich Steps Down as Speaker in Face of House GOP Rebellion," and Dan Balz, "For GOP Fighter; A Confrontation He Didn't Want," both in The Washington Post, November 7, 1998, A-1.

CHAPTER 16

1. Thomas L. Friedman, *The World Is Flat: A Brief History of the Twenty-First Century*, expanded and updated ed. (New York: Farrar, Straus & Giroux, 2006).

2. CNN, "The Budget Battle," http://www.cnn.com/US/9512/budget/budget_battle/index.html.

3. Faulkner campaign files (Obenshain 1978).

4. For a detailed critique of the failure of the Republicans to cut spending, see Stephen Slivinski, *Buck Wild: How Republicans Broke the Bank and Became the Party of Big Government* (Nashville, Tenn.: Nelson Current, 2006).

5. Citizens Against Government Waste, "2005 Pig Book Summary," http://www.cagw.org/site/PageServer?pagename=reports_pigbook2005.

6. David Broder, "The GOP's Whopper of a Budget," *Washington Post*; April 2, 2006, B7.

7. Dana Milbank, "Bob Barr, Bane of the Right?" *Washington Post*, February 11, 2006, A2.

8. Robert Weissman, "Hearings Loss: Oversight in the Republican Congress," *American Prospect*, November 1, 1998, http://www.prospect.org/web/page.ww?section=root&name=ViewPrint&articleId=4576.

9. Susan Milligan, "Congress Reduces Its Oversight Role: Since Clinton, a Change in Focus," *Boston Globe*, November 20, 2005, http://www.boston.com/news/nation/washington/articles/2005/11/20/congress_reduces_its_oversight_role/. In that article, Milligan writes:

> An examination of committees' own reports found that the House Government Reform Committee held just 37 hearings described as "oversight" or investigative in nature during the last Congress, down from 135 such hearings held by its predecessor, the House Government Operations Committee, in 1993–94, the last year the Democrats controlled the chamber. . . .
>
> In 1993–1994, under the chairmanship of Democrat John D. Dingell of Michigan, the panel's oversight efforts accounted for 117 pages in its activities report for the session, compared with 24 pages in the last Congress. The committee in 1993–1994 held 153 investigative hearings, compared with 129 during 2003–2004, and the more recent hearings have not targeted the Bush administration. . . .
>
> But the agenda was different during the Clinton administration. The government reform panel alone, for example, issued 1,052 subpoenas related to investigations of the Clinton administration and the Democratic National Committee from 1997 to 2002, and only 11 subpoenas related to allegations of Republican abuse.

10. The House Oversight Committee held numerous hearings on steroid use in base-ball and even held a hearing on "Why Most Nats [Washington Nationals] Fans Can't See Their Team on TV" on April 7, 2006. *Activities of the House Committee on Government Reform*, 109th Cong., 2nd sess., 2006, H. Rep. 109-739, 85, http://republicans.oversight .house.gov/Media/PDFs/Reports/109activityreport.pdf.

11. One of the most insightful ways to track this long history of the revolving door is reading obituaries of lobbyists. Most begin as members, or as staff to members or com-mittees, and then cash in on "K Street." See, for example, the obituary of Paul Nelson in the *Washington Post*, March 31, 2006, and the obituary of Richard Rivers in the *Washington Post*, May 9, 2006. An excellent series on the rise of Democratic lobbyist Gerald S. J. Cassidy and the Washington lobbyist culture can be found at http://blog.washingtonpost .com/citizen-k-street/.

12. Juliet Eilperin, "The Ties That Bind on Capitol Hill," *Washington Post*, August 7, 2003, A19. The Democrats continued to exempt these family linkages from lobby reform in 2007. See John Solomon, "Reforms Omit Lobbyists Married to Lawmakers," *Washington Post*, January 17, 2007, A1, A6.

13. *Washington Representatives*, 6th–25th annual editions (Washington, D.C.: Colum-bia Books, 1982–2001); and Jeffrey Birnbaum, "The Road to Riches Is Called K Street," *Washington Post*, June 22, 2005, A1.

14. An excellent overview can be found in David Margolick's, "Washington's Invisible Man," *Vanity Fair*, April 2006, 196–201, 247–252.

15. A separate 2004 Project on Government Oversight study revealed "300 cases in which officials left government to go work for the 20 largest contractors, with as many as one-third of those officials having been in key positions to influence spending decisions that benefited the contractors." Thomas D. Williams, "Project on Government Over-sight's Baker's Dozen," *truthout*, January 12, 2007, http://www.truthout.org/docs_2006/ printer_011207O.shtml.

16. Norman Ornstein, "Part-Time Congress," *Washington Post*, March 7, 2006, A17.

17. Many columnists flagged this growing rage during the summer of 2006. See, e.g., David Broder, "Simmering Rage within the GOP," *Washington Post*, July 27, 2006, A25.

18. "Trust in Government," *Washington Post*, June 2, 2006, A17.

19. "Seeing Corruption," *Washington Post*–ABC News poll, January 5–8, 2006.

20. Dana Milbank, "So $90,000 Was in the Freezer. What's Wrong with That?" *Washington Post*, May 23, 2006, A2; and Laurie Kellman, "Hastert Demands FBI Return Doc-uments," Associated Press, May 24, 2006.

21. John Yang, "Gays in a Conservative Closet," *Washington Post*, November 7, 1997, A23; and Jose Antonio Vargas, "Hill Republicans Air Out the Closet," *Washington Post*, October 20, 2006, C1.

22. George F. Will, "What Goeth before the Fall," *Washington Post*, October 5, 2006, A33.

23. Dick Armey, "Christians and Big Government," open letter, October 12, 2006, Freedom Works, http://www.freedomworks.org/informed/issues_template.php?issue_id=2731.

24. Richard McCormack, "Power Shift: What Happens If the Democrats Win the House," *Manufacturing & Technology News*, September 22, 2006, http://www.manufacturing news.com/news/06/0922/art1.html.

25. *Manufacturing & Technology News*, September 22, 2006.

26. For a poignant and insightful take on the collapse of hope and dreams, see T. S. Eliot's 1925 poem, "The Hollow Men," available online at http://www.cs.umbc.edu/ ~evans/hollow.html.

CHAPTER 17

1. David Dishneau and Matt Apuzzo, Associated Press, "Abramoff Laments 'Nightmare' in E-mail as He Enters Prison in Scandal," *Sun-Sentinel*, November 15, 2006.

2. Randy Hall and Marc Morano, "Murtha's Anti-War Stance Overshadows Abscam Past," *Cybercast News Service*, January 13, 2006, http://www.cnsnews.com/ViewPolitics .asp?Page=%5CPolitics%5Carchive%5C200601%5CPOL20060113d.html. For an overview of Abscam, see *Congresspedia*, s.v. "Abscam bribery scandal," http://www.source watch.org/index.php?title=Abscam_bribery_scandal.

3. See an excellent review of Representative Murtha's and the Democrats' quick fall from grace in John Fund's, "Meet the New Boss: John Murtha and Congress's 'Culture of Corruption,'" Opinion Journal, *Wall Street Journal*, November 15, 2006, http://www.opinion journal.com/diary/?id=110009248.

4. KSA Consulting, "KSA Legislative Personnel," http://www.ksaconsulting.net/ profiles.htm.

5. David Holman, "Murky Jack Murtha," *American Spectator*, February 2, 2006, http://www.spectator.org/dsp_article.asp?art_id=9359.

6. "Murtha Reportedly Called Dem Ethics, Lobbying Bill 'Total Crap,'" *Raw Story*, November 15, 2006, http://www.rawstory.com/news/2006/Murtha_reportedly_called_Dem_ ethics_lobbying_1115.html; and John Bresnahan, "Murtha Calls Ethics Bill 'Total Crap,'" *Roll Call*, November 15, 2006, http://www.rollcall.com/issues/1_1/breakingnews/16030-1 .html.

7. Daniel Reilly and Jim VandeHei, "Pelosi Falls Short on Election Promises," *Politico*, February 27, 2007.

8. David Broder, "Congress's Oversight Offensive," *Washington Post*, March 18, 2007, B7.

9. Jeffrey Birnbaum, "A Shift in Giving," *Washington Post*, April 10, 2007, A15; and Jeffrey Birnbaum, "In the Loop on K Street," *Washington Post*, April 17, 2007, A19.

10. John Fund, "Earmark Cover-Up; The Congressional Research Service Is Helping Its Masters Hide Wasteful Spending," Opinion Journal, *Wall Street Journal*, March 27, 2007; and Robert Novak, "Earmarks as Usual," *Washington Post*, April 19, 2007, A27.

11. Speaker Pelosi selected Daniel P. Beard, a senior adviser with Booz Allen Hamilton, to be the CAO of the House. The selection of a professional manager, along with the preservation of the management reforms and the retention of professional "career positions," proved, as of this writing, that the A Ring's efforts to "cement the sandcastle" were successful. Hoyer endorsed the management reforms numerous times. "He welcomed many of the changes the GOP put in place, and would preserve them, if the Democrats won. . . . 'We needed to get the ministerial operations of the House much more like a business.' Hoyer said." Juliet Eilperin, "House GOP's Impact: Transforming the Institution," *Washington Post*, January 4, 2000, A4.

12. Newt Gingrich, "Winning the Future: A 21st Century Contract with America," e-mail to various mailing lists, November 15, 2006.

13. Article I, Section 8 of the Constitution provides that Congress shall have the power

> to exercise exclusive legislation in all cases whatsoever, over such District (not exceeding ten miles square) as may, by cession of particular states, and the acceptance of Congress, become the seat of the government of the United States, and to exercise like authority over all places purchased by the consent of the legislature of the state in which the same shall be, for the erection of forts, magazines, arsenals, dockyards, and other needful buildings.

14. There is still no common or standard definition of "wasteful spending" for the federal government. Jenny Mandel, "Lawmaker Asks Overseers to Agree on Meaning of Waste," *GovExec.Com.*, January 18, 2007, http://www.govexec.com/story_page.cfm ?articleid=35898&printerfriendlyVers=1&.

★ INDEX ★

Note: Those listed under *Cast of Characters*, with a few exceptions, are not listed in this index as they appear so often in the text.

★ ABOUT THE AUTHOR ★

Scot M. Faulkner was the first chief administrative officer of the U.S. House of Representatives (January 1995 to November 1996). The business reforms he introduced into the U.S. House became a model for the operation of forty-four national parliaments worldwide and were named one of the Top 100 Innovations in American Government by Harvard University and the Ford Foundation.

Faulkner was the national director of personnel for the Reagan-Bush campaign of 1980 and served in the presidential transition and then on the White House staff. He has held executive positions at the Federal Aviation Administration and the General Services Administration, and served as country director for the Peace Corps in Malawi, Africa. He was also the global practice leader and designated spokesperson for the American Management Association.

Mr. Faulkner earned a Masters Degree in Public Administration from American University and a Bachelors Degree in Government from Lawrence University. He also studied at the London School of Economics and at Georgetown University.

He is currently senior partner for global operations with Phoenix Consulting Associates. He may be reached at www.scotfaulkner.com.